T. S. Eliot, Poetry, and Earth

Ecocritical Theory and Practice

Series Editor: Douglas A. Vakoch, California Institute of Integral Studies, USA

Ecocritical Theory and Practice highlights innovative scholarship at the interface of literary/cultural studies and the environment, seeking to foster an ongoing dialogue between academics and environmental activists.

Recent Titles in the Series

T. S. Eliot, Poetry, and Earth: The Name of the Lotos Rose, by Etienne Terblanche
Ecocritical Approaches to Literature in French, edited by Douglas Boudreau and Marnie Sullivan
The Green Thread: Dialogues with the Vegetal World, edited by Patícica Vieira, Monica Gagliano, and John Ryan
Interdisciplinary Essays on Environment and Culture: One Planet, One Humanity, and the Media, edited by Jean-Marie Kauth and Luigi Manca
Romantic Sustainability: Endurance and the Natural World, 1780-1830, edited by Ben P. Robertson
Ishimure Michiko's Writings in Ecocritical Perspective: Between Sea and Sky, edited by Bruce Allen and Yuki Masami
The Ecopolitics of Consumption: The Food Trade, edited by H. Louise Davis, Karyn Pilgrim, and Madhu Sinha
Writing the Environment in Nineteenth-Century American Literature: The Ecological Awareness of Early Scribes of Nature, edited by Steven Petersheim and Madison Jones IV
Persuasive Aesthetic Ecocritical Praxis: Climate Change, Subsistence, and Questionable Futures, by Patrick D. Murphy
The Forest in Medieval German Literature: Ecocritical Readings from a Historical Perspective, by Albrecht Classen
Ecocriticism of the Global South, edited by Scott Slovic, R. Swarnalatha, and Vidya Sarveswaran
Explorations in Ecocriticism: Advocacy, Bioregionalism, and Visual Design, by Paul Lindholdt
New International Voices in Ecocriticism, edited by Serpil Oppermann
Urban Ecologies: City Space, Material Agency, and Environmental Politics in Contemporary Culture, by Christopher Schliephake
Myth and Environment in Recent Southwestern Literature: Healing Narratives, by Theda Wrede
Ecoambiguity, Community, and Development: Toward a Politicized Ecocriticism, edited by Scott Slovic, R. Swarnalatha, and Vidya Sarveswaran
Transversal Ecocritical Praxis: Theoretical Arguments, Literary Analysis, and Cultural Critique, by Patrick D. Murphy
Feminist Ecocriticism: Environment, Women, and Literature, edited by Douglas A. Vakoch

T. S. Eliot, Poetry, and Earth

The Name of the Lotos Rose

Etienne Terblanche

LEXINGTON BOOKS
Lanham • Boulder • New York • London

Published by Lexington Books
An imprint of The Rowman & Littlefield Publishing Group, Inc.
4501 Forbes Boulevard, Suite 200, Lanham, Maryland 20706
www.rowman.com

Unit A, Whitacre Mews, 26-34 Stannary Street, London SE11 4AB

Copyright © 2016 by Lexington Books

All rights reserved. No part of this book may be reproduced in any form or by any electronic or mechanical means, including information storage and retrieval systems, without written permission from the publisher, except by a reviewer who may quote passages in a review.

British Library Cataloguing in Publication Information Available

Library of Congress Cataloging-in-Publication Data

The hardback edition of this book was previously cataloged by the Library of Congress as follows:

Names: Terblanche, Etienne, 1964- author.
Title: T. S. Eliot, poetry, and earth : the name of the lotos rose / Etienne Terblanche.
Other titles: Name of the lotos rose
Description: Lanham, Maryland : Lexington Books, 2016. | Series: Ecocritical theory and practice | Includes bibliographical references and index.
Identifiers: LCCN 2016006141 (print) | LCCN 2016010235 (ebook)
Subjects: LCSH: Eliot, T. S. (Thomas Stearns), 1888-1965--Criticism and interpretation. | Nature in literature. | Materialism in literature. | Ecology in literature. | Ecocriticism in literature.
Classification: LCC PS3509.L43 Z8747 2016 (print) | LCC PS3509.L43 (ebook) | DDC 821/.912--dc23
LC record available at http://lccn.loc.gov/2016006141

ISBN: 978-0-7391-8957-3 (cloth : alk. paper)
ISBN: 978-1-4985-3747-6 (pbk. : alk. paper)
ISBN: 978-0 7391-8958-0 (electronic)

∞™ The paper used in this publication meets the minimum requirements of American National Standard for Information Sciences—Permanence of Paper for Printed Library Materials, ANSI/NISO Z39.48-1992.

Printed in the United States of America

Contents

Acknowledgments		vii
Introduction: T. S. Eliot, Nature Poet?		1
1	Rock Solid Proof: Or, The Matter with Prufrock	31
2	Dislocation: Dearth, Desert, and Global Warming	51
3	Location: Mandalic Structure in *The Waste Land*	67
4	Immersion: The Authentic Jellyfish, the True Church, and the Hippopotamus	91
5	Dissolving: The Name of the Lotos Rose	113
6	Bad Orientalism: Eliot, Edward Said, and the *Moha*	131
7	The Tyrannies of Differentiation: Eliot, New Materialism, and "Infinite Semiosis"	155
Conclusion: Where Does the Truth of New Materialism Lie? A Response Based on Eliot's Poetry		185
Bibliography		205
Index		211
About the Author		221

Acknowledgments

My gratitude for permission to cite lines from T. S. Eliot's poems *The Waste Land*, *Four Quartets*, "The Love Song of J. Alfred Prufrock," "Rhapsody on a Windy Night," "Preludes," "Gerontion," and "The Hippopotamus," as well as from T. S. Eliot's *Selected Prose*, all as published by Faber & Faber Ltd.

Gratitude for permission to use excerpts from the Harcourt publication of T. S. Eliot's *Complete Poems 1909-1962*. Copyright 1936 by Houghton Mifflin Harcourt Publishing Company. Copyright © renewed 1964 by Thomas Stearns Eliot. Reprinted by permission from Houghton Mifflin Harcourt Publishing Company. All rights reserved.

I thank wholeheartedly colleagues who have inspired me over the years with discussion of Eliot's poetry, modernism, and ecocriticism. Without the connection that I have been enjoying with Michael Webster, Attie de Lange, Jewel Spears Brooker, Nicholas Meihuizen, Reinier Terblanche, and Thys Human, my work in these areas would have been impoverished beyond recognition. My heartfelt thanks to colleagues and friends Aaron M. Moe, Franck Liu, Dan Wylie, Heilna du Plooy, Ian Bekker, Laurence Wright, and Bernard Odendaal for their input into one's thought and life. My thanks to Douglas Vakoch not only for incorporating me in this book series, but also for his hard, synergistic work on my ecocritical collaboration across international boundaries. Thanks also to fellow lepidopterists who patiently support one's interest in natural history and "hard" science: Hermann Staude, Graham Henning, Dave Edge, Mark Williams, Silvia Kirkman, and my brother, inspiring fellow student of Earth, Reinier Terblanche.

I also wish to thank my school director, Wannie Carstens, my dean, Jan Swanepoel, and my vice-chancellor, Dan Kgwadi, for their willingness to provide me with a sabbatical's worth of formulating and polishing the book's materials. Here I need to thank especially my English department—Rakgomo Pheto, Lande Botha, Ian Bekker, Attie de Lange, Nicholas Meihuizen, Karien van den Berg, and Michele du Plessis-Hay—for their willingness to organize our teaching in such a way as to make the said sabbatical possible. A special word of gratitude to my honors students of 2014, Daniel Engelbrecht and Crizeldi Gray, for their input in response to the manuscript. Also to Christien Terblanche for minor but vital language editing of the materials, and for acting as a soundboard toward testing my ideas. We all need a trustworthy and bright first reader. In the same breath my thanks to the publisher's editors and proof readers Lindsey Porambo, Anthony Johns, and Hannah Fisher for instructive comments and encouragement. It has been a real pleasure to work with this remarkable team.

My immediate family deserves considerable praise and gratitude for their patience with their husband-and-father (and his books, insects, and journeys), their unconditional love, and much, much more: my beloved partner Christien and our children Brink, Reinier, Stephan, and Benjamin. My parents-in-law, Koos and Hannatjie Vorster, as well as my brother-in-law, Nico Vorster, embody invaluable and formative energies in my life, and I herewith honor their unconditional and open-hearted acceptance and guidance.

Introduction

T. S. Eliot, Nature Poet?

T. S. Eliot enjoyed a lifelong, profound relationship with nature. As a teenager he solo-sailed the perilous Dry Salvages off Cape Ann in Massachusetts; as a grownup he became unusually excited about spotting a kingfisher over the waters at Kelham; he intensely loved the blue Massachusetts ocean throughout his life, poignantly longed for a daughter of his own, wrote a passionate plea for culture's return to integrity with Earth,[1] and more. These facts about his life and prose are relatively well known, but the considerable critical output in response to his work does not suggest that his poetry cares about Earth. How does his poetry engage with it, and what can the current generation of Earth-bound readers learn from the twentieth century's most important poet? These interrelated questions will be the focus of this book.

By virtue of foregrounding matters earthly and poetic, the discussion to follow will enter the ever-burgeoning world of ecocriticism. It is necessary to situate it within the ecocritical enterprise, daunting as the task is, because the ecocritical field is far from homogenous. Its position can be outlined on two interrelated levels: that of ecocritical praxis (or engagement) and that of ecocritical theory. The praxis will be the analysis of poetry, hermeneutic work. In teacher's parlance the book indulges in "close reading." This phrase no doubt captures the nature of close examination and analysis of poems at the intersections of their meanings and forms, to a degree; the process of "close reading" therefore enjoys sexiness, contra the ongoing general feeling that such close examination of meanings and forms is regrettably "conservative." One in fact enters the poem as though entering a world, a world of forms, meanings, and dynamisms, so close can the reading be.

In Eliot's case the hermeneutic loop (reading the parts of the text in terms of the whole and vice versa) furthermore tows one into the pursuit of various allusions, not rendering a final solution to the interpretative problem, carrying one back to the signs on the page of the poem.[2] To this I wish to add here not only that his poetry tends to come to directness of affirmation through indirectness of skepticism, but also the fact that the poems may be said to signify on two main levels. The first is "internal" in the sense that it has to do with figures and meanings "within" the world that the poem creates. For instance, Gerontion's perception within "Gerontion" is of utter despair. The second level, however, may alter the situation. For, on the level of the reader, Gerontion's despair is instructive, even affirmative of meaning, while that external interpretation is valid to understanding the poem, and even intrinsic to such understanding. I do not think "Gerontion" the poem wants us to feel and think like Gerontion the character in the poem. In the cases of Gerontion as well as Prufrock, moreover, their loss of meaningful connection with Earth points exactly into the meaningfulness of that connection.

Given the scope of the argument here, the hermeneutic loop will also be interrupted by the narrower "extra-textual" concern regarding the relationship between poetry and Earth. Poems are traced anew in terms of their eco-*logos*, that is, their specific way of orienting themselves to and within the Earth process. Questions arise: How do these poems depict Earth? How do they actively depict their active participation in being on Earth? How do they portray the modern sensibility of one's relations with matter, being, and non-being? What critiques do they offer in terms of these relations, and how do (or don't) they affirm these relations? For instance, what does Prufrock's demise into a solipsistic world have to do with his disconnection from matter? Does *The Waste Land* deny or affirm one's being on Earth? Does Eliot's insistence on *dislocation* as the mode of the modern poet[3] have anything to do with *location* or place? These are the kinds of questions that arise in this manner of critical doing. In response to these questions, the book will demonstrate that Eliot's poems excel at an idiolectic eco-*logos* of their own, while the tracing of it illuminates one's understanding of modern nature engagement.

Related to this praxis is the book's theoretical position on the level of ecocriticism. But what is ecocriticism? At its heart probably still resides Cheryll Glotfelty's satisfying middle-of-the-road working definition. "Simply put, ecocriticism is the study of the relationship between literature and the physical environment."[4] It presumes that artistic literature offers imaginative avenues into understanding the relationship between humanity and Earth. In this spirit, the book's close reading is ecocritical, and the beginnings and ends of the various chapters will situate the various close readings in terms of this ecocritical purpose. As the chapters moreover approach an overall conclusion to the book, inferences made from Eliot's poems will be applied increasingly to general ecocritical matters.

But in accepting Glotfelty's definition it has to be added that the field continues to spiral out in various directions at great speed. This brings into focus a recent, even fresh ecocritical development known by some as "new materialism." Though the new material development has been burgeoning in other disciplines (notably political studies) over a slightly longer period, its recognizable inducement into literary studies has been as recent as 2012. When it comes to ecocritical theory this development will be the book's main focus. For, new materialism carries within its relatively limited new microcosm numerous important relations and intersections that have arisen in the macrocosmic development of ecocriticism over time. For instance, ecocriticism on the whole has been concerned all along with its relations to literary theories, and new materialism brings this into sharper view, since it concerns itself with the matters of the linguistic turn and a new material turn. The discussion here will explore these matters fairly substantially, and it must therefore touch on one or two issues related to poststructuralism and postmodernism, such as the linguistic turn in particular as well as corollaries such as "infinite semiosis," the role of culture studies in literary discussion, and so forth. These developments of the past forty-odd years variously inform and are at odds with ecocriticism, especially in new material mode. Mainly, one expects that renewed focus on the relative primacy of the *materiality* of experience finds itself juxtaposed in one way or another with the overbearing emphasis on the linguistic nature of experience. I return immediately to this crisis in ecocriticism, for it is a crisis. The fact is that Eliot's poetics as embodied in his poems sheds valuable light on these affairs. For instance, the prototypical "infinite semiosis" within "Gerontion" shows that "infinite semiosis" has to do with deep-seated cultural corruption that tends to dislocate language from its earthly roots, as the book will posit in greater detail.

The book will anchor itself from within Eliot's modern project toward new materialism and its postmodern relations on the basis that the boundaries between modernism and postmodernism in literature are continuous in many respects, while in the case of literature, postmodernism undeniably begins in modernism. Postmodernism therefore has much to learn from Eliot, and this goes for the problematic relations between postmodernism, ecocriticism, and new materialism in focus here. But new materialism is important in its own right, and particularly important for Eliot's poetry. The reasons for this include, firstly, that in new materialism, ecocriticism comes to the said intriguing crisis point at which decisions are made anew about the primacy of the linguistic aspect of (material) existence, or not. How skeptical should one be, in other words, about the primacy of material being? How skeptical should one be about the nature of matter? Does either the response dominated by the linguistic turn or that dominated by scientific materialism, reducing matter to inert muteness, do justice to matter? What has happened to more affirmative views of matter, such as imaginative poetic and religious ones? This list of questions indicates already that the said crisis point occurs at the intersections of skepticism and affirmation, two major topics of the argument to follow. Secondly, new materialism illuminates Eliot's poetry anew, as will be shown, because the sheer dynamism of earthly existence that his poetry entertains has not been examined substantially. Thirdly, Eliot's poetry casts direct light on the said crisis of ecological skepticism and affirmation to which new materialism brings ecocriticism, provided that one means "crisis" not in its popular sense of alarm, but in its original and more optimistic sense of a turning point. For, in his poetry (as mentioned), particularly in its oriental aspect, skepticism is an avenue into affirmation, including skepticism about concrete existence and its affirmation.

Briefly unpacking each of these three reasons will further clarify the book's position vis-à-vis ecocriticism. To begin with, what exactly is the nature of the turning point to which new materialism brings ecocriticism, or to which it is a response? General consensus about the starting point of new materialism involving its most pertinent breach with past thought is that Earth *evidences its own agency* with which human agency entwines.[5] In other words, Earth changes in and of itself, inducing changes in others; Earth is not in need of human will or deistic interference in order for it to move. Nor is it in need of linguistic interference in order to take its shape. This is of course as obvious as the fact that planets shift, seasons change, bacteria break down organic matter and much, much more—Earth enjoys these agencies without having need of humans to push them into motion, even as our very understanding of these matters surely involves human agency.

To my mind, this central tenet of the movement puts new materialism at relative odds with the advent of the linguistic turn that has dominated theoretical doing over the past decades in deconstructive, poststructuralist, and postmodern modes. With the linguistic turn I have in mind, as a working definition, the persistent notion that signs refer to themselves in a form of differentiation that consistently, even systematically, defers the real presence of a world outside and prior to signs. Concomitant with this is the occasional and ridiculous notion that human signs somehow create Earth. Though there is little doubt that signifiers such as words and sentences participate in creating Earth, as new materialism acknowledges, the notion that human semiosis precedes earthly change is untenable. It is clear that we live in an ancient space to which we have come only fairly recently, though our roots on the planet go back millions of years, and albeit further that our existence naturally goes back all of those billions of years to the start of Cosmos. Human semiosis is therefore at once naturally ancient and relatively recent, while the idea that human language in its particular modern forms is somehow infinitely or "strategically" dominant in creating experience is a drastic position of the recent past, a position made possible only by the linguistic turn with its pervasive postmodern notion that language is the way (though in a series of ways), or even the only way, in which we have access to a (therefore) thoroughly relative existence that denies materiality any claims to real presence, especially real presence as embodied in language.

Whatever the case, at the moment of writing new materialism is struggling to choose between its own coming into being as a response and even a reaction to these excesses of the linguistic turn on the one hand,[6] and its wish to see itself as participating in a seamless continuum with the linguistic turn on the other,[7] and here we begin to trace the outline of the said crisis. In the present book, not least because it focuses on Eliot's poetry, I will take this matter to a radical position. Instead of asking how or why language defers origins and original experience, I will entertain the prospect of *real presence* in existence and in art, asking how that presence distributes itself also in linguistic worlds in relation to earthly ones, as found in Eliot's poetry. The distribution of such presence in these two worlds within his poetry is of course a vital component of his eco-*logos*, and only a most ignorant and wilful reader will insist otherwise.

For, there is another important agency undermined by the linguistic turn: the real presence enjoyed by great works of literary art. A stock reflex of theoretical and culture studies discourse (made possible by the linguistic turn) has been to highlight the secondary, including trash, while eliding or belittling the primary and the great in art, as expressed best perhaps by George Steiner throughout his essay *Real Presences*. Reading this essay in extension, that is, with a view not only to art (on which Steiner focuses), but also Earth, makes one aware of two massive reductionisms underpinning current thought patterns. The first (again) is the view of matter as mute, inert "stuff" to be manipulated, as if Earth enjoys no agency of its own. The second is the view of signs as infinite, secondary signifier-materials to be proliferated virtually for the sake of proliferation in the process of avoiding profound meaningfulness, that is, presence. From this perspective, the reductionism in literary studies ironically does not look that different from the reductionism in material science, since they both embody the loss of spiritual perception of the corporeal, the concrete, *physis*, matter.

Skepticism is therefore in the process of corrupting itself. If skepticism— inherent to the argument here as it is to all modes of scientific doing— engages the critical act of postponing judgement about facts and phenomena out of respect for more complete understanding of their nature, it is healthy. This is modern (and postmodern) and, quite frankly, human, and it involves the overcoming of superstition, bigotry, and so on. Such is the value of this, that there should be no turning back from it. On the other hand, though it is hard to pinpoint the exact moment at which it has been doing so, skepticism has increasingly become a form of hollow cynicism about the value of existence, Earth, and literary art.

This dilemma comes to a relative crossroads in the Summer 2012 issue of *ISLE: Interdisciplinary Studies on Literature and Environment* devoted in its entirety to the introduction of new materialism to a literary (ecocritical) audience. At one extreme ecocritical skepticism is characterized by the brilliant but one-sided discourse of Dana Phillips. The stock targets of his skepticism are nature conservation, poor literature, and even (only occasionally) major literature. In the mentioned volume of *ISLE* it acquires the form of barely subtle cynicism toward aesthetics, the unconscious, and natural nature, including yet another instance of snapping at conservation with the concomitant elevation of the hypernatural, in this instance the "benign" lawn, as well as the bringing down of his favored straw man, Henry David Thoreau, on a stunted basis.[8]

Phillips's criticism is intriguing also because it occurs at an exceedingly pragmatic and agnostic end of (what used to be) American Transcendentalism, where it persistently flirts, as some corrosive forms of American guilt[9] will tend to do, with hypernature (humanly "made" nature) as an alternative to actual life; as if pristine nature, harmony, and wholeness had better not exist.[10] Recently, he professed in so many words his "bad faith" in literary art, as well as values in general, as worthwhile ecocritical focal points, stating further that one could not expect natural scientists to attend multidisciplinary events, because there is too little in it for them;[11] Phillips in fact elevates himself to the desired position that he ironically preaches, namely to stay as close as possible to what he perceives as natural science, even within the humanities. Necessary as this positioning can be, since it clears away ecocritical wooliness and rust, his skepticism remains partial. It avoids grappling with great literature in its own terms, while it is too persistent in denying meaningful perception of Earth's real presence. One imagines, in fact, that for him "real presence" will be just another "platitude," because real presence is *not* confined to logic, and therefore cannot, and need not, "defend" itself in logical terms. Instead, it is far more likely that logic is an offshoot and specific instance of a narrow and highly useful way of perceiving things, while wholeness and intuition are the contextual bases that make that necessary—but narrow—avenue with its re-presentation of things possible in the first place.[12]

Careful study of ecocritical writing in the shadow of the linguistic turn further shows that Phillips's skepticism is symptomatic of broader corruption in the current literary episteme which it carries, and which carries it. To formulate the problem is not difficult when one views it from the perspective of Eliot's poetry with its alive expression of *wholeness*, that is, the recognition that being-and-non-being continue intact (his phrase is "un-being and being" at the heart of "co-existence"[13]), that the universe conspires with all its opposites, forms, energies, creatures, and so forth, for the now moment to occur, and for one to participate in it—to which *Four Quartets* is a modern hymn. From this perspective the problem is that one's sinewy ability to differentiate and re-present, making judgements and laying down categories and static hierarchies, cannot overshadow the phenomenon of dynamic wholeness. Without that wholeness, which cannot be finally defined in terms of objects, differentiation cannot occur.

It is becoming increasingly clear, however, that postmodern ecocritical skepticism presents differentiation, the tendency to continue to split up all unity into as many constituents as possible, as the dominant force in human and earthly affairs, a problem that might be as wide as Western thought patterns of the past centuries of modernity,[14] again placing postmodernism in the same category as natural science in terms of such predominance. (Though natural science does assume a brute "unity" of matter, which is also problematic.) In contrast to this, it will be an axiom of the present book that differentiation is dynamically interdependent with wholeness. Since differentiation and definition are, however, equally critical to the outcomes of the book, I have given my working definition of wholeness above, which can be no more than a bare approximation. Here Eliot's major poems (*The Waste Land*, *Four Quartets*, "The Love Song of J. Alfred Prufrock," "Rhapsody on a Windy Night") enter strongly, for they are better able to express wholeness, also in terms of its absence—not least because they *are* poems, whereas my discourse must be limited to academic prose, though it participates in the poems. The argument here continues to return to that wholeness as found in the poems.

At stake is a certain *cortesia*[15] that would restore active respect for the sharp skepticism of the intellect *and* the actualities of harmony, wholeness, and presence found in, among other things, poetry. Such *cortesia* is willing to acknowledge the profundity of artistic literary gifts such as major poems, the more so in combination with response to Earth's wholeness, that is, its very continuation which, in the "final analysis," cannot be written out in so many words. In other words, the book assumes an easy authority in accepting the affirmation of great literary art such as *The Waste Land*. Not as if the affirmation is necessary, but rather as if it is already there, while one of course wishes to delve into it and respond to it.

These matters bring the book to an important sub-plot of its limited but important engagement with the postmodern narrative in which differentiation pretends to be the master of wholeness.[16] It is the notion that greater maturation will come not with an increasing dominance of differentiation, but with renewed connection between skepticism and affirmation, while this has considerable implications for ecocritical forms of skepticism, not least in the case of new materialism. Compared to postmodern theory, Eliot's poetry enjoys substantial, intriguing, compelling, and *active balance* between the two energies, skepticism and affirmation. Broadly (not absolutely) related to skepticism in his project are the actions of linguistic dislocation and poetic fragmentation, while his affirmative mode broadly relates to the actions *induced by* dislocation and fragmentation, actions made possible and steered by those actions, in a sense at the reader's end of the poetic bargain: recombination and location. His achievement of this active balance (therefore in a sense an asymmetrical, alive balance) may shed invaluable light on the current crisis of skepticism in ecocriticism, and this the book pursues, following these key modern poetic words (dislocation, fragmentation, recombination, location) in various chapters.

To return to the matter of skepticism within ecocritical new materialism, given the extremities of such skepticism of late: it cannot be a surprise that the same volume of *ISLE* in which new materialism is introduced to the literary audience sees a different major ecocritic, Greg Garrard, raising issues about the ecocritical limits of skeptical thought. Among other considerations his article offers a plea for affirmation of imagination, conservation, and the freedom of enjoying a *humanities* slant in the making of ecocriticism[17]—all of these are necessary interventions, however much the interventions must fumble initially in the wake of Phillips's commanding work boosted by the ballast of postmodern skepticism which, perhaps despite itself, may yet give impetus and shape to affirmation. For, as William Blake[18] has long since known, opposite positions, carefully and/ or passionately entertained, shape each other.

Now, Eliot's major poems along with one or two minor poems (especially "The Hippopotamus") and his intellectual prose together provide a highly useful mortar and pestle in which the chemistry of this ecocritical dilemma can be mixed into a new configuration, provided that one cannot reduce the poems to their usefulness thus, since their "usefulness" is inseparable from the poetic experience they offer *as poems*. Still, Eliot's poems succeed in using skepticism as an avenue into affirmation, especially with a view to the Christian and Buddhist religious imagining that he weaves into the very fabric of his poems. The affirmation is a kind of recognition. One recognizes the presence of experience, or the experience of presence, instead of skeptically finding to one's apparent satisfaction that things have been merely re-presented. Part of what makes modern poetry wholly compelling, in fact, is its use of the contemporary crisis in representation to come to new ways of *presenting* things, thus finding renewed affirmation of life's value amidst a seemingly totally nihilistic, lifeless, re-presented world. The turning point between skepticism (re-presentation, re-consideration, re-spect, difference, abstraction) and agency (presence, value, wholeness, embodiment) that the arising of new materialism marks will therefore gather impetus through close study of how skepticism leads into affirmation within Eliot's poetic project.

All of this accepts that new materialism illuminates Eliot's poetry as much as his poetry illuminates ecocriticism in its new material moment. What new perspectives does new materialism bring to his poetry? It makes one see, perhaps for the first time, the remarkable extent to which Eliot's poems reveal mindfulness of Earth as motion and change, unfolding and return. It heightens the recognition that his poetry presents human participatory change within Earth change to a degree that is quite reminiscent of the new material focus on agency, flow, a human process and history within an equally dynamic and probably much larger earthly process. I return to this immediately.

The argument to follow will continue to use this much-used word, "Earth," writing it in the upper case to indicate that it is a proper name, like "Venus," while underlining its importance across generations, millennia, cultures, and geographies. For the purpose here, the question is of course how Eliot sees its meaning. Careful reading of his poetry soon shows that he does not see it in the usual sense of a piece of rock wrapped in water, consisting of various objects made up of inert matter acting as a static backdrop for subjective human dramas, stories, and utilitarian interferences. It is in many ways to him not an object or set of objects at all. Since modern poetry views objects radically in terms of subjects and vice versa, as exemplified among other things in Eliot's much-discussed "objective correlative,"[19] this should of course be expected.

For him, mostly, Earth is change in which one changes, and his poetry seeks to express, follow, move with, and resonate within these changes. He also strives to express the sheer simultaneity of these changes. The wind wrinkles and slides on the sea: it is in the pattern of the connection between wind and sea that the motion of wind at last becomes clearly visible.[20] Simultaneously, it is in the becoming of the unity of these dynamic elements that perception arises. Earth is a becoming, not a cold, hard fact. For him, concrete existence on the planet is furthermore a mysterious-but-clear (or clearly mysterious) *dance* of persons, animals, crumbling houses, trotting mice, cracking words, yew trees, life-and-death (and so on), emerging as if from nowhere, from a still point that permeates all existence as an absolute and utterly open, active, peaceful awareness. As *Four Quartets* shows, earthly creatures, energies, and things continue to emanate from the still point, a holy point that can be defined and cannot be defined—and they continue to return to it.[21] As part of the process the stars are fixed and stable to look at, but they certainly also *drift*, blood is passed on from generation to generation along a dynamic, *trilling* wire. Blood enjoys a *dance* along the artery, the tree (certainly also a metaphor of Christ's mandalic cross) does not stand neatly still, it is a *moving* tree above which we move, while simultaneously the boarhound and the boar *pursue* their pattern. And "do not call it fixity, / Where past and future are gathered" (have critics taken satisfactory heed of this?). For, "there is only the dance," made possible by a Mind, an Awareness, the still point.[22] At the opposite end of the spectrum of motion, opposite to the optimistic motion in *Four Quartets*, one finds "The Hollow Men," where motion and act are split by a shadow of which the impact is the terror of stasis, underscoring the importance again of motion.[23] Critical moments of *The Waste Land* take great care to emphasize verbs: continuous verbs as hubs at the line-ends of the first stanza, for instance: "breeding," "mixing," "stirring," "covering," "feeding." Nature is a process, it is agentic with a drive of its own, the seasons change, and the changing seasons have various effects on and dynamic interrelations with humans. Toward the poem's conclusion a pattern of verbal enjambment moves the poem forward, related again to agentic nature: the limp leaves "waited," the black clouds "gathered," the jungle "crouched," the thunder "spoke," and, following the same verbal pattern of enjambment, one hears the key "turn," each in his prison "thinking" (of the key), and so forth.[24] The examples of a pervasive verbality in Eliot's poetry are numerous. It is not so much a poetry of bits of "what," but a *how*-poetry, like the poetry of his compatriots such as E. E. Cummings. "only consider How," Cummings advocates,[25] and in its very different way Eliot's poetry offers the same verbal invitation, being modern.

As the book will also demonstrate, Eliot's view of Earth as process includes humanity to the extent that fully to exist means that humans *immerse* themselves in the concrete changes that relate them to Earth, not unlike jellyfish and hippos. And at its very heart, the immersion has generous implications for the nature of language, for the immersion reaches a point at which signs *dissolve* into the Earth process, the process of being-and-nothing, as the book will further attempt to show. For, the Earth process surely is one of coming and going, existence and non-existence, being and nothing. Earth's continuation *is* the simultaneous event of now, here, and nowhere. One will oneself one day be nowhere on Earth in contrast to one's form now and here. So many forms of the now and here of the distant and immediate past now find themselves (from an earthly perspective) to be nowhere, and from this nowhere totally unexpected forms even of familiar creatures such as babies appear. And knowing this nowhere, that is, seeing without prejudice or preconception or fear, makes one see the very suchness of each thing now and here. Eliot employs poems such as *The Waste Land* and *Four Quartets* to evoke a renewed sensibility of this now-here-nowhere, in his unique manner.

In *Four Quartets*, then, a masterful poetic paradox offers his readers this clear and peace-giving glimpse into the nature of all movement, certainly including Earth's: *except for the still point,* the poem suggests, *there would be no dance, and there is only the dance.*[26] All is movement and all is stillness. One cannot return to this paradox enough, because in it resides, moves—at the very least for a moment—the baffling actuality of what it means to be alive on the planet. Concrete being continues to unfold rhythmically from the elusive, all-pervading still point, that non-pin-pointable point of which the stability is change, known variously as God, Being, IS, the Absolute, the great nowhere, Tao, or, simply enough, love. In one sense this means that the flow of existence cannot be reduced to the singularity of this or that form of being, hence being cannot be reduced to this or that. In this sense, being is nowhere and everywhere. As Eliot highlights in his layered way on more than one occasion, this means that one is not where one is, but elsewhere: that is how radical interconnected dynamism is for him—one is, quite literally, too, what one was, because one *is* only by benefit of one's forebears having been, and so forth. This generational awareness in Eliot emerges in his poetry, certainly also at the conclusion of *The Waste Land* that leans back conspicuously into our Indo-European past to take the present forward. Moreover, as part of the discovered or being-discovered pattern in *Four Quartets*, one has to do with a dynamic unfolding in the shape of a *continuous mandala* of wholeness at the chiasmus of eternity (stillness) and the busy dance of (one's) concrete life. This is the "lotos rose," among other things. Stillness and dance, space and concreteness, peace and motion, all of these and more are inseparable when seen from the complete perspective that the poem takes. That is why Eliot can say in the poem that all is always now, and that even his personal history occurs at the intersection of England, now, nowhere, and always.[27]

That the stillness and the dance continue to coincide utterly means that on the scale of existence on the planet as a whole, stillness and motion literally are simultaneous or synchronous. That is how radical one's participation in earthly existence happens to be: one is concretely part of the ongoing now moment at the dynamic, opening center of enormous opposites in simultaneity. Or, this is one way of attempting to translate into academic prose what Eliot succinctly presents in a poetic, even mystical image. Such academic prose responses must of course be undertaken, and they must fail as carefully as possible.

From my individual perspective, as I dance my dance through a lifetime, dancing with the planet as it dances, I breathe in or out, move forward or backward, stand still or move, and so forth. From the perspective of coexistence on Earth's significant soil—central to *Four Quartets*—I am part of a much greater movement that can be pinned down neither to this creature nor that rock, this breeze nor that wave, this heat energy nor that cold energy (and how rigorously cold the universe can be, making biological life virtually unthinkable!). There should be reverence for this, if only for the sheer enormity of matters and energies that conspire to make one's participation in a lifetime possible. Though the modern lifestyle has surpassed the superstition of praying to one of Earth's trees, it is in the process of rediscovering reverence for Earth's sheer being on a modern plane, and *Four Quartets* is a poetic node of that rediscovery. It centers on the ever-changing still point where opposites flower into now, about which mystics have been garrulous, and of which Eliot's poetry as a whole is a prime expression. The still point involves the amazing grace of continuation and one's participation in that continuation. Here, as intimated, Earth (and all existence) breathes in and out simultaneously, moves forward and backward in the same moment, and so on. *To sense this*, to realize one's participation in this impossibly actual real presence, this profound dance carried by stillness, among other things is to read *Four Quartets* with the serious attention it asks and deserves on the level of the eco-*logos*, getting immersed in the actuality of one's being to the point where signs no longer matter in the most positive sense. Let these bare notes act as a platform for discussing Eliot's sensibility of the changing, agentic Earth.

The otherness of nature's forms and creatures do occasionally strike one in reading his poems, even if Eliot is perhaps not as striking in this respect as are fellow modern poets such as Marianne Moore or D. H. Lawrence. From the hippopotamus to the horseshoe crab, from the anemone and rose petals to an old crab in a city pond, like most moderns Eliot is able to render a certain strangeness and distance between these phenomena and human perception, which distance embodies not only a modern attitude but also respect for others. But it is precisely breaking through this boundary, this distance, to establish renewed connection, which brings about the sense of real presence—somehow without losing the respect of distance and space! Indeed, George Steiner defines real presence as the transgression of personal egoic boundaries in encountering the other on a deeply meaningful level, for instance when one is listening to Gustav Mahler's music.[28] When the speaker in Eliot's "Rhapsody on a Windy Night" experiences an old crab grabbing the end of a stick that he holds out to the creature,[29] from an ecocritical perspective one has exactly this kind of transgression of entrenched subject-object boundaries. It is a moment of real presence, the real presence of the crab breaking through to the speaker, the speaker connecting to his own real presence in a world of urban paucity, and the reader experiencing the immaculate timing and moving, precise emotion rendered by the presence of the image within the context of the poem.[30] (I return on occasion to this moving moment within the body of the book.) The transcendence that occurs is therefore neither hierarchical nor fixed, totalitarian, nor positivist. It is instead enormously subjective, open, dynamic, participatory, and so forth. It is in the nature of the significant transgression of automated boundaries, those boundaries somewhat entrenched perhaps in a grown-up, linguistically dominated mind and civilization in which re-presentation begins to appear to dominate the presencing nature of experience.

The sense of enormous and sensitive interaction between one's self and that of another is part of what makes Steiner's discussion of real presence attractive and, as will be demonstrated further, this is also true of Eliot's sense of real presence as found in his major poems. In this view, real presence involves the transgression of one's taken for granted personal "reality:" one moves from the real into the deeper reality—I term it actuality—of the numinous recognition of one's participation in life. We "encounter the *other* in its condition of freedom," Steiner profoundly says.[31] This freedom Eliot in fact strategically employs in *Four Quartets*, as indicated by the critic William Kevin Penny, who illustrates that "adopting nonhuman imagery possessed of a highly numinous quality allowed the poet to more successfully map out meaning in *Four Quartets* within the context of his designated poetic and spiritual agenda."[32] He demonstrates how the use of natural images allows Eliot to transcend purely or merely linguistic patterns. This is part of the way in which Eliot shows how the enormous and delicate Earth on and in which we concretely dwell is exactly such an other whose freedom is of the greatest significance. To my mind, in the ultimate freedom of our dynamic connections with it, the experience is holy.

Original meanings of this word, "holy," come into play. That which should not be violated, that which is free from sin or evil, that which is worthy of reverence, that which is whole in its continuation. Earth is not inherently sinful, its process or agency has no aim of inflicting evil, and its existence is worthy of reverence, whether from a deistic perspective that says it is holy because it is created, or from a non-deistic perspective that says existence, coexistence, being, and nothing are utterly meaningful in any event. In Eliot's project, both positions pertain to his reverence for Earth, as will be demonstrated.

His poetic sense of this holiness is moreover secular. I must then hasten to qualify the word "secular." I do not mean it in its clichéd sense of that which is anti-religious or against institutionalized faith. I mean it in the Indian sense, as expounded lucidly by the current Dalai Lama, with whom Eliot's thought shows perhaps surprising affinities. The poet and the Dalai Lama agree, for example, that one cannot simply leave behind the everyday realities of one's own culture to adopt a religion soaked in habits, everyday norms, and histories of another.[33] This involves a cross-stitching in thought between East (the Dalai Lama) and West (Eliot), after all, and it is true of almost all the modern poets—W. B. Yeats, Ezra Pound, E. E. Cummings, Marianne Moore, William Carlos Williams, and even the "delayed" modern and Beat poet Gary Snyder—that they worked hard to incorporate, with sensitivity and a sense of difference, oriental materials into occidental forms; this pertinently includes Eliot, as Snyder has indeed been one of the first freely to admit.[34]

On this basis I take the momentary liberty of following the Dalai Lama closely when it comes to his particular definition of the secular, so different from the familiar, anti-religious one usually entertained, because it is close to the secular in Eliot's poetry. In his book *Beyond Religion: Ethics for a Whole*

World, the Dalai Lama advocates the sense of secularity that is not exclusive of religion on the whole but *inclusive* of religions other than one's own.[35] In his singular way, this inclusivity and therefore secularity functions in Eliot's poetry, as a first glance will confirm. He includes various religious materials in his poems, almost always with the respect that goes along with having "lived through" the materials, while not being able to discard them, since they are formative to his poetic being. This is true especially of his two most important poems, *The Waste Land* and *Four Quartets*.

His poetic secularity comprises radical inclusion of various forms of reverence for being ranging from the Christian to the Buddhist, right down to concrete being in the now-moment. "And all is always now," as *Four Quartets* demonstrates.[36] This secular sense of holiness involves the most ordinary, extraordinary real presence of living on and within Earth. Some will say in less theoretical parlance that this is to respect and enjoy "the gift of a lifetime." In extension of Steiner's terms, I would say further it is the freedom of concrete access to existence on the planet, with a certain ease and openness of concretely knowing what to do next. And though I am unqualified to enter theological discussion of Eliot's secular sense of holy Earth, I would venture that his poetry is secular in this positive, inclusive sense. Over and above this, he experiences religious connection with the concrete world. It is there in the poems, and the reading of this "thereness" in the poems is what is really important—the real work in the instance of this book.

All in all, the book therefore posits that a definition of Earth that would remain as true as possible to Eliot's thought as reflected in his poetry would see it as the real presence of a changing, concrete process in which one radically participates. Thought has no meaning unless it connects to this miraculous, ever-unfolding given of being. Or, its meaning *is* the extent to which it connects thus. This is why thought-becoming-poetry is important. Poetry makes possible the active embodiment—a unique linguistic concreteness in sound and pattern—of the connection between the thinking capacity and emotive and bodily experience. The ultimate "definition" of Eliot's Earth is therefore to be found not in theoretical abstraction, useful as this may be, but once more in the co-creating act of reading his poems.

From this angle, his poetry appears as a real cultural presence that presents the real natural presence of earthly being, not only in theme, but in poetic forms—and this combination of cultural and natural presence is not realistic, but actual. It includes a kind of realism in its *poetic* view, and that makes it actual rather than "realist." In it, no single viewpoint can pretend to give transparent access to reality. This of course radically includes rather than excludes the real. The active becoming of subjective awareness and objective reality emerges from the reading of his poetry and its engagement with Earth. For instance, a straightforward moment of brightness and joy occurs in *The Waste Land*, and it is a moment permeated by bodily participation in the embodying Earth. Marie, a woman of apparent German aristocracy, is reluctant to remember or desire things, unwilling to accept the cruel ache that comes with the new growth of spring, remaining loosely nostalgic in her longing for the warmth and forgetfulness of winter snow as she passes the hours with a little reading—but then a memory does come to her of an exhilarating, liberating moment:

> And when we were children, staying at the arch-duke's,
> My cousin's, he took me out on a sled,
> And I was frightened. He said, Marie,
> Marie, hold on tight. And down we went.
> In the mountains, there you feel free.[37]

Liberty is to participate in concrete being. Meaningfulness can be very plain—perhaps at its best, it is concretely plain. It is to be "in the moment," like the child Marie on the exhilarating sled down the slope. As the book aims to demonstrate, it is important to see that Marie's emplacement, her joy at being part of the concrete moment, occurs on a larger and more complex scale throughout Eliot's poetic project. For instance, the joy of emplacement further carries, or is carried by, a passage in *The Waste Land* that directly refers to real places in close proximity of each other within the London that Eliot experienced:[38]

> And along the Strand, up Queen Victoria Street.
> O City, City, I can sometimes hear
> Beside a public bar in Lower Thames Street,
> The pleasant whining of a mandolin
> And a clatter and a chatter from within
> Where fishmen lounge at noon: where the walls
> Of Magnus Martyr hold
> Inexplicable splendour of white and gold.[39]

Somehow, inside Magnus Martyr, those Ionian pillars painted white (with gold-painted spirals at their tops) do hold a concrete, inexplicable splendour. The fishmen (!) who in Eliot's day came from the fish market nearby to the bar immediately adjacent to Magnus Martyr joyously engaged in music and talking and eating. The noise was literally audible through the church wall. In line with this, the tone of the passage above that focuses on real spaces is one of warm celebration, and the celebration directly connects with an actual sense of place.[40] The poetic embodiment that Eliot gives to these places is attractive and elevating. The manner in which the word "hold" flows with delicate pausing into its rhyme word "gold," for instance, enjoys considerable immediacy. The rhyming of "mandoline" with the word "within" is poignant: the speaker's outer and inner worlds for once enjoy an equal music of joy.

However, at the other end of the spectrum of responses to modern being, Eliot's poetry of course reflects the world-weary nihilism of his era. Part of his poetic commitment is to pursue and express this. But even by such means he evokes the importance of nature in a passage of *The Waste Land*:

> The river's tent is broken: the last fingers of leaf
> Clutch and sink into the wet bank. The wind
> Crosses the brown land, unheard. The nymphs are departed.
> Sweet Thames, run softly, till I end my song.
> The river bears no empty bottles, sandwich papers,
> Silk handkerchiefs, cardboard boxes, cigarette ends
> Or other testimony to summer nights. The nymphs are departed.[41]

Through a peculiar indirectness this passage insists that pollution of the Thames boils down to a searing irony. Where we expect to find nature in a river we must deny it, because we have spoiled its naturalness for ourselves. The fact of the pollution is made all the more telling by denying-and-stating it. The bottles, papers, boxes, and cigarette ends strike one all the more, because they are disallowed by indirectness and disbelief (the latter in its root sense, too). The speaker, aware of the earlier, more joyous and intimate Thames of Edmund Spenser in 1596—and the even earlier, pagan, and integral Thames of the water nymphs—can hardly bear the reality of its contemporary pollution. The actuality of the Thames is therefore considerably affirmed, though. For the denial of the pollution makes one even more aware of how ugly the pollution is, hence doubly evoking the river's real presence as an ancient natural place. Eliot thus achieves greater directness by way of indirectness, and we will come across this again on a larger scale in his poetry; recognizing this is critical in coming to grips with his eco-*logos*.

In his 1939 prose essay *The Idea of a Christian Society* he is at pains to clarify for himself and his audience the imperative set of connections that he perceives between religion and nature, and this brings his engagement with Earth into further view. There he says that it may be observed "that the natural life and the supernatural life have a conformity to each other which neither has with the mechanistic life."[42] Something mechanical has come about in the relation between modern humanity and Earth, disrupting the conformity between belief and concrete existence. This machine-like disconnection has suffused the levels of sex, relationships, marriage, community, faith, an authentic inner life, interconnecting coexistence, the pureness of rivers, and so forth.

In *The Waste Land* one finds poetic expression of his concern about this collective modern disconnection between holiness and Earth, for instance in a striking, distressing scene of automated sex between a typist and a carbuncular clerk.[43] This is just one example among many that embodies Eliot's poetic expression of the bitter disjunction between modern culture, the meaningfulness of sign-making, and the concrete sensuality of the Earth-process.

In his manner Eliot is here participating in a long poetic tradition, including (at least in this respect) Romantic poetry, which "accords value to what is created by natural processes rather than by artificial human ones,"[44] finding it necessary to return to emotional and instinctive responses to being here (on or within Earth). Given that sex is very much an Earth activity permeated with concreteness and sensuousness, this scene between typist and clerk offers a modern admission about what has become of the connections between humanity and concrete being. The gain in automation and artificiality involves a loss in the meaning of sensuality, because it involves loss of the warmth of spiritual-concrete apperception.

This of course has to do with profit and myopic forms of progress. *The Idea of a Christian Society* mentions that "the principle of private profit is leading both to the deformation of humanity by unregulated industrialism, and to the exhaustion of natural resources," with the result that

> a good deal of our material progress is a progress for which succeeding generations may have to pay dearly. I need only mention, as an instance now very much before the public eye, the results of "soil-erosion"—the exploitation of the earth, on a vast scale for two generations, for commercial profit: immediate benefits leading to dearth and desert.[45]

What would Eliot have said about the monstrous scale of *current* Earth exploitation? One thinks of bottom trawlers working in the dead of night to pull up huge swathes of ocean floor in their broad paths, pulling up absolutely everything, leaving an instant "dearth and desert" behind their ever onward, profitable, blind keels. His passage above of course anticipates that the scale of destruction would increase. A further aspect of intrigue here are the striking parallels, hitherto unmentioned, between Eliot's thought and that not only of Aldo Leopold, but pertinently again Gary Snyder. With reference to the ancient oral tradition of the Ainu that made them part of Earth—not unlike Eliot's plea for a "social-religious-artistic complex"[46] with similar effect—Snyder writes that paradoxically, only then, in the last years of the twentieth century, could this Ainu view be understood for its real worth. "Millennia of rapacious states," he writes,

> spilling out of their boundaries to plunder the resources and people within reach created a false image of limitless space and wealth on the planet, available for whoever had the weapons, organization, and willingness to kill without saying thanks. Through no wisdom of its own, but out of necessity, industrial civilization in particular is now forced to realize that there are limits, and that there is a life-support system composed of millions of subsystems all working or playing together with amazing grace.[47]

These passages contain at least two nodes of connection between Eliot and Snyder. One is their sense of "amazing grace": that holy (whole) perception of Earth is necessary. The other is their concern for civilization that has lost touch with that grace to the extent of a thankless willingness to destroy it on a devastating scale. We thus begin to see the green Eliot at work in his prose. His phrase "dearth and desert" is the prose counterpart of desert images or desertscapes in *The Waste Land*, which the present book will bring into renewed focus.

Already in 1939, then, Eliot said that the scale of Earth exploitation was out of all proportion with conformity to nature, resulting in outer and inner wastelands. Desert within (loss of religious awe) causes desert without, leading to a horrible sense of powerlessness in the human realm, a pervasive sense of humanity (women especially) raped along with the raped Earth—as the said desertscapes in *The Waste Land* intimate.[48] The powerlessness of Philomela as her nails break in the bleak soil of the scene of her being raped by King Tereus, described in this poem in such a way as to evoke the horror of the materiality of the matter, is perhaps the most disturbing and important example of this.[49] In fact, one finds in Eliot's poetry one of the earliest and most searing critiques of patriarchal "progress," and he anticipates by some decades the ubiquitous feminist insight that human rape runs parallel to Earth rape, just as human damage runs parallel to Earth damage.[50] That is, in his poetry we see an "Eliot" much different to the "personal" one that has been demolished over the past decades of culture studies, especially when it comes to the sexism that dominated his era.

One further finds in *The Idea of a Christian Society* the continued surfacing of the important Buddhist sensibility that he developed in his formative years as a student at Harvard University in Cambridge MA, a sensibility that he never discarded.[51] It is healthy to recall that he specifically chose oriental philosophies above occidental ones, because he found the former to be more engaged with everyday life than the latter, just as he pertinently decided to follow poetry instead of philosophy, again because he found the former to be more engaged with everyday life than the latter. His Buddhism therefore embodies a choice for grounded life above thought patterns that disengage from reality.[52]

For instance, when he says that "a wrong attitude towards nature implies, somewhere, a wrong attitude to God,"[53] the Christian aspect of the comment is informed by the rich Buddhist tradition, which holds with greater emphasis than most religions that a culture's engagement with nature directly mirrors its spiritual health.[54] However, it is not only Christianity and Buddhism that come into the focus of *The Idea of a Christian Society*, but also the pagan roots of European history. Though he does not advocate a return to what has become popularly associated with Jean Jacques Rousseau's "noble savage"—he does not wish for a sentimental return to it—he does advocate modern perception infused with primitive insight and wisdom about the meaningfulness of concrete existence. He says that we should not sentimentalize the life of the savage, while we should

> practise the humility to observe, in some societies upon which we look down as primitive or backward, the operation of a social-religious-artistic complex which we should emulate upon a higher plane. We have been accustomed to regard "progress" as always integral; and have yet to learn that it is only by an effort and a discipline, greater than society has yet seen the need of imposing upon itself, that material knowledge and power is gained without loss of spiritual knowledge and power. The struggle to recover the sense of relation to nature and to God, the recognition that even the most primitive feelings should be part of our heritage, seems to me to be the explanation and justification of the life of D. H. Lawrence, and the excuse for his aberrations.[55]

The passage reflects important ecocritical imperatives. One may start with the word "humility." Eliot seems to be saying that it is humble to learn anew about a complex of religious relations with nature from primitive worlds of culture (presumably past and present ones, including (to my mind) those that crop up in one's dreams at night)—not unlike the thought in more recent important ecopoetic works such as David Abram's *The Spell of the Sensuous: Perception and Language in a More-than-Human World*; a book to which I occasionally return. Having enjoyed a thorough education in classical languages at Harvard, Eliot would consciously or unconsciously have known that humility has to do with a sense of fruitful soil: *humus*. The reciprocity of that sense of soil in *Four Quartets* is striking. Two key moments in the poem are the phrases "humility is endless" and "the life of significant soil."[56] The humility of matter, so to speak, is eternal. It is as real as the fact that it cannot be grasped. Humus, in this view, is everything but dull "stuff" lying in wait for humanity's necessary and unnecessary interferences of use. Instead, it is alive with significance of its own in which humanity partakes—again this approaches the new material sensibility. And to be humble is to stay connected to this sense of vibrant humus. For this poet, connection with a vibrant Earth is superior to the inflated "superiority" of a "civilization" that lacks all instinctive wisdom when it comes to relationships with and within nature.

The active integrity between culture and nature is therefore of critical importance to Eliot. This integrity is to him of a holy nature, as indicated. He indeed enjoys a considerable religious imagination.[57] It continues to seek and find the depth of dynamic wholeness. As the foremost Eliot critic Jewel Spears Brooker points out, the Sanskrit roots of the word "religion" signify wholeness: re-*ligare* means to re-tie or re-unify loose ends.[58] Eliot is an early recognizer of the fact that our society needs, for the sake of its own health, to re-bind and re-member its moving connections with the unfolding Earth. Of course, there will be thoughts that, since his religious imagination has to do with wholeness, it must be static, positivist, monolithic, or totalitarian. It is therefore important to reiterate that the establishment of such wholeness is dynamic and open. It is therefore far removed from the violent imposition of fixed ideas and ideals on organic unfolding. The argument to follow will further highlight this important recognition from time to time, because in the past the notion of wholeness has been confused with the notion of monolithic properties.

Even in his later prose, then, and from an ecocritical perspective especially, wholeness in the dynamic relations between modern humanity and ancient Earth are important. And examining in this way *The Idea of a Christian Society* is a first step toward the discovery that Eliot's sense of sacredness does not restrict itself to cultural affairs. It extends to nature, which (as indicated) he views to be of conformity to religion. He enjoys the sense of roots, as Snyder rightly says about him.[59] Concrete being in time is rooted in the timeless. All existence is a continuous Incarnation, and belief means little if it is not corporeal, permeating one's concrete life on Earth.

As has been indicated, a substantial dimension of his sense of Earth is oriental, and Buddhist in particular. Eliot is emphatically Christian (though emphatically not in any textbook manner), especially after his conversion in 1927, but the still point and its flow cannot be reduced to institutionalized images with fixed properties of God the Father within the protestant or even catholic Christian tradition, or their philosophical equivalents of logocentric patriarchy that subjugates concreteness under the origin of breath and speech. Incidentally, most of the spiritual presences in his poetry are female, hermaphrodite, or, if they are quite masculine, accompanied by a goddess or a mystery. One thinks immediately of the Sybil of Cumae, Madame Sosostris, Julian of Norwich, Mary, Tiresias, Dante and Beatrice, St John of the Cross and God's darkness, or Prajapati accompanied by Ganga. More importantly, the emphasis on Earth as consisting of changes—instead of consisting of fixed patriarchal properties—already brings one to the Buddhist strand in his poetic making. This is the strand that has most often been misunderstood by his critics, while it is imperative to understanding his poetic connection with Earth. Buddhism enjoys unique sets of wisdom about one's active embedding within Earth,[60] and his two major poems, *The Waste Land* and *Four Quartets*, carry important Buddhist sensibilities that embody special forms of communication about earthly emplacement, such as his use of blank space and meaningful fragments to revoke, in the present, a past characterized by greater culture-nature integrity.

One speaks here not simply of Buddhism as practiced in India or China *an sich*, but of important misunderstandings *as* understandings (in English) of oriental materials. One therefore speaks of what Steiner terms in his classic book *After Babel* "a general phenomenon of hermeneutic trust."[61] More or less, the reader enters into a pact with the poet that certain devices in a poem act as shorthand for what is perceived to be oriental meanings. The result is of course unique participation in a new form of Buddhism. It is therefore worth ensuring a brief outline of the nature of this modern Buddhist making and participation to which modern poets in general and Eliot in particular have given considerable impetus. In *The Making of Buddhist Modernism*, David McMahan notices that what many Americans and Europeans often understand by the term "Buddhism,"

> is actually a modem hybrid tradition with roots in the European Enlightenment no less than the Buddha's enlightenment, in Romanticism and transcendentalism as much as the Pali canon, and in the clash of Asian cultures and colonial powers as much as in mindfulness and meditation.[62]

It is useful to think of Eliot's Buddhism in similar terms, as a hybrid, not only of secular, ecumenical elements across faith traditions, but also in terms of Buddhism itself, since his particular Buddhism mixes and matches all kinds of elements related to Buddhist traditions, varying from Sanskrit understandings to the employment of blank space (as in Taoist traditions), and Zen-like paradoxes that open into renewed recognition of one's radical, meditative participation in Earth's process; these and more the book will continue to examine in close reading of the poems. Suffice it to say for a start in this respect that Buddhism is in his case a truncating umbrella term that encompasses a hybrid, modern kind of Buddhism-Taoism-Zen (henceforth simply "Buddhism") involving special employments of the said shorthand techniques to indicate meanings related to Earth connection; the shorthand, again, includes such phenomena as Sanskrit fragments reverberating within heightened blank space.

In his singular way, Eliot occupies the profound cultural world of "between," like those who occupy the space between East and West in one way or another, where English becomes a kind of Chinese, or Chinese a kind of English[63]—or where Sanskrit enters English anew. This means that such Buddhism is neither exactly the same as it is practiced in the actual East, nor a fabrication, and this is a cultural view of modern orientalism more refined than that of Edward Said, who condemns orientalism *even in art* as an evil fabrication. As McMahan finds, such Buddhism

> is neither unambiguously "there" in ancient Buddhist texts and lived traditions nor merely a fantasy of an educated elite population in the West, an image with no corresponding object. It is, rather, an actual new form of Buddhism that is the result of a process of modernization, westernization, reinterpretation, image-making, revitalization, and reform that has been taking place not only in the West but also in Asian countries for over a century. This new form of Buddhism has been fashioned by modernizing Asian Buddhists and western

enthusiasts deeply engaged in creating Buddhist responses to the dominant problems and questions of modernity, such as epistemic uncertainty, religious pluralism, the threat of nihilism, conflicts between science and religion, war, and environmental destruction.[64]

Again Eliot's poetry offers a unique, anachronistic aesthetic of this new Buddhist nature. Like Said, Eliot knows that Pound "invents" China for his time;[65] and so does Eliot "invent" singular Buddhist patterns that at once honor the ancient Buddhist traditions, discard with some Buddhist elements, and reinterpret and "picture" Buddhism in his individual way within the poems. His Buddhist use of fragments and blank space, for instance, is an idiosyncratic variant of such use found throughout modern poetry, with *its* broad emphasis on fragments and the significant use of blank space. As will be shown, Eliot's making of the new Buddhism enacts a maturing response to the epistemic uncertainties, threats of nihilism, and environmental destructions that the moderns face in their time. McMahan's useful general remarks suit their case well.

He emphasizes that the "recent forms of Buddhism have not simply dispensed with all traditional elements in an effort to accommodate to a changing world but have re-invented them."[66] This is so important, because Eliot's allusive re-invention of Sanskrit in *The Waste Land*, for example, does not simply get rid of traditional significances in favor of modern nihilisms, contrary to the view of some of his important critics such as F. R. Leavis.[67] Like all his allusions, they are at pains to cite *and* change their origins, and in this process they surpass mere nihilism, signifying rather a primordial love that permeates concrete existence in terms of being-and-non-being. Part of this is that he gives his own unique modern shape to Buddhist elements to point into the social maturation that comes with spiritual recognition of earthly being.

The critical confusion that has constantly led to the overlooking of his poetic re-invention of Buddhism and its affirmative environmental importance for his poetry and his readers arises, because Eliot's skepticism and indirectness are so intense. That very intensity is part of his Buddhist formation so that, ultimately, the skepticism results in a profound affirmation of all that is,[68] whereas it is easy for critics to remain blinded to the affirmation, because they continue to confuse his affirmative skepticism with the "standard" nihilistic sensibilities that have set in since the beginnings of the twentieth century (and earlier). However, Eliot is decidedly and by his own decision neither an epistemologist nor a skeptic in any "standard" occidental sense.[69] It is when one sees him as a kind of nihilist cynic that his Buddhism is misplaced. It will therefore be important in the pages here to re-locate Eliot's Buddhism as found in his poems with a view to its ecopoetic affirmation, carried rarely by direct optimism and often by the Buddhist forms of indirectness—indirectness related to everyday life![70]

The indirectness has to do with the recognition that Earth is constantly changing. Consequently, naming it with great finality of directness would be to denounce its most important aspect. Perhaps this is the reason why, in the broadest sense, including its Taoist and Zen forms, Buddhist perceptions of Earth emphasize its changing nature, perhaps more so than is the case in other traditions. As the book will show, the Buddhist energy in Eliot's poetry makes it possible to express Earth-as-process by means of indirect statements that ultimately confirm the significance not of some future spiritual existence but of sacredness here and now: the actual significance of reality. Another term for this is the real presence that I have gleaned in ecocritical manner from Steiner. In its way, the book synthesizes Steiner's conceptions of real presence and hermeneutic trust as part of following Eliot's poetry into its vibrancy and nuances from ecocritical, new material perspectives.

Against the background of these terms and methodological concerns, it is possible to sketch the outline of the chapters to follow. Chapter 1 examines the matter with Prufrock. By careful reading of "The Love Song of J. Alfred Prufrock" the chapter argues that his disconnection from meaningful matter, his displacement of the real presence of Earth and Cosmos, reduces the protagonist to a match stick glutton suffering from a Jungian kind of semiotic overcompensation or neurosis. His world consists of infinite, slippery signs unable to find earthly resonance, and the less earthly resonance he finds, the more he fills the void with signs. His failed materialism comments with intense, even unbearable, irony on the nature of the modern lifestyle and the matter with it.

Dislocation is in other words critical to understanding Prufrock's distorted materialism, a materialism uncomfortably familiar to readers of the poetry. Chapter 2 subsequently continues to pursue the dislocating theme and act in Eliot's project, showing that it is pervasive. Perhaps its most intense expression is found in fragmentation and desertscapes in *The Waste Land*; these the chapter carefully analyzes. It finds that the poem adumbrates the parallels between rape and Earth-rape, as well as global warming. Toward its conclusion, the chapter however asserts that Eliot's procedures of dislocation always already assume affirmation of *location*. His poetry dislocates language in order to restore it, or show with real presence the prospect of restoration and the ongoing affirmation that is inherent to Earth's continuity. Here the chapter engages on a broader theoretical front with dislocation in new material ecocriticism, critiquing the matters of one-sided skepticism and the concomitant lack of affirmation as exemplified in new material discourse.

If the main point with regard to Eliot's dislocation happens to be that it does not embody an end but a means to renewed *location*, one should consider the poetic embodiment of a deep sense of earthly emplacement in his oeuvre, as chapter 3 argues. It pays attention to the ready appreciation that *Four Quartets* is a poem of active location, but focuses in particular on how *The Waste Land* embodies location by means of Sanskrit mandalic patterns of culture-nature integrity rendered in modern Buddhist manner. Based on these findings, at its conclusion the chapter returns to new materialism and its ecocritical implications. It demonstrates that Eliot's poetry offers the huge verb, the verbality, that the major new materialist Jane Bennett finds lacking in the available English grammar,[71] arguing also on this basis that following Eliot's poetry is useful in determining the new material way forward.

But it would not be Eliot if he were satisfied only with a dialectic of dislocation implicating one of location. Neither would it be poetry in its fullness if this were the point at which the new material following of his poems had to reach its end. His poetry is intense, and intensity requires that location should be as complete as possible. Here comes into view the poet's radical sense of *immersion* in existence, that is, an intense form of location and culture-matter integrity, taken up in chapter 4, which reads the minor 1920 poem, "The Hippopotamus," against the background of his near-obsession with creatures of immersion such as polyps and jellyfish. It traces immersive imagery throughout his poetic project, to find that for Eliot, immersion in earthly being is by far more holy and elevating than the civilized (but actually barbaric) modern retention of a dislocating, "spiritual" aloofness from matter.

I say "spiritual" with reference again to the fact that the rationalistic privileging of language as "breath," a kind of reduced spiritual essence, may disconnect humanity from Earth. At least, this is what modern poets suggest in their voice *that are part of a system*[72] that places equal emphasis on the phonetic and the visual, not least through procedures of fragmentation. At its conclusion this chapter relates its preliminary findings again to new materialism, comparing the new material notions of enmeshment and entanglement briefly with immersion. By following poetry, it argues, new materialism allows its scope to include the more intense, poetic aspects of enmeshment embodied in immersion. The chapter points out also in this respect that actual citation from poetry offers value for new materialism, referring to the matter again of skepticism and affirmation with reference to Garrard's work, as well as that of the ecocritic, herpetologist, and nature writer Richard Kerridge, who makes the necessary point that theory meets its creative moment in close reading, in lingering in the moment of the text.[73] The chapter concludes that immersion in poetry is one way of getting immersed in being on Earth.

Eliot knows, as briefly indicated above, that immersion in being has radical consequences for the nature of language, as chapter 5 will maintain. It follows him into the deepest (and also most feather-light and humorously skeptical-affirmative) place in his project, the dissolving of signs into the sacred Earth process as found in *Four Quartets*. The chapter shows that the poem dissolves the usual grammatical categories in English, such as noun and verb, to induce a kind of melting in which sign-boundaries dissolve, while this semiotic dissolving pertinently evokes (or dissolves further into) the patterns of being-and-nothing at the heart of earthly being. At its conclusion the chapter relates this finding to Bennett's depiction of the role that empty space has played in the human understanding of its place on the planet. It finds that following poetry, Eliot's in particular, into the mythopoetic understanding of such vibrant being-and-nothing is valuable to the ecocritical pursuit of new materialism, since it connects with the most immediate nerve ends of one's concrete existence.

Based on the ecocritical close reading of the poems established up to and including this fifth chapter, the book will be in a position to bring its ecopoetic findings to a more general discussion. The timing of the emergence of new materialism is such that two broad strands concern it: the linguistic turn (poststructuralist poetics) to which it responds, as indicated, and culture studies, of which it arguably forms a subset. The former involves great emphasis on the proliferation of sign-differentiation to an extent that borders on believing that humans inhabit a world of signs, a semiosphere[74] of which the connections with the biosphere, Earth, and Cosmos are at best uncertain and ill-defined. Contradictorily, this involves progressive drifting away from what has been known as the "primary text"—canonized artistic work in literature that has survived the considerable testing of successive generations—in the understandably liberating quest to examine the "literariness" of most anything or everything, varying from Japanese jokes to fashion and soccer matches, as found in the culture studies "movement" that comes partly with, and partly after, the advent of theory. In new materialism this culture studies mode finds its resonance in the excruciating attention paid, in academic prose, to such phenomena as peak oil, food security rhetoric, the authenticity of fake meats, and so forth.

Switching around this chronology of theorizing followed by culture studies for the reason that Buddhism is vital to reading Eliot's eco-*logos*, in chapter 6 the book first examines the implications of Eliot's ecological orientalism for culture studies of the kind practised by Edward Said, surely a father of the movement. It will contend that Said undercuts his own heavy-handed, abrupt culture studies dismissal of Eliot's poetic Buddhism, based on his ill-informed opinion that it involves mere nostalgia for a bygone era.[75] It will demonstrate that he has mislaid an ally for his argument, because Eliot's poetic Buddhism is precisely an invaluable part of that which embeds his poetry in concrete existence, while rootedness in concrete existence is what Said uses as the main criterion for what should be viewed as valuable in all literature from his culture studies perspective.[76] Toward its conclusion this chapter contends that new materialism, an inheritor of the culture studies approach that makes it possible in the first place, should do well to keep the primary artistic text in mind to a greater extent than has been the case in culture studies as practiced by Said.

But what about new materialism's theoretical inheritance that stems from the linguistic turn to which it (new materialism) is a response? By this stage of the argument, analysis of "The Love Song of J. Alfred Prufrock" would have revealed that "infinite semiosis" does not only harbour potential advantages of infinite creative exploration via unique sets of differentiation such as strategic deconstructive analysis of phenomena. It may be a semio-neurotic reflex, so to speak, in the face of dislocation from the real presence of matter in the attempt to fill an impossible, infinite void—a void arising exactly from the lack of earthly and cosmological connection—with the noise of signifiers. The linguistic turn is drastically *subjective*. It always already occurs on the brink of collective solipsism, skirting it, flirting with it, lapsing into it on occasion. Perhaps the best example of this is the bafflement caused by Jacques Derrida's project, whose critically important work of our age on occasion seems impossible to understand, even to those trained in philosophy and logic.[77] Has there ever been a greater Houdini of intellectual positioning? One is not sure that his remarkable idiolect does not sometimes, and in a sense on the whole, form a solipsistic universe of peculiar close reading. The overall nihilistic sensibility—to which Derrida gave indubitable willing or unwilling impetus—which holds that most experience is mediated by semiotic differentiation, strikes me as inherently solipsistic in the way of Prufrock's experience.

Thus comes into focus the problem of infinite differentiation as a set of tyrannies, to be discussed in chapter 7: tyrannies in the sense that the postmodern wave in which differentiation must triumph over poetic wholeness will always already be violent as viewed from a perspective informed by Eliot's poetry. In his poetry, differentiation is a means, not an end. Fragmentation leads to new prospects of recombination and integration. Dislocation brings about new ways of locating signs within contexts larger than themselves, such as being on Earth, and so forth. On this basis the chapter suggests answers from Eliot's poetry about one or two pertinent questions before which new materialism overtly or inadvertently places itself. Will new materialism merely amount to an affluent of the postmodern reign called "infinite semiosis"—and that kind of postmodernism that insists on discarding modernism, to boot? Or does its explicit differing from the linguistic turn entail an advance away from the constraints, ennui, cynicism, and one-sided tyrannies of the poststructuralist hyper-emphasis on differentiation that strategically denies the wholeness of real presence?

In pursuit of answers to these questions, however provisionally, the chapter reads "Gerontion." It is a poem of houses within houses within houses, acting as a prototype of "infinite semiosis" and its corrupting premises and consequences. Having carefully traced the outline of this corruption, the chapter grapples with the tyranny of Derrida's influential notion, assumed by postmodernism, that there is nothing outside the text or, in its apparent better translation, there is no outside-text. Taking its lead from the ecocritic Laurence Coupe, the chapter finds this position to be not only at least as corrupt as the dry onion-like structure in "Gerontion," but also immature. From this angle, too, the book calls on greater maturity in new material ecocriticism that would balance skepticism, affirmation, and all that is actively agentic outside the text (to which the text may relate itself).

This book's conclusion will take this perception, based on the findings of the new material close reading of Eliot's poetry that precedes it, to the relative fullness of its implications for new materialism as such. It will synthesize the book's materials by showing how new material skepticism, especially as introduced to a literary audience in 2012 by Dana Phillips, Serenella Iovino, Serpil Opperman, and Greg Garrard, can be enhanced by mature affirmation of earthly being and closer engagement with primary, artistic literature with its mytho-poetic vibrancy; how the real presence of vibrant matter informs one's new material engagement with literature and ideas; how the modern hybrid of Buddhism of which Eliot gives such an astonishing example points into the importance not only of vibrant matter, but also *vibrant emptiness*, that is, the "room" or "space" of a generally shared human propensity toward reflection and meditation within which clarity comes about one's place in being-and-non-being, including especially the awareness that emptiness is resonant with all that has gone and all that will come and all that is in the present moment. It will posit that new materialism's impetus to advance the poststructuralist discussion may be boosted by forms of writing like Eliot's, since those forms of writing somehow are critically aware that differentiation can be tyrannical, while they are able on this basis to connect anew with Earth.[78]

The conclusion to be reached will be that Eliot shows how one may add to sign-making with a built-in prophylaxis that points through skilfull mytho-poetic signs into worlds at once inside and outside semiosis, where a sense of place finds poetic location, immersion, and dissolving. When the book has followed this poet's idiolect, his individual eco-*logos*, into these (again, often feather-light) profound implications for a burgeoning, brave, and welcome new materialism, it will hopefully have made its contribution to increasing ecopoetic understanding of Eliot's poetry, new materialism, and the vital modern, cultural, and human relationship with and within the changing Earth-ship.

NOTES

1. Peter Ackroyd, *T. S. Eliot: A Life* (London: Hamish Hamilton, 1984), 22; Helen Gardner, *The Composition of* Four Quartets (New York: Oxford University Press, 1978), vii, 38; A.

N. Dwivedi, *T. S. Eliot: A Critical Study* (New Delhi: Atlantic Publishers, 2002), 14. Robert Crawford suggested the possibility of reading Eliot's poem "Marina" also as suggestive of the poet's yearning for a daughter at the First International T. S. Eliot Summer School held in Bloomsbury, London, from 27 June to 4 July 2009, attended by the author. T. S. Eliot, *Collected Poems 1909-1962* (New York: Harcourt Brace, 1991), 106; T. S. Eliot, *Selected Prose*, ed. Frank Kermode (London: Faber & Faber, 1980), 290.

2. Jewel Spears Brooker and Joseph Bentley, *Reading* The Waste Land: *T. S. Eliot and the Dialectic of Modernism* (Amherst: University of Massachusetts Press, 1990), 154–158.

3. Eliot, *Prose*, 65.

4. Glotfelty, Cheryll. "Introduction: Literary Studies in an Age of Environmental Crisis," *The Ecocriticism Reader (Landmarks in Literary Ecology)*, eds. Cheryll Glotfelty and Harold Fromm (Athens: University of Georgia Press, 1996), xviii.

5. Serenella Iovino, "Stories from the Thick of Things: Introducing Material Ecocriticism," *ISLE: Interdisciplinary Studies in Literature and Environment* 19.3 (Summer 2012), 456.

6. Iovino, "Thick of Things," 452.

7. Serpil Opperman, "A Lateral Continuum: Postmodernism and Ecocritical Materialism," *ISLE: Interdisciplinary Studies in Literature and Environment* 19.3 (Summer 2012), 460.

8. Dana Phillips, "'Slimy Beastly Life:' Thoreau on Food and Farming," *ISLE: Interdisciplinary Studies in Literature and Environment* 19.3 (Summer 2012), 536.

9. *See* Annette Kolodny, "Unearthing Herstory," *The Ecocriticism Reader: Landmarks in Literary Ecology*, eds. Cheryll Glotfelty and Harold Fromm (Athens: The University of Georgia Press, 1996), 60.

10. However, human made nature always already presupposes non-human, born nature. *See* Kate Soper's important book *What Is Nature? Culture, Politics and the Non-Human*, throughout. And pristine nature actually still exists on Earth at the moment. In such places, for instance the Foja Mountains in Papua, the habitat sustains itself in breath-taking harmony; *see* Eric Dinerstein, *The Kingdom of Rarities* (Washington: Island Press, 2013), 43–44. Dana Phillips's insistence that ecocriticism must get rid of poetic notions of interconnectedness and harmony is based on his belief that natural science has gotten rid of these since the advent of A. G. Tansley's work in which he rightly pointed out the abuse of organismic terms within ecology proper; *see* Phillips, *The Truth of Ecology: Nature, Culture, and Literature in America* (Oxford: Oxford University Press, 2003), viii. Saying that interconnectedness and harmony are "platitudes," while nature is more chaotic and violent than these platitudes allow, however makes one wonder exactly how nature is able to continue if it is dominated to such a degree by chaos and violence. Phillips lacks a certain tact toward nature's intact continuation. *Even in those places* so hyperreal ("disturbed" is the scientific term) as to be hardly recognizable, if a single plant happens to grow there, there "lives the dearest freshness deep down things" (Gerard Manley Hopkins, *The Major Poems* [London: Dent, 1979], 64). The plant that actually grows there has within its being myriads of ancient, pristine processes that work in the most brand new way imaginable. The same is true of the human body, which, even in the most hyperreal circumstance, consists of a universe of interrelating, pristine functions as it continues to be. The actions of cells are indubitably ancient and remarkably present, in this sense pristine even if *despite* human smear, smudge, blear, and trade.

11. Dana Phillips, conversation emanating from questions posed by the author during question time after his keynote address titled "Collapse, Resilience, and Sustainability" at a conference of Auetsa (The Association of University English Teachers of South Africa) at Rhodes University in Grahamstown, South Africa, on 13 July 2015.

12. Iain McGilchrist, *The Master and His Emissary: The Divided Brain and the Making of the Western World* (New Haven: Yale University Press, 2012), 50, 92–93.

13. Eliot, *Poems*, 180, 181.

14. McGilchrist, *Master and Emissary*, 14.

15. George Steiner, *Real Presences* (Chicago: University of Chicago Press, 1991), 148.

16. McGilchrist, *Master and Emissary*, 14.

17. Greg Garrard, "Nature Cures? or How to Police Analogies of Personal and Ecological Health," *ISLE: Interdisciplinary Studies in Literature and Environment* 19.3 (Summer 2012), 497, 510, 512.

18. William Blake, *The Complete Illuminated Books* (New York: Thames & Hudson, 2001), 109. The citation reads: "Without contraries there is no progression."
19. Eliot, *Prose*, 48.
20. Eliot, *Poems*, 183.
21. Eliot, *Poems*, 177.
22. Eliot, *Poems*, 177.
23. Eliot, *Poems*, 82.
24. T. S. Eliot, *The Waste Land* (Norton Critical Edition), edited by Michael North (New York: W. W. Norton, 2001), 5, 18, 19.
25. E. E. Cummings, *Complete Poems 1904-1962*, edited by George James Firmage (New York: Liveright, 1994), 363.
26. Eliot, *Poems*, 177.
27. Eliot, *Poems*, 180, 181, 187, 201.
28. *See* Steiner, *Real Presences*, 4.
29. Eliot, *Poems*, 17.
30. Eliot, *Poems*, 17.
31. Steiner, *Presences*, 4.
32. William Kevin Penny, "Dialect of the Tribe: Modes of Communication and the Epiphanic Role of Nonhuman Imagery in T. S. Eliot's *Four Quartets*," *Harvard Theological Review* 108.1 (January 2015), 112.
33. Dalai Lama, *Beyond Religion: Ethics for a Whole World* (London: Rider, 2011), 20; T. S. Eliot, *After Strange Gods: A Primer of Modern Heresy* (London: Faber & Faber, 1934), 41.
34. Gary Snyder, *The Real Work: Interviews and Talks 1964-1979* (New York: New Directions, 1980), 57
35. Dalai Lama, *Beyond Religion*, 6.
36. Eliot, *Poems*, 180.
37. Eliot, *The Waste Land*, 5.
38. Which the author witnessed on a tour of Eliot's London guided by Wim van Mierlo at the First International Eliot Summer School.
39. Eliot, *The Waste Land*, 14.
40. As witnessed by the author on a tour of Eliot's London guided by Wim van Mierlo during the First Eliot International Summer School.
41. Eliot, *The Waste Land*, 11.
42. Eliot, *Prose*, 290.
43. Eliot, *The Waste Land*, 13.
44. Kate Soper, *What Is Nature? Culture, Politics and the Non-Human* (Oxford: Blackwell, 1995), 16.
45. Eliot, *Prose*, 290.
46. Eliot, *Prose*, 290.
47. Gary Snyder, *A Place in Space: Ethics, Aesthetics, and Watersheds* (Washington: Counterpoint, 1995), 97.
48. Eliot, *The Waste Land*, 8.
49. Eliot, *The Waste Land*, 15.
50. *See* Soper, *What is Nature?* 11.
51. Jeffrey M. Perl and Andrew P. Tuck, "The Hidden Advantage of Tradition: On the Significance of T. S. Eliot's Indic Studies," *Philosophy East & West* 35.2 (April 1985), 115.
52. Perl and Tuck, "Eliot's Indic Studies," 117.
53. Eliot, *Prose*, 290.
54. Paul Waldau, "Buddhism and Animal Rights," *Contemporary Buddhist Ethics*, ed. Damien Keown (Richmond: Kurzon, 2000), 86.
55. Eliot, *Prose*, 290.
56. Eliot, *Poems*, 185, 199.
57. I take the phrase from personal conversation with Jewel Spears Brooker at the First International T. S. Eliot Summer School held in Bloomsbury, London, from 27 June to 4 July 2009.

58. Jewel Spears Brooker, *Mastery and Escape: T. S. Eliot and the Dialectic of Modernism* (Amherst: University of Massachusetts Press, 1994), 161.

59. Snyder, *The Real Work*, 57.

60. Cheryll Glotfelty, "Introduction: Literary Studies in an Age of Environmental Crisis," *The Ecocriticism Reader: Landmarks in Literary Ecology*, eds. Cheryll Glotfelty and Harold Fromm (Athens: University of Georgia Press, 1996): xxii.

61. George Steiner, *After Babel: Aspects of Language and Translation* (London: Oxford University Press, 1975), 359.

62. David McMahan, *The Making of Buddhist Modernism* (New York: Oxford University Press, 2008), 5

63. Eric Hayot, *Chinese Dreams: Pound, Brecht, Tel Quel* (Ann Arbor: The University of Michigan Press, 2007), 27.

64. McMahan, *Buddhist Modernism*, 5.

65. Hayot, *Chinese Dreams*, 6.

66. McMahan, *Buddhist Modernism*, 6.

67. F. R. Leavis, "The Significance of the Modern Waste Land," *The Waste Land* (Norton Critical Edition), ed. Michael North (New York: Norton, 2001), 181.

68. Perl and Tuck, "Eliot's Indic Studies," 119–120.

69. *See* Brooker, *Mastery and Escape*, 173.

70. Perl and Tuck, "Eliot's Indic Studies," 115.

71. Jane Bennett, *Vibrant Matter: A Political Ecology of Things* (Durham: Duke University Press, 2010), 119.

72. Jacques Derrida, *Of Grammatology*, trans. Gayatri Spivak (Baltimore: Johns Hopkins University Press, 1997), 90.

73. Richard Kerridge, [Review of *Ecocritical Theory: New European Approaches*, eds. Axel Goodbody and Kate Rigby; *Environmental Criticism for the Twenty-First Century*, eds. Stephanie LeMenager et al.], *ISLE: Interdisciplinary Studies in Literature and Environment* 19.3 (Summer 2012), 597, 598.

74. Yuri M. Lotman, *Universe of the Mind. A Semiotic Theory of Culture* (Bloomington: Indiana University Press, 1990), 133.

75. Edward Said, *Reflections on Exile and Other Essays* (Cambridge: Harvard University Press, 2002), 247.

76. Said, *Reflections on Exile*, 252.

77. Dino R. Galetti, "Searching for a Logic in Derrida: Assessing Hurst's 'Plural Logic of the Aporia,'" *Journal of Literary Studies / Tydskrif vir Literatuurwetenskap* 26.3 (September 2010), 107.

78. Eliot, *Poems*, 41; Daniel Albright, *Quantum Poetics: Yeats, Pound, Eliot, and the Science of Modernism* (Cambridge: Cambridge University Press, 1997), 226.

Chapter One

Rock Solid Proof

Or, The Matter with Prufrock

What is the matter with Prufrock? This main character in Eliot's first great modern poem, "The Love Song of J. Alfred Prufrock" (1917), has been bothering his audience, frustrating and exhausting it for nearly a century. Prufrock will not go away. He is a central consciousness that comprises some of the thorniest traits of what it means to be a modern human being. His surname is one of his interesting characteristics. It sits richly in the mouth on full pronouncement, and somehow remains enormously bland. The poet got this apparently plain affair from advertisements appearing in the first decade of the twentieth century in St. Louis, Missouri, of Prufrock-Littau, furniture wholesalers,[1] but reading the surname carefully in terms of the poem soon reveals more. It shimmers with subliminal suggestions contained by fragments such as "proof" and "rock," as if he desperately seeks rock solid proof of his existence, while he remains a prudent frock, disenabling him from salvaging the necessary connection with physical existence.

Prufrock's materiality does not sit well with him. His sense of it is extremely limited in general, and his particular embodiment within the concrete universe is a dilemma for him. On the one hand, he finds little or no significance in concrete acts and objects and, on the other, signs swamp his experience. He desperately lacks instinctive, earthly, and emotional responses to his existence. The poem therefore offers a vital poetic grip on the matter of the modern material psyche. As is evidenced by the searing contemporary difficulty that centers on engaging Earth, which we glibly term the "ecological crisis," the contemporary psyche is at odds with matter in some way or another. Prufrock offers a detailed glimpse into this modern horror.

For Eliot, as the whole of his poetic project will show again and again in other poems that are as brightly fragmentary and allusive as "The Love Song of J. Alfred Prufrock," connection is essential to love. To love is to connect, and when love as connection fails (whether on the levels of life, others, oneself, history, society, a sexual mate, marriage, myth, religion, nature, and so forth) barren wastelands of non-love and insignificance arise. Fertility, prosperity, joy, elevation, wonderment, and so on, become impossible or distorted, and deserts of language, soul, mind, body, and Earth encroach and dominate one's experience of being. Perhaps the most straightforward "small scale" example of this is divorce: a crucial relationship disconnects, and a wasteland results for family and children especially. On larger scales, such wastelands of disconnection are known to humanity. Simple and age-old as this motif of disconnection and resulting wastelands appears, it is very much part of Eliot's complex poetic world.[2] In ecocritical terms, surely the vast wasteland resulting from human progress points at some form of disconnection between the human sense of meaning and the meaning of Earth.

Of course, our linguistic connections with concreteness are not completely rationally definable, but they are no less real as a result of that. Let us just say that it is worth examining whether Prufrock, he in need of rock solid proof of his concrete being, may be the victim of disconnection from concreteness and the concomitant inability to love. As the critic Christopher Ricks mentioned at the first T. S. Eliot International Summer School in 2009, one can well imagine a title such as "The *Tax Returns* of J. Alfred Prufrock," while "The *Love Song* of J. Alfred Prufrock" sounds improbable. One is not likely to fall in love with him, Ricks asserted, although he is "not necessarily a bad person"—which led to a burst of laughter in the audience.[3]

One cannot avoid the rude and itching question: what were we laughing at? Assuming for the moment that laughter results from self-recognition, I think that part of the reason was that one knows in general that Prufrock uncomfortably reflects our own awkward orientation in life and love. And the disorientation has to do with connections to matter: dislocation at the exact points in being where essential location or placement with one's concrete condition should occur. Let me therefore take a closer ecopoetic look at this strangely compelling poem, beginning with the realization that the word "matter" appears with striking effect on two occasions in this text. One of its meanings is the notion of a problem: "the matter" as found in questions such as "what is the matter, what is the source of your dis-ease?" The poem never succumbs to a mere definition of this matter, preferring to keep it afloat in passages here and there, hence making it all the more intriguing and informative:

> And would it have been worth it, after all,
> After the cups, the marmalade, the tea,
> Among the porcelain, among some talk of you and me,

> Would it have been worth while,
> To have bitten off the matter with a smile,
> To have squeezed the universe into a ball
> To roll it towards some overwhelming question[4]

This passage offers a glimpse into how un-dramatic this "dramatic" monologue can be. Prufrock sighs with the despair of ennui and static uncertainty, but the very sigh seems false, and the very awareness of the falseness offers no redemption from a secondhand view of his lifetime on the planet. The problem, the "matter," cannot be bitten off with a smile (line 5). Plainly it cannot be overcome or solved. He can neither incorporate nor digest, embody, or integrate the matter of his material existence. Even when he bites into marmalade with tea (line 2) he fails to link up with life. Even when he indulges in some prospective sexual "talk of you and me" (line 3) he knows in advance that no real union is possible. Even if he were to possess the imaginative or scientific strength to squeeze the universe into a ball (line 6) it would not have changed his life into meaningfulness.

This is so unlike the truly marvelous Andrew Marvell poem to which the image alludes! There the lover's urgency to roll abstractions into a ball has to do exactly with density and the felt weight and excited, playful, bright anticipation of connection and consummation.[5] There the erotic metaphor finds poetic embodiment. In the case of Prufrock it merely finds the compelling isolation of a sort of pure "languageness." He feels that he has been set free by his modern linguistic sensibility veritably to roll one "piece" of language toward another "piece" of language. The misplaced Marvellian metaphor is rolled toward a question never asked; just ponder the prospect of this for a moment! Though he appears to be so safe in his house of signs—for it is a world of signs he inhabits—he therefore ends up in very thin semiotic ethers.

By creating the tension of this difference between poetic embodiment and bland "metaphoricity" precisely in terms of the allusion, Eliot, who is not Prufrock, brilliantly delineates a great and elusive difficulty of our ecocritical day. By rendering a kind of "pure" metaphor, one that appears to drift loose from its material moorings at last, he paradoxically shows that the pure or completely linguistic metaphor can never exist. The pureness that arises as a result of its near-complete dislocation from matter, concomitant with pointing at matter's absence, serves simply to heighten the awareness exactly of matter. Everywhere the concrete referent seems to have been dodged by our bright protagonist. But this merely serves to make his awareness of that from which he wishes to escape at all costs—the matter—all the more conspicuous.

Perhaps the sheer language-like nature of this ethereal Prufrockian maneuver is more striking to a modern or postmodernist audience than it should be. But in a world such as ours, in which signs seem to have taken over from concrete nature,[6] the maneuver should be examined as closely as possible. In any event, the "overwhelming question" introduced with considerable airs at the poem's beginning[7] at one stage actually plops wonderfully semiotically, wonderfully concretely, down on poor Prufrock's plate—although he (or the poem) has still not given us the semantic content of that question, of course:

> There will be time to murder and create,
> And time for all the works and days of hands
> That lift and drop a question on your plate[8]

Again the metaphor approaches its pureness. Any concrete rendering of the last line in this passage would go along with the expectation that something more tangible gets dropped on a plate: a thick, juicy steak, perhaps, or a delicately tossed salad. The linguistic space there is usually reserved for something tangible and edible: "lift and drop a [. . .] on your plate"—anything—an egg, a bunch of noodles, even cakes and ices—but not a semicolon or a question. On the other hand, assuming for the moment that the implied plate is purely figurative, one follows the metaphor. Some kind of trouble (question) ends up within one's domain of responsibility and digestion (plate). But the metaphor so particularly does not resonate with any conceivable situation. The image strikes one as deliberately "symbolist" in Eliot's inherited French poetic sense. It somehow remains excessively metaphorical, denying the link between language and matter's actual materiality just a crucial fraction too much, as if the relations between linguistic "things" speak purely for themselves, without any reference to any concreteness whatsoever. The shadow of the metaphor's material root—something edible, if not edifying—lingers in the excesses of the metaphor's "purely" semiotic aspect.

This approaching of a situation of pure semiotics again increases the awareness of matter in its various senses, certainly also of concrete experience in a dynamically physical Cosmos. These pure metaphors and "bits" of language therefore point acutely into their own impossibility, and they commit the pointing at the moment of their becoming-possible in the semiotic sphere. We should infer that total escape from concreteness is that which is not linguistically possible. We have here the opposite of the loosely "deconstructive" notion that Earth cannot escape text, for even this assumption can be true only to the extent that text can never escape Earth. Even the remotest Prufrockian sign has to unveil the primacy of an unfathomable physical being. An analogy is this: If one adopts an ultimate ironic position, proclaiming "Earth does not exist," the irony gathers its meaning only to the extent that it does exist. Similarly, Prufrock's "inhabitation" of severely reduced, uncannily overwhelming language is the result of a severe disconnection from earthly being, thus highlighting the importance of earthly being on the level of the reader, if not for Prufrock himself "within" his disconnected world.

And so the deprived Prufrock swims in his solipsistic soup consisting of disconnecting language objects. Throughout the poem, a plethora of severed objects imprint their isolated selves on the reader's sensibility: ices, butt-ends, a necktie, skirts, eyes, novels, hair parted behind, a head brought in upon a platter, an unspecified room somewhere, Michelangelo, downy arms, and so forth. The downy arms have no body attached to them. Michelangelo drifts into conversation and out of it again for reasons that are not entirely obvious or grounded in the poem's erected spatiality—he is a gamma ray beamed into Prufrock's world with little more context than Prufrock's thought. Ultimately, we have the image of a life measured away piece by piece in those famous coffee spoons:

> For I have known them all already, known them all—
> Have known the evenings, mornings, afternoons,
> I have measured out my life with coffee spoons[9]

In one sense Prufrock's world therefore consists of what appears to be a collection of very discreet objects, including time objects. It is an "objectified" world. In another sense, the inverse condition holds sway. Since the space in which all this occurs is only a semiotic one—Prufrock's language dominated mind—it does not involve an objective reality with its sometimes irreversible patterns in time. Again, where there might have been consumed meat or vegetables, there has remained only a hopelessly undetermined question. Or: thin Prufrock's soul to which he is the mere witness lives in quiet, bored, and meaningless desperation outside material concerns, while questions have become as tangible as lettuces. All he has left to digest are ideas, severed linguistic objects, thoughts, and a question without stated content.

But being a linguistic consumer to such a degree has serious implications for him. His sense that he has known all already, that he has incorporated everything to the point of world-weariness, at bottom threatens to consume the last crumb of significant experience that would have been available to him. In fact, a horrid switch is implied in the other passage in which the poem mentions matter:

> Should I, after tea and cakes and ices,
> Have the strength to force the moment to its crisis?
> But though I have wept and fasted, wept and prayed,
> Though I have seen my head (grown slightly bald) brought in upon a platter,
> I am no prophet—and here's no great matter[10]

We find vital clues here about Prufrock's matter, the matter with him. His dislocation from deep spiritual meaning has brought about a drastic dissociation from the meaning of material existence. "I am no prophet—and here's no great matter" (line 5) carries this subtle implication in terms of the poem and Eliot's project overall. As a result he has turned into a consumer to the extent that he has only himself left to consume. His own head is brought in to him on a platter for consumption.[11] Apparently so sophisticated and sensitive, Prufrock turns out to be an all-consuming barbarian. He is the very prototype of the bored postmodern consumer of delicacies who turns into the auto-cannibal created, among other things, by his ennui. In its turn the ennui stems from the fact that the material world has turned into "mere" matter, consisting of materials used and wasted without the sincerity of hunger, urgency, or profound meaning. One has mere pieces of things or objects ultimately drifting disengaged in one's thought, and even though he appears to recognize the horrible self-communion that this entails, he still cannot see beyond his own thoughts about it. In Jewel Spears Brooker's words, matter in the poem

> is a troublesome topic, an overwhelming question, substance that occupies space and can be served on a platter, something like toast or a communion wafer or the head of John the Baptist or the head of Prufrock. And "matter" is "mater" or mother, the great Ur-Womb, the original that both generated and is the universe.[12]

On three interrelated material levels, then, Prufrock experiences trouble: that of "matter" as a problem, that of disconnection with *Mater*, and the resultant problem that matter turns into pointless "stuff" to be gathered, discarded, even eaten—but never enjoyed; up to the point at which his own head is brought in upon a solipsistic platter. For him the trouble begins, therefore, when what used to be saturated with symbolic, numinous, or spiritually significant kinship between self and the ur-Womb of Cosmos in Europe's past turns into mere "connections," mere *relations* in the most epistemological sense, among his perceptions of existence. Depth of the great mother turns into the shallowness of "material linguistic objects."

The beginnings of these material troubles crop up already in Eliot's simpler poem "Preludes" (1917). Indeed, the troubles will creatively plague the poet throughout his oeuvre. In "Preludes," the pronouns do not make sense. They dislocate the poem by displacing the reader's usual deictic expectations. We read of cityscapes and people, and more intimately of a certain "you," a "he," and an "I"[13] without certainty about what their antecedents are—the personas they are meant to refer to remain unclear in the final interpretation. How they are to be related, and the relations between them, is therefore of equal uncertainty. Relation, linkage, connection as such becomes the poem's problem. And yet, in a faintly Romantic way, which at once also shows a breach with the Romantic ideal of complete harmony with nature, at its conclusion the poem does make clear where this problem arises, in ways reminiscent of Prufrock's disconnected love song:

> His soul stretched tight across the skies
> That fade behind a city block,

> Or trampled by insistent feet
> At four and five and six o'clock;
> And short square fingers stuffing pipes,
> And evening newspapers, and eyes
> Assured of certain certainties,
> The conscience of a blackened street
> Impatient to assume the world.
>
> I am moved by fancies that are curled
> Around these images, and cling:
> The notion of some infinitely gentle
> Infinitely suffering thing.
>
> Wipe your hands across your mouth, and laugh;
> The worlds revolve like ancient women
> Gathering fuel in vacant lots.[14]

The soul in this modern city can barely retain its relationship with sky (line 1). It is as if the thinnest of glues was holding it artificially there—a striking description of urban tension. Perhaps this stretched soul is the infinitely gentle and suffering thing of the lines further down, or perhaps it is the very universe suffering, or modern humanity, or a deity of some kind. But the certainties are no longer at all sure, to the extent that the speaker can no longer find a place in Cosmos. In a modern city like the one here described, agency therefore belongs as much to the street as to the persons who are aware of it (line 9). Disturbingly, it enjoys an impatience of its own to which one had better oblige as one hour slides into the next, apparently purely on the basis of an arbitrary number that labels the given moment (line 4). The best one can do if you were a persona in this poem is to find some form of clinging to this turning world, knowing well that it and all the worlds—including planets and thoughts—have been depleted of their vibrancy (penultimate and final stanzas).

The "ancient" (final stanza, line 2) way of life, importantly maternal or female according to its image in the poem, concomitant with its significant and broadly poetic function of orienting one in the world, has nowhere to go. It has to gather bits and pieces of warmth and sustenance in deserted spaces. It is as if Cosmos itself has slowed down, lethargic in its desertedness, now that humanity has lost its full, energy-giving, symbolic, and earthly union with it. For, humanity has suppressed its reciprocal projection to and from the worlds, and no doubt all of this has involved considerable modern gain in the movement away from superstition, but it has equally involved an immense loss of meaning, particularly in terms of active and ongoing emplacement, including the loss of a sense of vibrant orientation and meaningfulness in one's cosmological and local dwelling.

This kind of trouble further entails that one such as Prufrock "enjoys" at once a vast sense of expansion and contraction. His subject has swollen to the extent of devouring Cosmos on the whole, including himself, while it has shrunk to a near absolute closure that shrinks away in the process of closing down-and-away from a sincere sense of actual cosmological participation. Also in this respect he presents a remarkable foreboding of the ecological crisis. Never before has there been such emphasis on subjecthood as in our day and age, and never before have we been so far removed from significant linkages with nature. This is clear from our treatment of Earth and animals in particular, which would have seemed monstrous to previous generations, as Jacques Derrida shows in the whole of his 2002 essay "The Animal That Therefore I Am (More to Follow)."

These levels of disorientation—not simply when it comes to deeper meanings of participating in (one's) natural being, but also when it comes to the apparently mundane questions centering on how to go about living in nature—are not easy. They probably are the reason why Prufrock has to "buy time" and even "infinity" by living within the endlessly differentiating walls of solipsism. The walls of a fully idiolectic ego, so new a thing under the cultural sun when it appeared in this poem early in the twentieth century.

In "Preludes," then, a certain "he" finds his soul stretched tight against the sky, as we have seen; for Prufrock, again according to an impossibly linguistic metaphor, the "evening is spread out against the sky / Like a patient etherized upon a table."[15] And critics say this is the metaphor with which modern poetry begins, but it has not been mentioned that Prufrock's sky is sick, because ironic imagery finally threatens to take the place of sky. Only a slight, superficial sense of understanding, of standing under and within the atmosphere, has remained. The slender surface of this understanding is uncanny. It is at once too expansive and too reductive, so that one has little or no control over it, even though it continues to appear that one's control is idiolectically very nearly omnipotent. In terms of that all-encompassing omnipotence, the matter is therefore intensely ironically "cosmological" in scope. In this respect, one of the few clear progressions in the poem shows a dramatic reduction from the question "Do I dare / Disturb the universe" to "Do I dare to eat a peach?"[16] The verbs in these formally duplicated expressions sit in equivalent positions: in the world according to Prufrock, simply biting into a peach is tantamount to disturbing not only this or that, but the entire universe. Even though he appears in this manner to have squeezed the universe into a peach-shaped ball after all, the verbal equivalence shows two further and rather less pleasing, interrelated meanings. He has been reduced to the embroidered shyness and somewhat apprehensive contemplation of wondering about whether he does indeed dare to bite into a peach, instead of actually finding the expansiveness of universal significance. Simultaneously, the connections with and within the physical *Mater*, which he persistently invokes by denying it, take their revenge, since even the "mere" act of biting into a peach registers as a disturbance of the responsive universe, while there is a real sense that this fills Prufrock with considerable fear of some sort of retribution, rejection, overwhelming question, or limitation inherent to his concrete moment in history.

He approaches here the feeling that all participatory taking from Cosmos is dangerous, reminiscent of the foremost Afrikaans poet Ernst van Heerden's excellent poem in which a person walking in the countryside topples over a rock, accidentally killing a lizard. This sets off a cosmological chain reaction that reaches all the way down to the dinosaurs, and Cosmos grumbles grumpily and threateningly in answer to the loss of one of its delicately created creatures.[17] Prufrock's fear of interfering with Cosmos, however, lacks the instinctive depth that the speaker of this lizard poem experiences. His fear is a kind of endless sensitivity, a neurosis.

Prufrock's daring and disturbing peach-biting further alludes (deliberately ridiculously) to Genesis and the fall of humanity when he and she eat of the fruit of knowledge—however, from this angle it becomes apparent that Prufrock's greatest sin is *not* to bite into that fruit, thus cancelling the very prospect of good, evil, and moral existence. All of this appears to presuppose his version of the much-discussed first law of ecology, that everything is connected to everything else. It seems that even his most organically normal little "aggressive" deeds (such as eating) will reverberate through the life web and, perhaps in the ludicrous hope that he will somehow avoid (his very) life itself, he prefers not to bite, but instead to feel superficially bad about the prospect, continuing his sensitive incarceration in a world of signs that appears to be only too willing to come to his salvation around every possible corner. In this sense he is a prototype perhaps of what we now term "political correctness," opting for words as a barrier against real atrocities.

His sensitivity therefore is an inevitable self-delusion. His words are restricted and knotted in by the fact that their only relation to any materiality is that of their own relatively immaterial materiality. He in fact presents a persona so scared of the nihilism induced by the "materialism" into which he has been born that he must perpetuate "meaning" at all costs in order to feel safe, that is, meticulously and cautiously erecting a sign-buffer between himself and actual participation in life. But, in uncanny manner once more, the safer he feels, the more slippery things get, because his existence cannot find any ground. The addition of each sign keeps his dilemma at bay, while it simultaneously adds to it, postponing the rock solid proof and connection that he seeks. Ironically, it is the very objectivity, the scientific nature of that materialism, which keeps the proof of engagement away, as a passage in the poem that one may label "Prufrock's entomology" reveals:

> And I have known the eyes already, known them all—
> The eyes that fix you in a formulated phrase,
> And when I am formulated, sprawling on a pin,
> When I am pinned and wriggling on the wall,
> Then how should I begin
> To spit out all the butt-ends of my days and ways?
> And how should I presume?[18]

The all-knowing eyes that pin him down suggest entomological practice, which works with formulae and pinning of insects. Only now *everyone* seems to be entomological: people share the same scientific gaze. And this gaze reduces individuals to specimens. It treats everyone with equal sameness. In a sense, persons are discreet collections of bits and pieces of matter arranged in recognizable and observed patterns, and little more. For Prufrock, everybody knows that we are always already aware of our scientific "essence." Incidentally, now, nearly a century after the poem's publication, scientists have proven that the material value of our scientific or objective or merely material "essence" amounts to disappointingly little. As Saul Bellow indicates with brutally ironic humor in his novel *Ravelstein*, contemporary science has calculated that the mineral stuff of which an individual human body consists is worth about sixty-two American cents.[19] So how should one presume?—one may ask even more pertinently with Prufrock today. Simultaneously, though, he makes the error of believing that this is meaning. The entomological imagery shows that he himself suffers from the projections that cause his pain. He has known "the eyes" already, known them all (line 1). But the knowing consists of viewing things—even eyes—in the most isolated, fragmentary, incisive, and freezing "scientific" way. The eyes, frighteningly, are objects.

The matter of belief enters the fray again in this instance of the poem. The entomological image is a parody of crucifixion. He wriggles against the wall, pinned down there by formula-obsessed and therefore unbelieving eyes. (Incidentally, as the image dissolves from entomology into crucifixion, it moves away from actual entomological practice in which insects are not pinned alive onto walls.) The scientific angle or aspect of the (entomological) view disqualifies the depth of meaning that used to be associated with crucifixion. The loss of both religion and a deep, collective poetic sense leads again to self-denial, excruciating self-absorbance, as in the mentioned case of Prufrock's cannibalism, but this time in terms of mutual self-crucifixion. In this new nature dominated by human "nature," concrete communion simply is no longer possible, as far as he can see. Is the supposedly excruciating pain that he feels therefore actual, or merely a further instance of the emaciating solipsistic soup that fills his Cosmos into its anemic corners? The poem keeps one wondering about this.

One infers that Prufrock anticipates deconstruction in its strategically logical sense, since he, like it, may be entirely objective, entirely subjective, not objective at all, and not fully subjective either.[20] These recognitions of course center on his peculiar materialism. But this means that Prufrock suffers from two equally binding sets of one-sidedness. He is merely subjective, and equally merely objective—and neither of these positions is healthy. What he lacks in this way causes his dis-ease and disorientation: there is little or no unity and dynamic interaction between his inner (subjective) world and the outer (objective) one. He is the victim of a doubly complicated cultural monolithics induced by the loss of subjective-objective integrity. As demonstrated, on the cosmological level this is the consequence of the disintegration of culture-nature connection. Perhaps surprisingly, he is therefore at once too materialistic and not very materialistic in any full sense. This peculiar problematic in large part gives the poem its disturbing glow.

Speaking of culture-nature unity: what about sex in this poem? Is it not the opium of those progressive masses whose lifestyle and world view happen to be at a considerable distance from natural contact—that little bit of nature, regularly visited and bulkily advertised, that has to serve as the sole remaining link with at least some sort of concrete and perhaps mystical union? Pitifully, to one such as Prufrock who is casually (or only apparently casually?) incapable of meaningful relationships, sex has turned into something to be kept at bay, leaving him not impotent, but unable to make a move in its unifying direction that would have revealed either his potency or his impotence:

> Would it have been worth while
> If one, settling a pillow or throwing off a shawl,
> And turning toward the window, should say:
>> 'That is not it at all,
>> That is not what I meant, at all.'[21]

He can therefore be thrown off by the merest anticipated whim, and he stalls at the exact moment that may have been a turning point. As he well knows, he is unable to act in such a way as to cause the turning point to turn, lacking the "strength to force the moment to its crisis,"[22] never mind through it. As the rest of the Prufrock poem further meticulously reveals, he happens to be a modern "Georgie Porgie, pudding and pie" who may consider partyish high-end Bostonian interest on careful occasion, while he will never be foolish enough to gamble on any real moment of sensually reaching out to an other. At this point in Eliot's project we are far removed from *The Waste Land* of 1922 in which "blood shaking" a heart and the "awful daring of a moment's surrender / Which an age of prudence can never retract" are redemptive factors in the context of a stylized and dry lifetime.[23] Another aspect of Prufrock's matter is therefore that he is so prudent as to be nobody's fool. Still, he senses that if only he could be foolish for once, risking comedy outside his caution, he might break out of his dilemma. He knows that he is

> Politic, cautious, meticulous;
> Full of high sentence, but a bit obtuse;
> At times, indeed, almost ridiculous—
> Almost, at times, the Fool.[24]

The well-timed placement in this passage of the word "almost" (lines 3 and 4) embodies the important bleak parts in his safe-guarding semiotic wall. They mark moments of "weakness" that very nearly allow escape into a world of participation in wholly concrete existence. If he could overcome his self-consuming self-"preservation" and high sentence to be the Fool, he would find humor, as well as the paradoxical wisdom associated with the stock figure in Elizabethan literature of the jester, advisor to the king, keeping the latter's feet solidly on the ground with earthly reminders of humility and a self-ironic sense of one's place in the larger scheme of things.

As in the cases of the words "Prufrock" and "matter," the word "Fool" enjoys meaning on more than one level in the poem. It gathers flickering suggestions related to the tropes of Christ and salvation, as well as the underground man out of step with society's rhythms. Were he to be the Fool for once, also in the (eluding) image of Jesus who is God become flesh at last, he could establish the comedy of concrete engagement. And as Fyodor Dostoyevsky has shown in unsurpassed manner throughout his work, in the modern world with its coercion of measurements the Fool has the ignorant courage to fall out of step with the often shallow and rigid rhythms of society.[25] He or she may therefore skip the beat of some of society's worst ailments, perhaps even finding a way back to original meaningfulness. Such a person "understands" in the particular sense of "standing under": knowing that there is much more to life and, in this case, Earth, than the normal and somewhat abstract pathways earmarked for a successful career. But Prufrock is unable to enter the divine earthly comedy. In this sense, we focus here on the angle in the oeuvre furthest away from the ending to *Four Quartets* in which all manner of things shall be well:[26] there, and in that case, exactly because one is a radical part of nature's changing timelessness in time.

With Prufrock we consequently end up soon enough in concerns central to ecocriticism, ranging from dislocation to materialism, meaning-and-nature dissociation, and waste in and of a lifetime—as well as the literally near universal consumption of those familiar coffee spoons in considerable stretches of the global village! And of course, only modern time makes a persona of this nature possible. As such he may cast intriguing light on the supposed postmodern condition with its huge tendency to proliferate and consume signs, known also as the linguistic turn, which patently begins in poems such as "The Love Song of J. Alfred Prufrock." But not the least of the problems here is that, as wise persons have indicated in many cultures and ages, thought or language is often considered to be "infinite," something that displaces the real presence of earthly engagement and the entry into utter meaningfulness, with the result that there are supposedly always more ideas to be had and toast and marmalade to be digested in the process of measuring one's life away within the apparent protection and "noise" of impenetrable layers of differentiation. The slippery slope of irony here is that we have supposed Earth to be unfathomable, while semiotics has nearly replaced even that position. For, there is now so much of it that any single person will be beleaguered by its sheer vastness. It is as if signs have become bottomless in the immensity of their production. Each coffee spoon of coffee therefore seems so different, while it is trapped in sameness.

Consider therefore one potential important difference between "The Love Song of J. Alfred Prufrock" and postmodernism (that is, literature after modernism): as far as this poem goes, the loss of connection with nature's real presence is tangible and painful, still a crucial dilemma, unlike the postmodern presumption that the loss either means little, or acts as an avenue into newly superficial ways of understanding things, continuing the feast of nihilisms. We therefore again approach the realization that sign-proliferation can be a form of neurosis, apparently providing pleasurable and profitable *compensation* for disconnection in the broadest sense, while one clings to the compensation, never taking responsibility for the problem of disconnection from matter. This loss emerges most strongly in the poem at a moment in which the extra-textual world becomes visible in its most poignant, felt, and straightforward line, near its conclusion, and with a stretch of blank space above it, and below, as if its placement on the page is an icon of its brittle sense of isolation: "I do not think that they will sing to me."[27]

Prufrock is speaking of the mermaids whom he has heard in the waves, "singing, each to each,"[28] but in all likelihood not to him. The tone of this sober little line, "I do not think that they will sing to me," also strikes one in the poem's overall context. It embodies the sum and *Gestalt* of the modern recognition that a radically shared awareness that used to hold that Earth and ocean were magical seems to have disappeared from our lives forever. A brittle and moving pathos carries or is carried by this line, and the pathos centers on the demise of full physical significance. That Eliot enjoys remarkable affinity for the ocean[29] perhaps adds to the poignancy here for the scholar of his poetry.

The mermaid image offers another important example of how Prufrock's dehumanization occurs in direct correlation with his inability to locate Earth's spiritual presence. Mermaids link with symbolic energies of kinship between humanity and Earth's oceanic spirit. Among other things, they are half human and half fish, seamlessly. They also have access to the spiritual and earthly kingdoms at once. In his way, Eliot here comes very close to William Wordsworth's sense in his sonnet "The world is too much with us, late and soon" that we need renewed identity with soil and water of the kind that our forebears enjoyed, seeing spirit in matter, and matter in spirit—in the case of that poem, among other pagan things, what used to be the knowing that waves were morphing gods such as Proteus.[30] Prufrock's sense of the mermaids marks a modern condition that finds itself one or two crucial steps further away from that kind of integrity. And those one or two crucial steps change the entire matter of one's relationship with the universe, as indicated. But what is to be done about this, if anything can be done at all?

Though neither Eliot[31] nor his contemporary scientist-artist Carl Gustav Jung,[32] to whom I will turn immediately, thinks that it would be wise to return to the noble savage in the popular manner that has become attached to Jean Jacques Rousseau, as indicated previously here with reference to Eliot, they do think that it is important for modern consciousness, with *its* undoubted gains, to find and establish renewed connective integrity with our ancient natural past, and nature in particular. Human inheritance, despite all latter-day appearances, does not exclude, neither genetically nor in terms of one's personal and the collective unconscious, those energies that we now think of as primitive. One's dreaming at night shows that all those primitive feelings are immediately alive in every individual human still; it is just that they frequently are suppressed or ignored by modern layers of being, unless one is fortunate to undergo the discipline of Jungian therapy or something similar. As Eliot advocates, these primitive feelings should be integrated into our modern sensibilities if we are to restore ecological health.[33] As his poetry shows, what one thinks of as sophisticated can be horribly barbaric exactly to the extent that it denies instinctual, primitive connectivity with Earth. In any event: it is not, as far as is known at this stage, that Jung directly influenced Eliot. It appears that their *Zeitgeist* and their sensitivity toward it compelled them to reach one or two related conclusions about humanity's modern materiality. One could say that the relative lack of direct influence between them makes these similarities more remarkable, not less.

This potential link between Eliot and Jung requires a brief cautionary detour. Jung is himself clear that his discipline of analytical psychology cannot be used simplistically to reduce works of art to materials for its consideration.[34] When I make use of the Prufrock poem here to illustrate certain psychological aspects of ecocritical concerns, which Jung's work happens to illuminate with fine precision, I therefore view the poem's first and last use to be the sheer presence of it as a remarkable poem. This I honor by citing from it, while carefully analyzing and describing its forms, and hence its poetic impact. Given this, consider that one of its important secondary uses established in this chapter is how it highlights the psychology of modern Earth engagement. It is here that Jung may come into the equation, as part of a broader conclusion to this chapter. "The psyche," he says,

> is the greatest of all cosmic wonders and the sine qua non of the world as an object. It is in the highest degree odd that Western man, with but very few—and ever fewer—exceptions, apparently pays so little regard to this fact. *Swamped by the knowledge of external objects, the subject of all knowledge has been temporarily eclipsed to the point of seeming non-existence* (emphasis added).[35]

For Jung the psyche is wonderful, mainly because it allows individual, wholly participatory, conscious reflection of nature's processes and seemingly ordinary realities.[36] To be sure, this is marvelous. I have experienced it in a special sense sometimes in the singing silence of the grasslands near my home, in looking at a bright jewel of moon above the dimly melodic line of a mountain along with my toddler son on my arm, or in getting out of my car to see the Milky Way set on the horizon roundabout midnight in the full clarity of an African semi-desert, the Karoo. But we see how one such as Prufrock is very far removed from such marveling. He is gnawingly aware of all kinds of things, but one consequence of this is indeed that he gets swamped by them in a "revenge of the objects,"[37] the latter of which Jung appears to have had anachronistic knowledge. Contradictorily, inflation of Prufrock's subject appears to be all-inclusive, once more, gliding with the greatest of ease through or among any set of objects, appearing to digest and incorporate them, while leaving Prufrock utterly, utterly starved. He is that rare thing, the first victim of infinite self-reflexive semiosis resulting from earthly severance—that is, a matchstick glutton. It is no wonder he confesses:

> I have seen the moment of my greatness flicker,
> And I have seen the eternal Footman hold my coat, and snicker,
> And in short, I was afraid[38]

To my mind, the crisp and slightly ridiculous sound in this context of those rhyming words "flicker" and "snicker" add a sickening note to his realization that his "greatness" is no greatness at all. And the reason, as indicated, is that he is no *Mater*-understanding prophet, although, to the reader, he paradoxically and probably is. What he needs is immersion in concrete being: the immediacy that comes with active participation such as Marie's journey on the sled in *The Waste Land*. Then his death might have made meaningful sense. And he kind of knows this:

> I should have been a pair of ragged claws
> Scuttling across the floors of silent seas[39]

That is, he should have been part of life's waters to the faultless degree that an oceanic creature is part of its aquatic element in and of Cosmos.

Disturbingly, a brief closer look at this image of immersion uncovers the fact that that which would have bound the claws together, the body, is missing. The claws scuttle impossibly on their own. Does this mean that Prufrock is part of his central self to such an extent that he can see only his claws as he scuttles, as may be the case for an actual sea crab or lobster inside itself? This does not appear to be so. Rather, it appears that even his innermost wish to be part of existence surfaces in an image that destroys its integrity. There is no body to keep things together in ontological immersion. What is more, imagination itself has been hollowed out or removed by lack of natural engagement. Such is the fate, according to "The Love Song of J. Alfred Prufrock," of those existing at a time that drastically denies matter any inherent spirit. One could say that this dilemma has disembodied the protagonist. His life enjoys no real presence. Prufrock therefore finds only the dismemberment of his lifetime, and cannot re-member the life-giving links with mermaids or myths symbolizing the human breathing with and within Earth. Instead of immersion and aquatic union, he finds only severed objects, as indicated. In later poems, the lack of water and immersion turns into Eliot's remarkable desertscapes to be discussed in the next chapter. Perhaps strangely, Jung seems to have known about the desertification that comes with loss of the vibrant sense of matter. He says that today

> we talk of "matter." We describe its physical properties. We conduct laboratory experiments to demonstrate some of its aspects. But the word "matter" remains a dry, inhuman, and purely intellectual concept, without any psychic significance for us. How different was the former image of matter—the Great Mother—that could encompass and express the profound emotional meaning of Great Mother. In the same way, what was the spirit is now identified with intellect and thus ceases to be the Father of All. It has degenerated to the limited ego-thoughts of man; the immense emotional energy expressed in the image of "our Father" vanishes into the sand of an intellectual desert.[40]

As I have shown, Prufrock is a striking poetic example of just this kind of degeneration into the "limited ego-thoughts of man," to such an extent that he is blinded by his limitless clinging to those limits, without the awareness that they in fact could be the avenues into his greater relationship with nature *since they are limits*, that is, since they are the very boundaries where culture potentially may meet nature. And the complete absence of a father figure in this poem is probably no accident. It is as if he has no instincts to guide him toward action. In Jung's words, to my mind again suitable in Prufrock's case: no one "has yet become a good surgeon by learning the textbooks by heart. Yet the danger that faces us today is that the whole of reality will be replaced by words. This accounts for that terrible lack of instinct in modern man."[41] Prufrock's inability to make a sexual move is merely the most superficial symptom of this neurosis that wants to replace reality with words. What Jung could not have foreseen entirely is the extent to which the postmodern era spanning roughly the latter quarter of the twentieth century would indulge in Prufrock's greatest problematic, his infinite semiotic shallowness, and the overt or covert belief in that shallowness as a philosophical "value." The whole affair has been threatening to turn into a collective linguistic neurosis.

We could therefore say that anachronistically, this poem adumbrates the two most important literary movements of the twentieth century's last quarter: postmodern infinite semiosis on the one hand, and ecocriticism on the other. What is highly useful and absorbing, is that the two problematics occur together in this one poem. For a moment at least, they present two sides of a single toxic matter: lack of contact with Earth gives rise to profound insecurity, and in its turn this gives rise to an infinite and slippery compensating "sound" of monotonously reassuring, supposedly infinite sign-proliferation. From this angle, ecocriticism is a response to postmodern non-connection with nature, and, as indicated, the recent advent of new materialism marks this in its way.

This recognition offers an excellent perspective on the current state of literary critical affairs. It seems at the moment as if ecocriticism wants to perpetuate, at least in some respects or instances, the infinite patterning that it inherits from poststructuralism.[42] While the creative playfulness and infinite potentials of thinking that go along with this are harmless and joyful enough—ensuring careers, among other things—the patterning may do well to remain skeptically, self-ironically aware of its disconnecting tendencies. And so Prufrock raises the critical question as to whether it can simply be assumed that theorizing and its proliferation of view-finders among readers is always a good idea or not. The remainder of the book will return to this complex issue from time to time, especially at its conclusion. Thus Eliot's project offers a spellbinding critique of the notion that we can go on discriminating (against) the unity of nature *ad nauseam*, into some infinity or flattening continuum of discreteness and banal, barbaric, or eternal difference. In Jung's words,

> Man's advance toward the Logos was a great achievement, but he must pay for it with a loss of instinct and loss of reality to the degree that he remains in primitive dependence on mere words.
>
> This rupture of the link with the unconscious and our submission to the tyranny of words have one great disadvantage: the conscious mind becomes more and more the victim of its own discriminating activity, the picture we have of the world gets broken into countless particulars, and the original feeling of unity, which we integrally connected with the unity of the unconscious psyche, is lost.[43]

In exact resonance with this, as demonstrated, Prufrock emerges in English poetry early in the twentieth century as a poetic embodiment of ecopoetic loss, in particular the loss of an original sense of wholeness with and within nature, a loss marked precisely by infinite digression into discriminations, or word-like objects that continue to cut experience off from existence. The mermaids will not sing to him, because his words have been stripped of that symbolic unity or integrity where the downward animal-energy and the upward human-energy (and their cross-stitching opposite energies), as well as the deep oceanic aspect and the dry terrestrial one, continue to meet. What Prufrock shows emphatically is that human energy cannot take proper shape without animal energy. The only alternative, which he is forced to inhabit due to the "materialism" that absorbs him, is the endless monotony and linearity—the infinite monotonous continuum—of his sign-production. But how does Eliot's reflecting of this Prufrockian mode of modern dislocation that he sees around him in his historical moment—such as the fragmentation for which he is both so famous and infamous, as well as his remarkable desertscapes—fit into the picture of the modern sign's uncanny inability to connect humanity and Earth? The next chapter seeks answers to these questions, in the knowledge that it has to do with the loss and rediscovery of location, that is, being in and of the great *Mater*.

NOTES

1. Hugh Kenner, *The Invisible Poet, T. S. Eliot* (London: Methuen, 1965), 3.
2. Jewel Spears Brooker, *Mastery and Escape: T. S. Eliot and the Dialectic of Modernism* (Amherst: University of Massachusetts Press, 1994), 247–251.
3. Christopher Ricks, "T. S. Eliot's *Othello*," morning lecture given at the First International T. S. Eliot Summer School.
4. T. S. Eliot, *Collected Poems 1909-1962* (New York: Harcourt Brace, 1991), 6.
5. Andrew Marvell, *The Complete Poems,* ed. Elizabeth Story Donno (London: Penguin, 2005), 51.
6. Fredric Jameson. *The Prison-house of Language: A Critical Account of Structuralism and Russian Formalism* (Princeton: Princeton University Press, 1972), ix.
7. Eliot, *Poems*, 3.
8. Eliot, *Poems*, 4.
9. Eliot, *Poems*, 4.
10. Eliot, *Poems*, 6.
11. Brooker, *Mastery and Escape*, 133.
12. Brooker, *Mastery and Escape*, 133.
13. Eliot, *Poems*, 14.
14. Eliot, *Poems*, 14.
15. Eliot, *Poems*, 3.
16. Eliot, *Poems*, 4, 7.
17. Ernst van Heerden, "Dood van die Akkedis" [Death of the Lizard], *Groot Verseboek* [Great Book of Poems], ed. André P. Brink (Cape Town: Tafelberg, 2008), 312.
18. Eliot, *Poems*, 5.
19. Saul Bellow, *Ravelstein* (New York: Penguin, 2001), 163.

20. *See* Dino R. Galetti, "Looking for a Logic in Derrida: Assessing Hurst's 'Plural Logic of Aporia.'" *Journal of Literary Studies/ Tydskrif vir Literatuurwetenskap* 26.3 (September 2010), 84.
21. Eliot, *Poems*, 7.
22. Eliot, *Poems*, 6.
23. Eliot, *The Waste Land*, 18.
24. Eliot, *Poems*, 7.
25. C. A. Bowers, *Critical Essays on Education, Modernity, and the Recovery of the Ecological Imperative* (New York: Teachers College Press, 1993), 47.
26. Eliot, *Poems*, 209.
27. Eliot, *Poems*, 7.
28. Eliot, *Poems*, 7.
29. Peter Ackroyd, *T. S. Eliot: A Life* (London: Hamish Hamilton, 1984), 22.
30. William Wordsworth, *Collected Poems* (London: Wordsworth Editions, 1995), 307.
31. *See* Eliot, *Prose*, 290–291.
32. Carl Gustav Jung, *The Earth has a Soul: C. G. Jung on Nature, Technology & Modern Life*, ed. Meredith Sabini (Berkeley: North Atlantic, 2008), 125, 199.
33. T. S. Eliot, *Selected Prose*, ed. Frank Kermode (London: Faber & Faber, 1980), 291.
34. Carl Gustav Jung, *Modern Man in Search of a Soul*, trans. W. S. Dell and Cary F. Baynes (London: Routledge, 2002), 157.
35. Jung, *Earth Soul*, 176.
36. Jung, *Earth Soul*, 83.
37. *See* Jean Baudrillard, *The Ecstacy of Communication*, trans. Bernard Schütze and Caroline Schütze, ed. Sylvére Lotringer (New York: Semiotext(e), 1988), 87, 92, 94.
38. Eliot, *Poems*, 6.
39. Eliot, *Poems*, 5.
40. Jung, *Earth Soul*, 85.
41. Jung, *Earth Soul*, 138.
42. *See* Serenella Iovino, "Stories from the Thick of Things: Introducing Material Ecocriticism," *ISLE: Interdisciplinary Studies in Literature and Environment* 19.3 (Summer 2012), 450, 451; Serpil Opperman, "A Lateral Continuum: Postmoderism and Ecocritical Materialism," *ISLE: Interdisciplinary Studies in Literature and Environment* 19.3 (Summer 2012), 460–470.
43. Jung, *Earth Soul*, 72.

Chapter Two

Dislocation

Dearth, Desert, and Global Warming

Prufrock's disconnection from Earth remains a hitherto neglected motif that runs throughout Eliot's poetic project. The poet's notion of the dissociation of feeling and thought[1] has received much attention, but in the same essay crops up his equally crucial notion of *dislocation*. The stem of this noun has to do with place, *locus*. As we have seen, Prufrock is dis-located. He enjoys no nourishing link with his earthly being. He suffers from a matter of matter. And part of the problem is how to place, emplace, or locate language once it has been severed from its earthly roots, of a sacred sensibility of Earth's real presence. For Eliot, his historical and social milieu therefore means that poets

> must be difficult. Our civilization comprehends great variety and complexity, and this variety and complexity, playing upon a refined sensibility, must produce various and complex results. The poet must become more and more comprehensive, more allusive, more indirect, in order to force, *to dislocate if necessary*, language into his meaning (emphasis added).[2]

Forced into extreme levels of indirectness by the complicated nature of his or her modern milieu, the poet must with difficulty (causing difficulty) and even with rebelliousness respond with necessary forcefulness to achieve meaning. The forcefulness dislocates language, dislodging it from its usual grammatical anchorage and poetic traditions, because everyday grammar and poetic traditions such as less fragmented poetic lines can no longer reflect the fractured ontology of ordinary experience. Fragmentation precisely reflects that ontology, even as the fragments retain skillful, unforgettable poetic form. In poems such as *The Waste Land* and "The Hollow Men" the results of this forceful linguistic dislocation are conspicuous. The poems teem with procedures of extreme fragmentation: dislocated, decontextualized, allusive bits and pieces of language. The problem of dislocation therefore finds its way into the very fibers of language. The poem embodies the problem of modern language, instead of merely treating the existential dilemmas that cause that problem.[3] But does the "great variety and complexity" of "our civilization" have anything to do with the matter of disconnection from Earth? We have seen that in Prufrock's case, it no doubt does. On a less sardonic or humorous scale, a scale that is more serious and larger in scope, it is to *The Waste Land* that one should turn to examine this question. For in this poem the sense of dislocating language reaches its most intense levels. The poem fragments language to the extreme. Careful reading shows that the conclusion of Section IV in the poem, "The Fire Sermon," may perhaps mark the lowest point of fragmentary despair in the oeuvre, rivaled only by similar moments in "The Hollow Men":

> 'On Margate sands.
> I can connect
> Nothing with nothing.
> The broken fingernails of dirty hands.
> My people humble people who expect
> Nothing.'
>   la la
>
> To Carthage then I came
> Burning burning burning burning
> O Lord Thou pluckest me out
> O Lord Thou pluckest
>
> burning[4]

The speaker cannot connect things, and the poet shows this in extremely disjointed language, language that is skeptical about its ability to do its work—though the said skepticism paradoxically enables the language to do its work of reflecting the fractious nature of modern experience. Even at this end of linguistic limits, Earth is not far away from Eliot's concern. To begin with, the passage refers directly to a place that he knows personally: a seaside resort at the Thames estuary in Margate (line 1).[5] This sense of place reverberates in the other lines. The most striking is the manner in which he renders the allusion to the Philomela legend in which she is raped by King Tereus in Ovid's *Metamorphoses*: the "broken fingernails of dirty hands" (line 4). As if from nowhere, the image beams into the field of significance with brutally concrete realism. The rhyming of "hands" with "sands" (line 1) further suggests her terrible ordeal of being pinned to the soil. The fragment viscerally embodies the disturbing knowledge that the raping of Philomela involves an alienated physical closeness to and psychological distance from Earth.

It is little wonder that the next fragment, equally beaming onto the page as if from nowhere, "la la" (line 7), alludes to the Thames daughters or nymphs, mystical figures from the pagan past who used to embody an utterly close reciprocity between human perception and the natural existence of the river. The fragment pitifully evokes a lost, sacred sense of Earth. Eliot takes it from Wagner's opera *Tristan und Isolde*,[6] with the consequence that the disconnection between pagan reverence for the Thames on the one hand and the fractured modern sense of it on the other simultaneously alludes to severance between male and female (Tristan and Isolde); severance symbolized by the very fragmentation that the fragment carries. Again, Eliot foreknows by some decades the major, common ecocritical insight that rape of women and rape of Earth diagnose the same stunted patriarchal cruelty.

King Tereus has indeed forfeited his authority, because he has used his power in the most inhuman way against the female world. According to the legend as presented originally in Ovid, the cycles of violence as a consequence of his rape spiral out of all control, to the point where each participant turns into a bird. Philomela turns into a nightingale and Tereus into a hoopoe.[7] Paradoxically, this "lower" animal-rank at last brings a metaphorical return to peace. The brutal violence comes to an end. However, Eliot's deliberately concrete fragment-image that alludes to the legend—broken fingernails, dirty hands—signals the considerably intense ironical recognition that no such escape into a more tranquil realm of existence appears to be possible in modern, fragmented time. The soothing link with nature seems to have gone amiss. As the poem suggests elsewhere, in the wasteland where the sun beats relentlessly on a heap of broken images, even the cricket brings no relief in the coolness of night-time.[8]

The little piece from Augustine's *Confessions*, "To Carthage then I came" (line 8) centers on that ultimate earthly and mystical connection, sex—to which Prufrock cannot respond, as indicated. To Carthage Augustine comes only to enter into a cauldron of unholy loves:[9] all kinds of sexual promiscuities, Manichean complications of body-soul divisions, and a soap-opera-like disillusionment. He burns with desire that cannot be fulfilled, a theme not unlike themes carried by the rock songs of our day. Hence the apparently idiotic fragment "Burning burning burning burning" (line 9) followed by utterly fragmentary images of the Lord plucking out the eye of desire (lines 10, 11) so that peace could arrive at last. One "final" and wholly isolated instance of the fragment-verb "burning" breaks down as the passage and the section in the poem conclude (line 12).

The implications are almost too serious to fathom when one considers the context to which the fragments allude, the Buddha's fire sermon. In it, he finally identifies the flames of desire (in the eye, in mind, in body, in feelings, in spirit) as the root cause of human suffering. Extinguishing desire brings not only open-ended peace, but complete, active, and open affirmation of one's coexistence with all that exists, as is commonly accepted about Buddhist belief. But what happens to this important recognition if, in modern urban existence, desire itself no longer truly occurs, but only automated sex as the rest of the poem reveals? The very *prospect* of calmness becomes impossible. There can be no true coexistence. In his way, Eliot is making a profound ecological point about the dis-admission of a resonant consciousness of coexistence, and coexistence surely is at the root of the meaning of the word "ecology."

Not even that intense verbal phrase—"to burn with sexual desire"—enjoys authenticity in modern time according to this fragmentary procedure. That is, not even evil, the evil of temptation, is possible any longer. The worlds of good and evil have dissipated, leaving humanity in doldrums between religious dispensations, doldrums in which, according to Eliot,[10] truly human behavior has become very nearly obsolete, since the moral carpet has been pulled from under current culture. Sex becomes material in the most boring sense. Even *this* vital connection with Earth has been dis-located, misplaced. Language, itself having lost some of its vital sexiness as a consequence, can at best reflect this loss in images reminiscent of broken fingernails in the unforgiving sand.

But it is not only the earthly setting that suffers from disconnection as reflected in dislocating language. Time suffers, too. Eliot's poetic city comprises not only a strange sense of fragmented space, but also a singular sense of suspended time with no link to timelessness. Time dislocated from any sense of eternity becomes pointless—just as little or no reverence for concrete being and coexistence on Earth means that matter turns into so much dormant, dull powder, which Eliot refers to when *The Waste Land* states: "I will show you fear in a handful of dust."[11] A nagging awareness, if not a similar fear, is reflected in the wealth of clock time images in Eliot's poetry. Though it has rightfully been said that modern poetry in English begins with his striking image of the sky stretched out like a patient etherized on a table in "The Love Song of J. Alfred Prufrock,"[12] as mentioned, it may as well begin with the poetic line reading (simply enough) "Six o'clock" in "Preludes":

> The winter evening settles down
> With smell of steaks in passageways.
> *Six o'clock.*
> The burnt-out ends of smoky days. (emphasis added)[13]

Drab as the scenery is, and melancholy and without prospect as the tone is, the images around that little fragment "Six o'clock" at least still echo the prosody of past poetry. Even beautiful, in fact, is the traditional four-beat in the first two lines to which line 4 returns. In accordance with the four-beat tradition, in line 3 one expects another four-beat, or a pentameter, or at least, and most likely, the balladic three-beat. The two-beat there is therefore strikingly out of prosodic step, it falls short of traditional aesthetic notions of poetry, and it closes with a finality of consonants that immaculately clinches the abrupt and finalistic—and immensely abstract—indication of the time of day. In other words, the line's brevity and its richness in "closing" (voiceless) consonants mime the absurd closure that comes from the lack of satisfactory time, and the threat to a meaningful lifetime. It is as if the consonants mime time bitten off by an invisible and somewhat industrial, cold, and precise "presence."

Maddening, of course, is the sheer lyricism and unforgettable exactness and skill of Eliot's poetic voice as he renders the fragment. This maddening quality of his poetry is no little part of his poetic appeal, especially in modern days. In any event, the fragment reading "Six o'clock" continues on a slightly larger scale in "Rhapsody on a Windy Night." Time fragments embody its main structuring principle. Most of the stanzas begin with one of these such as "Twelve o'clock" (the poem's first line) and "Four o'clock" (the second line of the last stanza).[14] It tells the "story" of a citizen walking to his flat or rented room in the deep of the night, and concludes:

> The lamp said,
> 'Four o'clock,
> Here is the number of the door.
> Memory!
> You have the key,
> The little lamp spreads a ring on the stair.
> Mount.
> The bed is open; the tooth-brush hangs on the wall,
> Put your shoes at the door, sleep, prepare for life.'
>
> The last twist of the knife.[15]

The knife is precisely that which has cut up the speaker's existence into meaningless fragments, and in the context of the poem overall, modern time is a knife that severs and isolates. The knife may well refer further to the speaker's analytical and perhaps paranoid memory that has been talking to him throughout his walk via the streetlamps and the fragmentary and chillingly precise measurements of clock-time. Memory has been reduced to a number on the door like thousands of other such numbers in the city. The key has been reduced to a literal replica of other keys. It has no symbolic meaning. For a moment the phrase "little lamp" holds the potential of something softer and more enlightening (as in the case of the Second Symphony by Eliot's contemporary composer, Gustav Mahler).[16] But even though it throws a circle, one is again struck by the absence of any symbolic extent of the image toward wholeness, or the stair as a metaphor of ascendancy and transcendence, sexually or spiritually.

The problem is that the stair is no more than a stair, that one mounts it for no apparent reason, and that the door has a number only on the most literal level. Similarly, brief numerical indications of time become iconic of no real time: lack of eternity, depth, freedom, and actual time to spend in a significant way. The clock and the streetlamps and the civilized mind—something terrifically rationalistic and mechanistic—cut life short. To speak with Prufrock again, one sees that existence is so sophisticated as to be not primitive, but barbaric in its denial of those who continue to suffer from semiotic hunger: the hunger for significance.

At least, this is the young Eliot's impression of the city, and he uses fragments as icons to mime and express it, thus very much succeeding in making his impression a felt, immediate, under-the-skin one to his reader. In other words, there is an iconic level of embodiment at work through the use of fragments. The fragments mime the concrete experience, paradoxically involving embodiment after all. Linguistic embodiment must stand in for the lack of *actual* embodiment, that is, a sense of being-alive within one's concrete surroundings and one's body. The fragments therefore hauntingly signify dis-location. Nothing is as disorienting to the speaker of the passage under examination than modern "orientation": the automated "finding" of one's abode, one's door, one's key, and one's promising but meaningless toothbrush.

These fragmentary procedures of dislocation also on the level of emplacement, I believe, are linked in a profound and perhaps mysterious way to the poet's employment of desertscapes. On reading Eliot again and again, it may well appear to one at some point that these remarkable desertscapes, which have not been discussed to the extent that they deserve, arise on the metaphorical plane of his poetry like a mirage from his fragmentary procedures briefly described above, that is, the enormous image of those desertscapes acts as a distinct, vivid, and disturbing icon of precisely the kind of isolation and dislocation that the fragments signal. Has there ever been a composer, in English or elsewhere, of such constant and unsettling desert images? And why are desert images so exceptionally conspicuous not only in his case but in major modern poetic discourse overall, for instance in the cases of Ezra Pound's earlier cantos in *Cantos* and W. B. Yeats's profound condensation of his era in "The Second Coming"? But first consider Eliot:

> Here is no water but only rock
> Rock and no water and the sandy road
> The road winding above among the mountains
> Which are mountains of rock without water
> If there were water we should stop and drink
> Amongst the rock one cannot stop or think

> Sweat is dry and feet are in the sand
> If there were only water amongst the rock
> Dead mountain mouth of carious teeth that cannot spit
> Here one can neither stand nor lie nor sit
> There is not even silence in the mountains
> But dry sterile thunder without rain
> There is not even solitude in the mountains
> But red sullen faces sneer and snarl
> From doors of mudcracked houses
>   If there were water
> And no rock
> If there were rock
> And also water
> A spring
> A pool among the rock
> If there were the sound of water only
> Not the cicada
> And dry grass singing
> But sound of water over a rock [17]

The verb "singing" in the penultimate line of this passage is just one of the intense ironies at work here. The passage overall embodies perhaps the most profound moment of chanting in modern verse. Such repetition and lyricism to signify such desertification and lack of completeness! The grass is singing with a kind of madness induced by one-sidedness. The opposite pairing of dryness and moisture, in mythical traditions frequently associated with maleness and femaleness, has turned out to be one-sided according to this image. If only, the passage chants: if only the opposite in the pair was available for the sake of wholeness, an escape from stasis into the dynamism of health, fertility, growth, and the meaningful combination of male-female opposites would come about.

But dryness and sunshine, the "male" aspect, has been forced onto existence to the extent of insanity; a compelling moment of Eliot's poetic critique of patriarchy. If one goes further to associate the said masculine "dryness" in mythical conception[18] with rationality, objectivity, or "reason," then we have in this image a veritable diagnosis and anachronistic prognosis of what we term "global warming"—the desertification of the Earth's habitable surface. Too much emphasis on the patriarchal forms of reason, as well as the progress that comes with it, the image says, confirms one-sidedness to such an extent that fertile soil disappears literally and spiritually. Reason becomes one-sided, it becomes strange—a form of "reason."

Today, it is becoming increasingly clear that Eliot and this image have been right all along, and continue to be so, as we see rain forest turning into desert, to name an obvious but no less disturbing example. As indicated, Eliot's prose clearly signals his concerns about soil erosion, and how myopic materialism in his time would lead to "dearth and desert" for future generations.[19] One infers that desertification is on Eliot's mind and in his unforgettable poetry long before it becomes a buzz word of global climate change. He reveals the inner metaphorical aspect of the outer, climatically concrete dilemma, in Prufrock as much as in fragments and desertscapes of *The Waste Land*. In fact, his poetry richly suggests that the outer dilemma of what we now term global warming with its soil erosion results from some sort of profound dislocation from the natural world within the inner human realm.

But could Eliot really have known, purely on the basis of this recognition, of the desertification to come? The inner as well as the outer: the desert within, reflecting itself increasingly unbearably in the concrete one without? How should one go about finding a causal or logical explanation for the exactness of his premonitions in this regard? Perhaps we should insist that poets enjoy extra antennae that enable them to sense the future to a slightly greater, but still telling, degree.[20] Or perhaps we should acknowledge, as Eliot does on more than one occasion, sometimes despite himself, nature's spirit: its meaningful energy, which moves one. If so—with this wager on Earth's enormous freedom to influence everything, including poetic thoughts—the fragments and desertscapes under scrutiny offer iconic and metaphorical premonitions of the increasing "dearth and desert" that follow on the persistent progressive "rationalization" of earthly destruction, rape, provocation, mutilation. As such the fragments and desertscapes will then combine to act as a warning from Earth, for Earth has long since found its voice in poetry, also via language-embodiment (images and sounds) and the unconscious.

I find no problem in reading a modern poem in this way—modern poetry has never shied away from religious depth.[21] I find myself shuddering in the face of the warning, especially when I look around me at an apparently diminishing, hurt, reeling Earth who may well "decide," in its way, to shake off a humanity that may collectively refuse to live along with its process. I think that this is part of what Eliot had in mind in 1939 when he warned that "the exhaustion of natural resources" and the concomitant "material progress is a progress for which succeeding generations may have to pay dearly."[22]

As the physicist and Gaia-theoretician James Lovelock indicates in a more pessimistic and urgent context, it appears that we (not the royal we, but those of us alive on the planet today) have neither the wisdom to live with Earth, nor the cleverness to manage it or outmaneuver the changes we induce in it. We do not even have the cleverness to predict the short term future of the weather much, and can at best make vague generalizations about climate change.[23] Surely under these circumstances healthy instinctive wisdom would say: Earth is immeasurably stronger, more beautiful, and nuanced than your individual or collective ego (center of consciousness), and it is your inclusion in its process that gives you your strength and refined shape. Do not therefore see yourself as outside, above, or against it, and carefully stop actions that continue to put it in defense against you, for if you continue, things will surely happen that will make Kali and Durga look mild.

This wiser materiality Eliot suggests already in the earlier parts of the previous century. And, at least in part or at some point, Earth suggests it "through" his poetry in terms of its (Earth's) agency. Around—and on a bodily level within—us, we begin dimly to perceive and warn one another about nature's destruction that goes hand in hand, according to Eliot, with poverty of the collective soul. Again, the consequence of desertification within is desertification without. One is therefore in fair agreement with the ecocritic Robert Pogue Harrison who writes in his 1993 book *Forests: The Shadow of Civilization* that modern poetry "at its best" is

> a kind of spiritual ecology. The wasteland grows within and without and with no essential distinction between them, so much so that we might now say that a poem like Eliot's *The Waste Land* is in some ways a harbinger of the greenhouse effect. Or better, we can say that the greenhouse effect, or desertification of habitat in general, is the true "objective correlative" of the poem.[24]

Without any apparent direct influence to explain the situation in causal terms, Ezra Pound and W. B. Yeats render their profound desertscapes more or less at the same time as Eliot does. It is possible that a more-than-human[25] collective agency works through these poets' individual egoic agencies to affect the collective human agency of their moment: the poem is able to cause culture-nature impact. Pound's *Cantos* sets out with a series of cantos demonstrating a modern hell of urban "sterility and decay"[26] similar to that of *The Waste Land*. A second series of cantos describes a post-war hell that leads to purgation.[27] These cantos express a searing desertscape quite comparable with Eliot's. For example, canto XVI begins with these lines:

> And before hell mouth; dry plain
>   and two mountains;
> On the one mountain, a running form,
>   and another
> In the turn of the hill; in hard steel
> The road like a slow screw's thread[28]

The image serves to "deromanticize war and revolution." In the process, it supplies a more "objective," modern perspective on landscape. The steel mountain and road like a "screw's thread" (final two lines) suggest the industrialism William Blake protests against.[29] There is something awfully metallic, harsh, and symmetrical about the landscape. It is as hard and symmetrical as metal, and there is the intriguing "doubleness" of two precise mountains and precisely two mountains.

What kind of gaze, stare, or seeing is operative in such harsh symmetry? Clearly, it is a manner of seeing that projects onto the landscape the perspective's entrenched steeliness, symmetry, aridity, and harshness, so that the *gaze* is itself hard, objective, objectifying (so to speak), and somewhat metallic and mechanistic. Nature solidifies under the scrutiny of this inflexible and isolating poetic manner of "seeing." An isolated Blake (the "running form" of line 3) runs in a desertscape of almost blindingly heliocentric, desertified outlines—but little flexibility, very little moisture, and only starkly antithetical moisture occurs when it is found (as happens to be the case further into this canto when it renders sudden aquatic images to which I return immediately).

It is therefore as if the difficulty warns that it is entrenching itself, or has been entrenching itself, irrevocably. Reflecting it (which is healthy) is also to continue to entertain the danger of projecting it. The eye begins to suffer that which it sees, and the landscape suffers that which the eye projects. This canto therefore formally and perceptibly illustrates the difficulty that it critiques. That is, it suffers from and further *entrenches* the dilemma of the difficulty of how to see the landscape with a steely modern eye.[30] This is the case even if this same canto subsequently and swiftly switches to the sudden awareness of the necessary fluidities that should complement the said desertscape, in order to encounter, still journeying, the stark, almost mechanically induced opposite of the desert's dearth:

> The plain, distance, and in fount-pools
>   the nymphs of that water
> rising, spreading their garlands,
>   weaving their water reeds with the boughs,
> In the quiet,
>   and now one man rose from this fountain
> and went off into the plain.[31]

This poignant poetic glimpse of pure aquatic bliss and a moment of tranquility stands in blatant contrast with the textual desert that precedes it. The powerful simplicity of each line and its condensed nature may be read as Chinese or Sino-English ideograms of a kind,[32] and they underscore the absence of moisture that characterizes the preceding arid mindscapes within this canto overall. Are the "dry" images in the desertscape of this canto, cited above, equally ideogrammatic? An accentuated image-per-line approach also marks its textual existence. Two mountains, a running Blake, and the corkscrew image "isolate" themselves in a way similar to (say) the reeds with boughs in the aquatic image above. And yet the desertified images reveal dissociation from nature in a "hardened," abstract manner. Given the general immersion of the Chinese ideogram in a cosmological and utterly interrelated perception of natural existence,[33] Pound's "arid ideograms" with their dislocating energy are peculiar, even impossible. They are modern icons, interferences from nature that proclaim a dangerous "realm" in which signs will be no more than Earth-dislocated entities. But perhaps the most striking single desertscape occurs in Yeats. It is worth considering his "The Second Coming" of 1920–1922 in its entirety with a view to its imagery of desertification:

> Turning and turning in the widening gyre
> The falcon cannot hear the falconer;
> Things fall apart; the centre cannot hold;
> Mere anarchy is loosed upon the world,
> The blood-dimmed tide is loosed, everywhere
> The ceremony of innocence is drowned;
> The best lack all conviction, while the worst
> Are full of passionate intensity.
>
> Surely some revelation is at hand;
> Surely the Second Coming is at hand.
> The Second Coming! Hardly are those words out
> When a vast image out of Spiritus Mundi
> Troubles my sight: *somewhere in sands of the desert*
> *A shape with lion body and the head of a man,*
> *A gaze blank and pitiless as the sun,*
> *Is moving its slow thighs, while all about it*
> *Reel shadows of the indignant desert birds.*
> The darkness drops again; but now I know
> That twenty centuries of stony sleep
> Were vexed to nightmare by a rocking cradle,
> And what rough beast, its hour come round at last,
> Slouches towards Bethlehem to be born? (emphasis added)[34]

Mythology associates the desert with a place of spiritual testing and awakening, for example in Christ's heroic journey, and this is part of the reason why the desertscape in this poem is so appalling and striking. In the absence of meaningfulness, the desert becomes a symbol not of spiritual growth, but of a pitiless democracy in which the same sun shines relentlessly on a people of "sameness," of monotonous and blunt, chimeric existence.[35] That the image has a human head and an animal body points at a disjunction between humanity and our animal aspect. There is only rationality and only sex, but no proper integration between them, for example. Prufrock's dilemma finds strange resonance here in "The Second Coming." Just as Prufrock is unable to hear the mermaids, the chimera in "The Second Coming" is one of human-animal disjunction.

It is somewhat hair-raising to think that Yeats works on these lines at the very same time in which Eliot's "stony rubbish" comes to him in the form of his desertscapes. "The Second Coming" is published in 1921, *The Waste Land* in 1922. Simultaneously, both Pound and Yeats are distinctly aware of fragmentation as part of their social milieu and their aesthetic procedure. Their work and thought are permeated by a fragmentary sensibility of a kin with Eliot's, even if, undoubtedly, they are highly individualistic artists, each of whom stylizes his work with fragments in a different way. In at least three major cases around 1910 and 1920, then, awareness of fragmentation, fragmentary icons, and desertified metaphors arise in globalizing English poetry. Of course one is free, as a result of the real advances made since superstitious days, to claim that this is "mere" coincidence. But is it?

Assume for a moment once more that these emerging desertscapes could be a kind of Earth-warning about climate change. It then follows that the human dislocation from Earth and its corollary thought-feeling and male-female dissociation presuppose their opposite conditions: human location on and in Earth as well as mindful association of thought, feeling, maleness, and femaleness. In other words, the poems suppose emplacement and inner integrity—an integrity of active emplacement in dwelling on Earth. Were it not for the actuality of these conditions, Earth would have nothing to warn us about, and there would be nothing to be skeptical about.

Eliot's extreme skepticism as embodied in his dislocating technique in the poems therefore dialectically calls upon the *affirmation* of location. Considering new materialism from this perspective, his poetry would indicate that skepticism about nature (and literature) can become one-sided if it remains merely, "purely," or excessively skeptical. With this recognition, we enter current ecocritical terrain of direct relevance to the burgeoning of new materialism, as indicated in the book's introduction. For in this burgeoning, the question comes to bear of whether ecocritical skepticism can go too far on both of its levels, the level of literature and the level of nature. In the *ISLE* volume on new materialism, Greg Garrard expresses concern that "ecocriticism may be at something of a crisis point," because of "the growing nature-skepticism in the field."[36] He fears that ecocriticism indulges too much in criticizing environmentalism, while this may lead to downplaying the political and ethical energies that are the *raison d'etre* of the field. His further concern is that in establishing more secure relations with biological sciences, new materialism may render redundant the vital "mystico-phenomenological" aspects of ecocritical engagement with literature.[37] In short, and strangely, the literary practice of ecocriticism may become reductive in a natural-scientific manner!

It is into this crisis point that Eliot's poetry has always already taken us, for, if only emptiness remains where meaningful connection with Earth once breathed, one turns into a kind of Prufrock wriggling on the pin of a reductive scientific outlook. However, the intense irony at the other end of this spectrum is that the linguistic turn, which responds to the reduction of meaningfulness by turning within (into the relational world of subjective signs) is equally reductive, for the reason that it complicates referentiality to the point of grossly and sometimes subtly denying the life-giving connections between signs and Earth. That is, the Prufrockian dilemma occurs again, this time because signs referring to signs somehow have to compensate for the loss of meaningfulness induced by scientific reductionism. The living connections between Earth and signs therefore become reduced twice—in two sets of separateness—as the humanistic sphere reacts to the scientific. Matter is mute, therefore signs are only signs. C. P. Snow's famous "two cultures" play themselves off in this newly refined split between matter as (scientific) "stuff" and signs as self-referring husks. In a very real sense, the counter of "infinite semiosis" to the reductionism of scientific materialism is Prufrock writ large, involving an immense desertscape of meaninglessness.

It is becoming rapidly clear that new materialism, if not ecocriticism, finds itself barely alive between these two reductionisms. That so (relatively) *much* ecocriticism does get published, is not the point. The crisis in the relationship between humans and Earth calls for this, and more. But there is an increasing and debilitating lack of instinctive affirmation to go along with ecocriticism's rightfully inherent skepticism. The disjunction, the dis-location of signs and nature reflects itself on more than one ecocritical front. There is the growing sense that apathy about nature parallels and potentially reinforces apathy about literature, and vice versa.[38] To be sure, environmentalist skepticism—even cynicism—about national parks, for instance, soon morphs into literary disgust, for instance in the insistent journalistic emphasis on secondary materials as being of greater interest than real works of art;[39] and I would be the first to acknowledge that modern literature, with its mixture of "high" and "low" (popular) elements, is part of the beginning of the problem.

What is really bothersome, however, is how literary discussion has come to the point where it is necessary to be petty in cynicism about big-hearted, profoundly impacting works such as (say) Henry David Thoreau's: blaming him in an entire article for not using the words "shit" and "piss," for instance,[40] as if anyone would publish a serious work containing those words in the nineteenth century. One gains the impression of teenagers feeling self-consciously forced to hammer at their fathers. More seriously, as has been indicated, the much-discussed ecocritic and new materialist Dana Phillips's thought has become increasingly caustic and immodest, despite its eloquence and vital illuminations, because it is one-sided, showing up the ineptitude of this or that poorly written text. When he comes to a good text, such as Thoreau's, he seems therefore able only to put him up and tear him down as his straw man, based at once on in-depth knowledge of this writer and the thinnest of pretences.[41] But surely the care that his own texts demonstrate in terms of their relative rhetorical aesthetics would point at the prospect of engaging openly with natural texts of masterful aesthetic impact.

Classics-bashing and/ or classics-ignoring and/ or persistent focus only on the secondary and trash will probably not take ecopoetics forward, and neither will parks-bashing or the notion that Earth may as well be hyperreal. It is easy to scorn that which has been built up and sustained with care, such as classical canonical literature, but will the act of scorning ever match the materials scorned? And, on a much larger scale, will the act of violating Earth ever match Earth? Are we not entertaining the dislocation of great literature at the risk of losing sight of the affirmation, freedom, and openness that it brings? Are we not mutilating Earth at the risk of losing freedom? I have in mind such apparently simple things as the fact that a great poem has the subtle power to open up a mind, sending it in new directions by one or two degrees, of which the ultimate consequence is immeasurable. I have in mind that Earth continues to produce a new day of which humanity has hardly begun to taste the fullness. After all, skeptics can be skeptical only because substance exists, even if substance must struggle to *define* itself in objective or left-brain terms of re-presented rational relations between thought-objects. In a sense, it is powerless to do so. Wholeness cannot *defend* itself rationally: it is that which IS. Rationality is much more astute at defending itself in its own terms. But can it function without empathy and other contexts larger than itself?[42]

In the case of Eliot, by way of a counterparadox, the indirectness that comes with dislocating language always already continues to suppose location: affirmation of living on Earth, and affirmation of alive literature and poetry that respond to this within their time. There are no cardboard boxes in the Thames, as indicated, only because they actually float down there. By momentarily refusing the Thames its modern existence, he underscores just how important that existence is. More direct forms of the affirmation of place certainly balance the said indirectness within his oeuvre overall. A world of uncovering Eliot's sense of location calls for examination.

NOTES

1. T. S. Eliot, *Selected Prose*, ed. Frank Kermode (London: Faber & Faber, 1980), 64–65.
2. Eliot, *Prose*, 65.
3. Michael Edwards, *Towards a Christian Poetics* (Michigan: Eerdmans, 1984), 109.
4. T. S. Eliot, *The Waste Land* (Norton Critical Edition), ed. Michael North (New York: W. W. Norton, 2001), 15.
5. *See* Michael North's note (number 2) in Eliot, *The Waste Land*, 15.
6. *See* Michael North's note (number 7) in Eliot, *The Waste Land*, 14.
7. Ovid, *Metamorphoses*, Gutenberg e-Text, trans. Henry Riley www.gutenberg.org/files/21765/21765-h/files/Met_IV-VII.html, retrieved 26 December 2013.
8. Eliot, *The Waste Land*, 5, 11.
9. Augustine, "From *Confessions*," in Eliot *The Waste Land*, 58.
10. Eliot, *Prose*, 236.
11. Eliot, *The Waste Land*, 6.
12. Eliot, *Poems*, 3.
13. Eliot, *Poems*, 13.
14. Eliot, *Poems*, 16, 18.
15. Eliot, *Poems*, 18.

16. Gustav Mahler, *Symphonie No. 2: Auferstehungs-Symphonie* [Resurrection Symphony], dir. Leonard Bernstein, New York Philharmonic, 1988.
17. Eliot, *The Waste Land*, 16.
18. J. C. Cooper, *An Illustrated Encyclopaedia of Traditional Symbols* (London: Thames & Hudson, 2013), 57, 109.
19. Eliot, *Prose*, 290.
20. C. A. Bowers, *Critical Essays on Education, Modernity, and the Recovery of the Ecological Imperative* (New York: Teachers College Press, 1993), 121.
21. Etienne Terblanche, *E. E. Cummings: Poetry and Ecology* (Amsterdam: Rodopi, 2012), 56.
22. Eliot, *Prose*, 290.
23. James Lovelock, *The Vanishing Face of Gaia: A Final Warning* (New York: Basic Books, 2009), 9, 10, 53.
24. Robert Pogue Harrison, *Forests: The Shadow of Civilization* (Chicago: University of Chicago Press, 1993), 149.
25. *See* David Abram, *The Spell of the Sensuous: Perception and Language in a More-Than-Human World* (New York: Vintage, 1997), 8.
26. Leon Surette, *The Birth of Modernism: Ezra Pound, T. S. Eliot, W. B. Yeats and the Occult* (Montreal: McGill-Queens University Press, 1994), 30.
27. Surette, *Birth of Modernism*, 33, 42.
28. Ezra Pound, *Cantos* (London: Faber & Faber, 1990), 68.
29. George Kearns, *Guide to Ezra Pound's Selected* Cantos (New Brunswick: Rutgers University Press, 1980), 70, 71.
30. Terblanche, *Cummings*, 217.
31. Pound, *Cantos*, 70.
32. Surette, *Birth of Modernism*, 24.
33. David Hinton, *Mountain Home: The Wilderness Poetry of Ancient China* (New York: New Directions, 2005), xiii; Ezra Pound, *ABC of Reading* (New York: New Directions, 1987), 19–23.
34. W. B. Yeats, *Yeats's Poetry, Drama, and Prose*, ed. James Pethica (New York: W. W. Norton, 2000), 76.
35. *See* Jewel Spears Brooker, *Mastery and Escape: T. S. Eliot and the Dialectic of Modernism* (Amherst: University of Massachusetts Press, 1994), 238.
36. Greg Garrard, "Nature Cures? Or How to Police Analogies of Personal and Ecological Health," *ISLE: Interdisciplinary Studies in Literature and Environment* 19.3 (Summer 2012), 497.
37. Garrard, "Nature Cures?" 510, 512.
38. Charles Bergman, "Nature Is the Story That We Live: Reading and Teaching 'The Ancient Mariner' in the Drake Passage," *ISLE: Interdisciplinary Studies in Literature and Environment* 19.4 (Autumn 2012), 674.
39. George Steiner, *Real Presences* (Chicago: University of Chicago Press, 1991), 7.
40. Dana Phillips, "'Slimy Beastly Life:' Thoreau on Food and Farming," *ISLE: Interdisciplinary Studies in Literature and Environment* 19.3 (Summer 2012), 536.
41. Terry Gifford, "Recent Critiques of Ecocriticism," *New Formations: Earthographies: Ecocriticism and Culture* 64 (Spring 2008), 16.
42. *See* Iain McGilchrist, *The Master and his Emissary: The Divided Brain and the Making of the Western World* (New Haven: Yale University Press, 2012), 177.

Chapter Three

Location

Mandalic Structure in The Waste Land

Somewhat hidden but profoundly important moments of locating signs in their earthly context occur in *The Waste Land*. The poem's title evokes the expectation that it will in some way or another entertain issues of place, of land. As we have seen, desertscapes are indeed central to its searing sense of dislocation, certainly also on the level of earthly life. One may assume that the next point of interest when it comes to land and soil in Eliot's work is delimited by *Four Quartets*. I will dwell on this poem, for the assumption is useful and truthful, but to my mind the slightly more exciting instance of affirmative location occurs already in *The Waste Land*, with the result that this poem forms a vital moment in the poet's development toward earthly acceptance in *Four Quartets*.

This recognition becomes apparent already, however, in the poem's procedures of dislocation. One may look again at the fragments that embody dislocation to see this. Each fragment is valuable as fragment. One thinks of Jewel Spears Brooker's instructive thought experiment. If a bomb were dropped on Bloomsbury with its British Museum and other vital cultural spaces, and one were to move around to pick up fragments from the disaster, each fragment would be of enormous value in itself, because it would offer a concrete link with the meaningful past.[1]

Similarly, each Sanskrit fragment is a concrete linguistic link with Europe's early, spiritually significant history, a history in which culture-nature balance and integrity were a greater part of religious and philosophical life, at least from the current perspective, than is the case in modern time. To be able to arrange these Sanskrit fragments into any kind of pattern at all—perhaps like putting together only part of an ancient vase from its chips, enabling a view of its overall shape—then adds considerable further significance to the fragments. And in Eliot, fragments always imply their participant transcendence into greater wholes within an overall sense of wholeness that acknowledges the absolute as inclusive of all experience.[2] For example, in the Prajapati story that predominates the final passages of *The Waste Land*, Eliot painstakingly arranges the fragments into a pattern consisting of the sound/syllable *Da*, followed by a stretch of blank space, a Sanskrit interpretation of the command, and an English gloss—all repeated thrice. In this pattern, I believe, resides the slightly hidden but important structure of affirming location, where concreteness and matter return to a sense of significant emplacement, there where the real presence of culture combines with the real presence of nature:

> Then spoke the thunder
> DA
> *Datta*: what have we given?
> My friend, blood shaking my heart
> The awful daring of a moment's surrender
> Which an age of prudence can never retract
> By this, and this only, we have existed
> Which is not to be found in our obituaries
> Or in memories draped by the beneficent spider
> Or under seals broken by the lean solicitor
> In our empty rooms
> DA
> *Dayadhvam*: I have heard the key
> Turn in the door and turn once only
> We think of the key, each in his prison
> Thinking of the key, each confirms a prison
> Only at nightfall, aethereal rumours
> Revive for a moment a broken Coriolanus
> DA
> *Damyata*: The boat responded
> Gaily, to the hand expert with sail and oar
> The sea was calm, your heart
> would have responded
> Gaily, when invited, beating obedient
> To controlling hands[3]

I wish to stress once more the *pattern* into which Eliot casts these lines, since its neglected formal arrangement points into earthly location. Each of the *Da*s above is marked by a long stretch of blank space (lines 2, 12, 19). These blank stretches steer a constant return to the syllable, with the result that it becomes the formal center of the passage, as depicted diagrammatically in figure 3.1.[4]

This is how, on the formal poetic level, Eliot is giving embodiment to the historical recognition of Sanskrit roots. If the usual way of perceiving history

DA

DA

DA

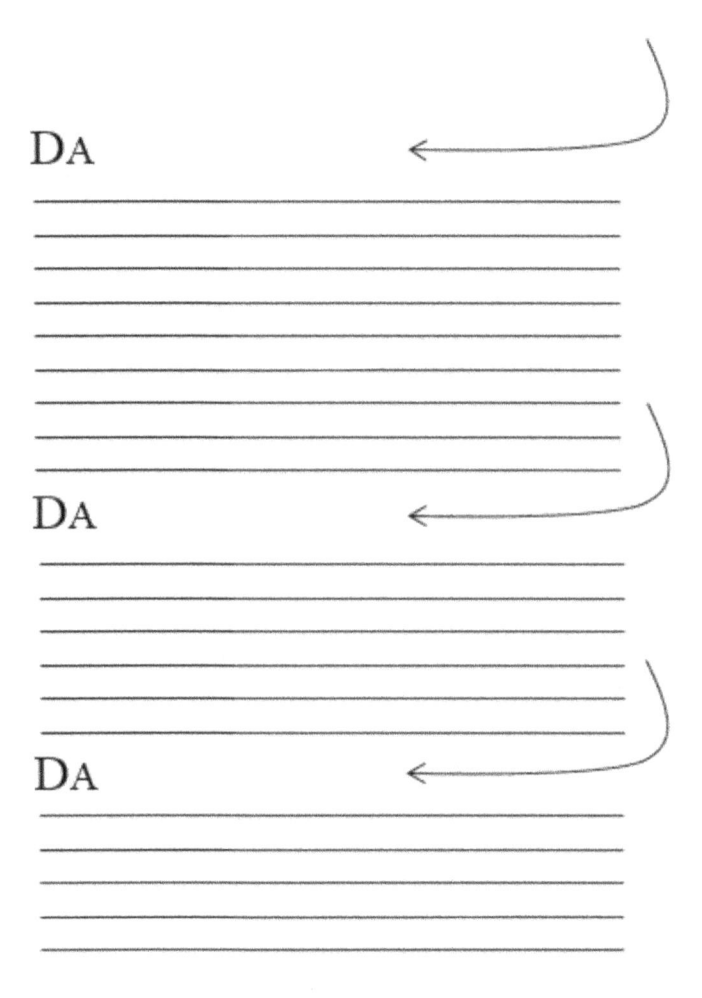

Figure 3.1. Sanskrit syllable at the center of its passage

takes the shape of linear progression from the past into the future, the poet disrupts it to show that, from the present into the past, there is the prospect of renewed recognition of cultural origins, including cycles that revolve around a significant center. It is little wonder once more that the delayed modern poet, Beat poet, and green writer of considerable impact, Gary Snyder, mentions in an interview that Eliot enjoys "the sense of roots":[5] and here we have its embodiment in his poetry. For, a structure that shows lines moving to a center is mandalic. Intriguing and informative mandalas have been recognized in *Four Quartets* by critics such as P. S. Sri and Northrop Frye,[6] but the Sanskrit mandalic structure in *The Waste Land* has not been discussed. Taking *Da* as the center of this particular mode of cyclical centering as presented in the figure 3.1, an ideal diagram of this structure may be presented as in figure 3.2.

This pattern suggests that the historical distance between Sanskrit and English implies their connectedness. And in this connectedness, Sanskrit is the historical, linguistic, and cultural root, as is commonly accepted. In the words of the Eliotian critic Michael Edwards, Sanskrit in the poem acts as a metaphor of "primitive, wise and single speech" that "reaches back to a pre-lapsarian condition, before the dispersal of languages."[7] The mandala concretizes the integrity at the root of language use. Mandalas furthermore are ancient and new symbols of cosmological centering. They convey emplacement: being at the center of (one's) being. They will often appear as if by themselves in situations of high stress, disruption, and despair, to return a sense of order and wholeness.[8] At the moment of the emergence of the mandalic pattern in *The Waste Land*, both Europe and Eliot were in the dire psychological situation of a detrimental, horribly fractured nature. They were trying to get to grips with and move through many wastelands, including the Great War and its aftermath. It could be said that under these personal and collective circumstances, mandalic structure arose in *The Waste Land* to compensate for the dire individual situation, and for the collective. By formally arranging the pattern into mandalic shape at the conclusion of this poem with its considerable collective impact, the poet has consciously and/

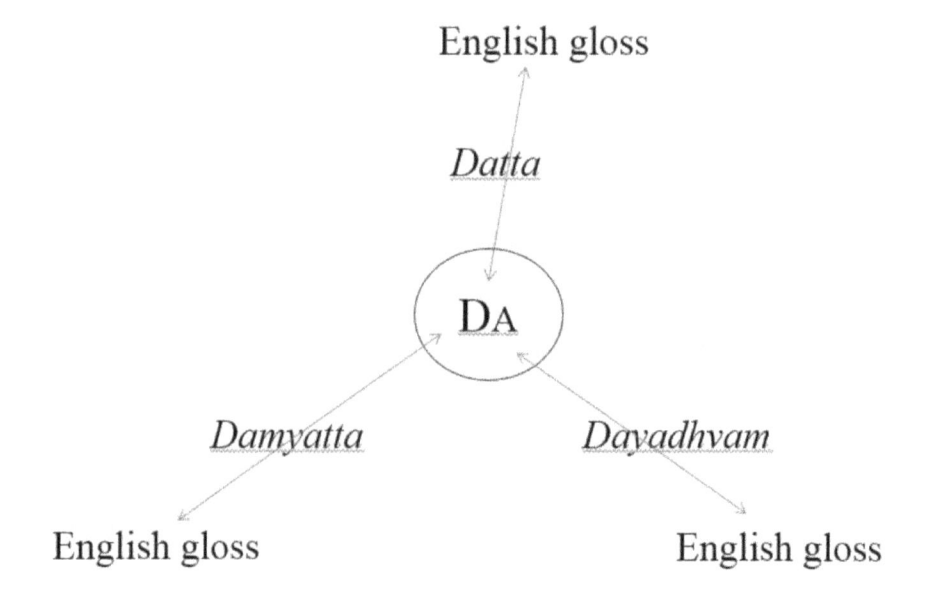

Figure 3.2. Sanskrit mandala in *The Waste Land*

or intuitively rendered a poetic form that dramatizes an emergent return to/ of wholeness.

But we have seen that *The Waste Land* has to do with Earth. It adumbrates global warming by pointing into the dearth and desert that follows upon individual and collective disconnection from the planet, within. Its drastic fragmentation and desertscapes reflect modern loss of meaningful concreteness, especially the instinctive knowledge that Earth is to be revered, that femaleness is to be actively respected, and so forth. Since the poem therefore anticipates what we now term global warming and the ecological crisis—since it in fact describes these with alarming poetic beauty—one may deduce that its mandalic pattern has an earthly center. And such is indeed the case. For instance, the syllable at its center, *Da*, is onomatopoeic in a special manner. It involves a charged sense of poetic embodiment. It is meant seamlessly to combine a natural event on the one hand and utter meaningfulness in the human realm on the other. It enjoys an attractive and impacting simplicity as it renders the noise of a loud clap of thunder. The miming of the macro-event of a peal of thunder on the relative micro-scale of pronouncing it in the mouth is very effective. Pressure builds up against teeth in the sound [d] and finds very open release in the sound [a], beautifully miming pressure building up in clouds to be released with a kind of maximum effect as the thunder claps.

On the level of culture, those who hear this *Da*! in the Prajapati story as found in the *Upanishads* instantly recognize that it carries important spiritual recognitions related to being on Earth. Prajapati is the thunder god. Thunder is a meaningful presence. The same immediate connection between natural sound and meaningfulness continues as each *Da* gets interpreted as a command. In these commands, onomatopoeia mimes the scattering of rumbling sounds that often follows upon a loud *Da*! of thunder: [data] (*Datta*), [dayadvam] (*Dayadhvam*), [damyata] (*Damyata*). The effect seems to be that though the sound of thunder is somehow "diluted" as it comes into the various spheres of interpretation, it does not lose the resounding of its original authority. What happens in nature echoes immediately in the world of the human soul. In short, Earth's elements and events have immediate spiritual, cultural significance. The emergence of mandalic patterning in the poem therefore marks a return to a center that is able to make spiritual, wise sense of earthly existence. This is what Eliot points into, in which—if one is willing—the poem participates, into which it *enters*. Viewed from this angle, the poem is an entrance: an entrance-ment—the poetic evocation of an originary experience in modern days.

The linguistic aspect also comes into its own as part of this mandalic motion. It should be impossible, given the corrosive nature of history, to juxtapose pieces of language as ancient as Sanskrit next to pieces of language as modern as Eliot's English. Things, especially linguistic things, just do not last this long, unlike animal fossils—though even the latter are extremely rare. That the linguistic "fossils" in this instance, the Sanskrit elements, can be understood today, adds to the wonder of the juxtaposition. The thought that so many generations have had to be sustained by thunder, rain, and spiritual perception in order for an Eliot to put the two languages next to one another, adds further to the wonder of it. That one of the languages is the modern offspring of the other completes the sense that something remarkably continuous is at the center of the Sanskrit mandala.

Somewhat contrary to this, it is true that the English glosses bring ambivalence and irony to bear on the Sanskrit commands. Yet, in typical fashion of Eliot's indirect method, they do not obliterate the original sense of those commands. As the ecocritic John Elder[9] points out, Eliot's sense of their meaning is not what we would ascribe to them today. The commands indicate active participation in the ongoing process of coexistence on Earth, rather than possession or narrow instruction. In this special Sanskrit sense, *Datta* should be translated as Give! It does not mean the handing down of an object from a superior to an inferior person, however. It means that one gives one's lifetime "back" to the life that one has received. One's life is woven into all life as a kind of ongoing gratitude for being alive. This would be one way to formulate its general Buddhist sense, which is a sense of vibrant coexistence and interconnectivity. Furthermore, the dominant image throughout the poem of a seed or corpse falling and dying in order to bring healing and fertility to society and the land finds its feather-light Buddhist resonance in *Datta*. One gives nothing less than one's entire life, as *Four Quartets* would make clear in commenting on *The Waste Land*. This is feather-light in the sense that one simply lives, accepting the gift of life, going ahead humorously to participate in it by way of actions as apparently ordinary as washing the dishes, carrying water, or walking.

Does the gloss refute this? To be sure, it is in ironic relation to it. One would not expect otherwise from modern life, and Eliot does not enforce the ancient sense of the command onto the modern English version that he endows it with. He does something more profound. He contrasts the ancient and the new, while he simultaneously shows the actual continuity between the two worlds. For instance, the sexual act depicted in the gloss to this command, Give!, does not have the kind of innocence one would expect from a truly spiritual moment (lines 4–7 in the passage above). The relation between Sanskrit command and English gloss is in this particular way ironic. On the other hand, at least this act is able to burst through the artificial glossing-over of a dry old lifetime on the planet: the kind of lifetime brought about by expected behaviors "rewarded" with a neat little obituary in the newspaper (lines 8–11 above). It is an act that confirms the prospect of real morality, since it places its actor in a world of actual (lived) good and evil and the necessary shaping toward moral maturity—as Eliot insists in a different context.[10] That is, the gloss goes beyond Prufrock, since an age of prudence can never retract the act.[11] In surrendering to life itself, its actuality, at least for a moment the speaker confirms that it is possible to Give! oneself to life, beyond modern constraints and expectations of "good" behavior. Eliot shatters the notion of such false, mechanistic "goodness" that would exist as if "outside" concrete life itself.

The second command in Eliot's sequence, *Dayadhvam*, should be translated as Sympathize! It distinctly does not mean passing around the tea as one looks down pitifully at someone who has been less fortunate than oneself. Its Buddhist and *Upanishad* meaning—for Buddhism is based on the Upanishads[12]—takes one back, rather, to an original meaning of the word. It resides in its stem, "sym": a companion in a walk, a fellow traveler. The word "sympathy" has root meanings such as co-incidence, the meaningful occurring-together of events, forms, energies: living together. "Sympathy" is to "feel (in) co-incidence with" another, and (in active, participatory humility) all others.[13] Again a profound consciousness of coexistence is the point, including the recognition that one cannot be alive outside coexistence. Coexistence makes one existence possible and actual. Now, the gloss to this command is a key moment in the poem; I return to it. Suffice to say for the purpose here that it is a brilliantly economical description of a problem that has occupied us anew in the twentieth century with its linguistic turn, the problem of language with all its refinements, relations, and spaces acting as a trap that persistently elides the real presence of meaningfulness. Language as an isolating phenomenon that excludes *communitas* with fellow beings, energies, elements, and in general the more-than-human world.

The final of the three commands, *Damyata*, could be translated as Control! In Buddhist terms, this means active control of one's desires, so that one's participation in life will be mindful of one's being along with the Being of all within the now-here-nowhere.[14] It is to be free from desire and compulsion, as Eliot phrases it in *Four Quartets*,[15] since one no longer needs to "control" anything, because one feels at one with life, having been freed from one's constant will toward being in command of the world with a view to satisfying one's instant desires. In this instance the gloss (final five lines of the passage above) very nearly offers a straightforward English version of the command. The speaker realizes that someone would have responded gaily to his controlling hands, like a yacht handled by a skilled operator, which Eliot certainly is, having sailed Cape Ann, as mentioned. He nonetheless does not pursue this path, controlling his desires for the sake of *not* "controlling" someone else for myopic "automated" sex, that is, in order to avoid the modern "English" action implied by the word.

The ironizing effect of the glosses can therefore not be used to argue that the Sanskrit elements are the pointless husks of past meanings in a current world of "infinite semiosis." On the contrary, they serve to highlight the importance of the Sanskrit roots for the conditions of modern existence, by virtue of that ironic contrast. The modern "explanations" of the Sanskrit elements are indubitably ironic, but the continuities-in-contrast with Sanskrit are serious. The mandalic patterning of these contents in fact underscores just how seriously one should take the ancient connectivity with nature that has managed to stay alive at the center of modern languages such as English. For modern culture from an ecocritical perspective, nothing is as sobering and healthy as an incorporating glimpse of its cultural roots.

It has been argued, though, that the poem as a whole makes of the Sanskrit pattern a mere whimper in response to life, a purely nihilistic "cop-out," in colloquial parlance. Critics such as F. R. Leavis and A. D. Moody in fact come very close to saying so themselves. Only the formality of their language prevents them from it. I will return to their take on the Sanskrit in *The Waste Land* when I discuss Edward Said's view of Eliot's orientalism in chapter 6 of this book. Nonetheless, the consideration as to whether the tone and structure of the poem as a whole is not simply too heavy with skepticism or nihilism for us to take the poem's mandalic affirmation of earthly existence at relative face value, is important enough. Many gifted readers of the poem have enjoyed this "closure" on their interpretation. It can and should not be wished away.

Yet the poem leaves entirely open the more affirmative reading made here. It resides in particular in the semantic elements *in their arrangement*, as I have been arguing: that is, their form, their manner of embodiment. The fact that thought and language change experientially when they become (into) poetry, is the key to this insight. In a sense, in other words, reading a poem is to perform it, guided by formal elements such as arrangement, contrast, and continuity. Part of performing it in this way—even in moments of individual reflection—is the recognition of affirmation in the poem. The mandalic structure set out above in this respect ties in with the related matters of what Eliot calls the "mythical method," as well as a kind of narrative structure toward the poem's conclusion. As he makes clear in his notes to the poem, the main formal aspect that he foresees for the poem is what he terms the said mythical method. He has in mind the anthropologist James G. Frazer's *The Golden Bough*.[16] Albeit in his different field of anthropo-mythology, Frazer follows a method analogous to that of Charles Darwin.[17] He takes many versions, bits, and pieces of scattered myth in Europe—like pieces of fossilized material—and arranges them to figure out a monomyth, just as Darwin uses scattered evidence and fossils to come to a single explanation for life's many different forms on a reductive material level.

The mandalic structure that I have indicated with a view to modern English and the Sanskrit fragments in *The Waste Land* indeed follows a similar method of constructing past significance—for the sake of the present—from various bits, pieces, flickering meanings, and so on. He does it to re-locate the modern sensibility in terms of its ancient, wiser roots. This mythical method involves a break away from usual narrative methods, for the reason that the story of Europe had torn itself apart around the time of the composition of *The Waste Land*, making it impossible to write ahead as if all its narrative wires from the past were still intact. Eliot insists on this in his essay on James Joyce's *Ulysses*.[18] It is in view of this that he further feels the poet has to be difficult and dislocate language into his meaning, acknowledging that a neatly symmetrical and linear continuation of "our story" has become impossible. Hence his urgent return to a "vertical," myth-bound technique that continues to fathom the depths of the wiser past in terms of the present. The patterning of the *Da* syllable indeed contrasts its mandalic structure with the linearity of the glosses, as indicated.

Yet *The Waste Land* does have a kind of mythological narrative structure, and one may fruitfully focus on this in the attempt to refute the idea that the Sanskrit patterning amounts to little more than nihilistic whimpering in the absence of meaningfulness. After all, those who insist that the Sanskrit comes to inert nothing view the poem as the story of the tensions between the ability and inability to cope with nihilism. Will the poem in the end overcome nihilism, after it has stacked up so much skepticism?—this is assumed to underlie the story. The more affirmative answer to this story, which comes with ecopoetic reading of the kind adopted here, tells it in terms of "twoness" and "threeness" (henceforth without quotation marks). The former roughly presents the dualistic limit of language, which can act as a major part of the language trap, since it has to do with the limits of human understanding. The latter presents the renewed recognition of the unity of opposites, which opens into meaningfulness through and beyond language.

The Waste Land throughout builds up considerable tension around the inability to reconcile opposite conditions. The Sybil of Cumae has eternal life, but she is trapped in a world where it leads to disaster; male and female worlds cannot meet, leading to automated pointlessness; arid mindscapes yearn for the moisture that would complement and resolve them, but cannot find it; and so forth. Toward the poem's conclusion, in the Sanskrit sequence, Eliot dexterously shows how opposites involve the language trap. This entails a brief revisiting of the second command and its gloss:

> *Dayadhvam*: I have heard the key
> Turn in the door and turn once only
> We think of the key, each in his prison
> Thinking of the key, each confirms a prison
> Only at nightfall, aethereal rumours
> Revive for a moment a broken Coriolanus[19]

Coriolanus symbolizes the outcast, he who has lost social connection.[20] And the passage alluding to incarceration in *The Divine Comedy*[21] (lines 1–2) states the linguistic dilemma central to Eliot's work. On the level of mature or relational experience, re-presented meaning and the real presence of meaningfulness have split apart. The very distance that language creates between oneself and experience turns into a wall that persistently blocks deeper meaning, that is, the meaning of connection, unity, or integrity. Prufrock's dilemma thus enters into *The Waste Land*, and the command *Dayadhvam*, Sympathize!, resonates on the level of the modern human condition. The gloss is a superb rendition of this dilemma, since it incorporates both aspects of it, thereby giving full expression to its slippery and uncanny nature. Paraphrased, it says that one who has been incarcerated will have on his mind above all else the notion of a key: the prospect of escape into freedom. "We think of the key, each in his prison" (line 3). But by employing the relatively royal "we," Eliot makes this yearning for escape into an abstraction, a universalism of the kind to be found in generalized thought, that is, in the "heart" of linguistic experience. And it is when one sees this that the subsequent line makes its frightening sense: "Thinking of the key, each confirms a prison" (line 4). In linguistic-dualistic terms—in terms of thought as thought—there can never be an escape from the duality, and thinking of the key has both effects in equal measure. It may confirm the prospect of escape, and it may equally well confirm the disaster of incarceration, for a key has both propensities. In this sense it is itself a form of incarceration, leaving no escape from the one-sidedness of its dual insistence.

The world of twoness is thus different from threeness. In the former, binary can only lead to another binary, and so on *ad nauseam*. This kind of twoness consists of two separated conditions of one-sidedness. It does not allow the opposites to connect and dissolve. It would be as if one were always to crave sex, never to find the solution of its actual consummation. Each leg in a pair of opposites remains forever isolated or distanced from the other. For example, patriarchy demands narrow maleness, which leads to suppressed femaleness, which in its turn narrows maleness even further, and so forth. The example of Eliot's desertscape studied in the preceding chapter springs to mind (if that be the metaphor!). There is only rock, but no water. Connection and relief, the dissolving of the tension, is impossible. The world turns infertile, loveless, without magic. Differentiation turns into tyranny when it is sustained indefinitely. Grown-up life becomes the hell of merely going through the motions.

However, twoness is always ready to return to unity in threeness. The one-sided splitting finally gets healed as it finds relief in the renewed recognition of oneness. A sense of rejuvenation and liberty is the consequence. In some cases, and perhaps at its very root, the returning from duality to unity certainly also involves a certain fourness: the continuing unfolding of the four seasons from an elusive center, the center point at the chiasmus of the four directions, and so forth. (Fourness therefore involves an archetypal unity at the center of four corners, elements, and the like.) Whether threeness or fourness or both, the return to unity is crucial to human survival, as has been shown amply in the analytical psychology of Carl Gustav Jung, for instance, and as confirmed increasingly by recent neurobiological and other psychological studies.[22] *The Waste Land* is a lyrical dramatization of such emergent threeness, for the sake of the greater collective good of its community at a time of near-impossible distress and splitting-apart also for its individual maker. Again, the most civilized continent on Earth, Europe, was tearing itself apart in the most barbarous slaughtering of millions of young men; the basis for morality had been severely destabilized by Sigmund Freud's illuminating but also reductive analytical-materialist thought; Charles Darwin's evolutionary theory appeared to have cut off biological existence *in toto* from meaningful real presence, since the great questions—where do we come from? who are we? where are we going?—then all seemed to have received materialist, reductive answers; and so forth. Simultaneously, Eliot was moving through an enormous psychological crisis of his own, in which his relations with the world threatened to split off.[23] *The Waste Land* takes great trouble to reflect this separation of opposites and the concomitant fracturing of living societal connections, which fracturing leads to wastelands such as automated sex, rape, destruction of Earth, and so on, as mentioned. And at some point the condition of twoness characterized by one-sidedness becomes unbearable. This is the next phase in the story that I tell about the poem here. Just prior to its entering into the Sanskrit pattern at its conclusion, which pattern insists on repeating things thrice within accentuated blank space, the poem dips into images of near-secular-madness.[24] It counts carefully as it does so:

> Who is the third who walks always beside you?
> When I count, there are only you and I together
> But when I look ahead up the white road
> There is always another one walking beside you
> Gliding wrapt in a brown mantle, hooded
> I do not know whether a man or a woman
> —But who is that on the other side of you?[25]

"When I *count*, there are only you and I together" (line 2); and there appears to be some sort of familiarity and safety in the mental act of counting, something to hang on to here at the brink of insanity. It evokes familiar personal relations determined by the neat rationalism of grammar, that is, relations between first and second person. But instead of the *grammatically* usual third person, in this instance the "third person" promises something that appears to the speaker to be insane: the prospect of meaningfulness beyond the opposing relations kept so tidily by the usual grammar. Something frightening occurs beyond the relation between "you" and "I," including that which is beyond the safe assumption that people are either male or female (line 6). In other words, the speaker is facing the dilemma of trying to exist between the rational and irrational worlds. "On the other side" (final line) of the automated grown-up understanding dominated by linguistic relations between different phenomena is terror. The prospect arises of that which is neither simply you or I, nor simply male or female. The prospect of threeness is at this stage highly uneasy. As the poem works its way to the Sanskrit patterns of threeness at its conclusion, at this early stage of counting on the road to Emmaus, the spiritual and healing prospect of that threeness (through and beyond the ordinary twoness, offering an escape from language) is therefore perceived as a hallucinatory threat of terrific proportions. It bewilders the speaker completely. It is even as though he wishes the prospect away, despite the fact that his healing lies exactly in the actuality of that very prospect, given that the remove between opposites within language is the root cause of the spiritual problem that the poem poses.

The next and final phase of the story occurs when the poem slips into the *Da* sequence with its emphasis on a third dimension that moves through and beyond twoness. Three is essential to the Sanskrit story. It would be incomplete if only two claps of thunder or two commands were entertained. It has to enter the world of threeness, hence the repetition of everything thrice. Eliot's formal emphasis on this by way of mandalic structure is therefore no accident. It is no less than the modernization of the ancient emphasis on the third position as the position of wisdom. It is, so to speak, not to lose sight of the first ground of one's experience, but to find it *again* from a dualistic, grown-up perspective. When the poem concludes—very openly in blank space—with its Sanskrit benediction of *shantih*, it moreover repeats the word thrice. In the notes to the poem, Eliot says that *shantih* is the oriental equivalent of "the Peace which passeth understanding."[26] In the most secular (inclusive) sense, this is to acknowledge real presence at the point where opposites meet and are surpassed. The dualistic language trap that the entire poem carries with so much dexterity and weight, dissolves. As such, (linguistic) understanding is surpassed by actual understanding as the insistence on duality (twoness) at last enters the active relief of threeness.

This further entails a kind of dissolving of language into charged blank space. The final sign (*shantih*) in the poem carries no full stop. Again this is no merely modern technical fancy. As we will see below, the fact that full stops should be read carefully along with blank space as the poem concludes is underscored by the poem's penultimate stanza, prior to the *shantih* benediction. Paradoxically, language is thus able to escape from itself by moving beyond one of its extreme limits, namely the condition of opposition. Another paradox in this regard is that language enters into itself more deeply by escaping in this way, because it becomes the momentary embodiment of real presence, dynamic wholeness, the renewed sense of knowing the numinous in terms of one's place for the first time.

However, this is not simply a return to the original unity prior to the separation of the world into relations, hence the need for the term threeness. It is a grown-up return to it, so to speak, in the nature of what Jung calls the archetype of the wise child,[27] and not simply the naïve child who still has to go through the pain of differentiation. It would be as though all our most civilized knowledge and healthy primitive feelings combine again. This is precisely what Eliot campaigns for in his prose when he calls for a return to a social-religious-artistic complex that would carry the modern community forward away from Earth-destruction. As he clearly says there, "even the most primitive feelings should be part of our heritage."[28] In the Sanskrit narrative and its mandalic structure underscored here, one finds poetic embodiment of the said complex.

By way of indirectness, then, taken to its near-absolute extreme in the fear of a "third" who moves always "on the other side of you"—the other side of "two"!—*The Waste Land* opens the avenue for the return to embodied threeness in Sanskrit. The embodying is simultaneously utterly modern and ancient: modern because it comes to the reader via fragments and charged blank space, as in the case of modern poetry in general ranging from that of Ezra Pound to E. E. Cummings and Paul van Ostaijen, and ancient because it accentuates the original wisdom into which English can point, of the concrete mystery and integrity of being-and-non-being as presented by characters-and-blank-space, black *shantih* immersed in whiteness. This concrete mystery—so clear, so differentiated, so *not* in need of any mystification—of course moves at the very heart or center of what it means to be alive on Earth, as the Sanskrit forebears have long since known in their refined and substantial way.

The story therefore comes to an affirmative conclusion in open-ended threeness. We have seen how the Emmaus passage (beginning with "Who is the third who walks always beside you?") prepares the way into Sanskrit threeness. This is narratological in the sense of prolepsis and analepsis, that is, the anticipation of what is to come and the referring to what has occurred. But healing is not possible without full acknowledgement of the dark, thick, nihilistic tension that prevents it in Eliot's time. This must somehow crumble for nihilism to give way to healing. Does the story of the poem acknowledge this? Just prior to the final line with its three instances of *shantih* in open space occurs a stanza that mimes and tells about the collapsing of the nihilistic denial of all significance:

>London Bridge is falling down falling down falling down
>*Poi s'ascose nel foco che gli affina*
>*Quando fiam uti chelidon*—O swallow swallow
>*Le Prince d'Aquitaine à la tour abolie*
>These fragments I have shored against my ruins

> Why then Ile fit you. Hieronymo's mad againe.
> Datta. Dayadhvam. Damyata.[29]

    These cruel fragments emerge from various texts and periods in European history. They all have to do with power and its concomitant violence and lack of meaningful connection, that is, plainly put, lack of love. The chaotic arrangement of the fragments presents the madness that comes along with the "disembodiment" that underpins the violent side of history: murder, revenge, mutilation, rampant ambition . . . raw power, the absence of humaneness, indeed the absence of being-human, a certain callousness and non-presence in "human" action; indicating, much as in the case of the Philomela legend that has been discussed here, that "authority" without care and connection is mere, brutal power, power that severs and dissociates thoughts from feelings and realities from liberty. In this view, power is the terrific form of dislocation, since the value of human understanding disconnects itself from concrete deeds. The result is unfathomable cruelty.

    The passage in other words turns Friedrich Nietzsche's *Wille zur Macht* on its head.[30] The will to power has the dire consequences that the passage refers to by bundling its references to violence into one distorting mixture. "London bridge is falling down" (line 1) reminds of a nursery song. Though violence often features in such songs, it is usually meaningless. But in the context here, as in the case of "Here we go round the prickly pear, prickly pear, prickly pear" in "The Hollow Men,"[31] the effect is disturbing, because the context is anything but childlike. The subsequent fragment sees Arnaut Daniel diving into the flames of purgatorio (*"Poi s'ascose nel foco che gli affina"*), speaking to Dante, warning him about the pain caused by sexual attachment (line 2). The next line returns to the raped Philomela plaintively asking: when shall I be the swallow? When will this hell of powerlessness end? When will there be love, actual, meaningful connection, and not the cutting out of my tongue after having been raped, leading to a massive vicious circle of revenge and counter-revenge, Procne cooking her own son and that of Tereus for him to eat? Then follows a fragment alluding to a prince in his ruined tower as found in Gerard de Nerval's sonnet of dispossession (line 4). These insane moments come to glaring insanity when Hieronymo declares that he is "mad againe" with some dramatic effect (line 6). Convincing his son's murderers to act in a play with him, Hieronymo murders them and then himself.[32]

    These fragments the poem's multiple speaker shores against his ruins (line 5). The word "shores," which in a preceding stanza acquires the positive meaning of that place where Earth and water meet at last,[33] now acquires a deeply negative meaning, of skepticism about existence as such, raw skepticism. One hangs on to last little bits of destructive, fragmentary imagery that somehow serve as the set of flickering little bridges (or their prospect) into a more meaningful textual and religious past. Also trapped into this stanza now are the Sanskrit commands "Datta. Dayadhvam. Damyata." In some editions of the poem they are printed without any blank spaces between them whatsoever, but only full stops (line 7). They, too, momentarily embody only the flickering of past meaningfulness.

A broader psycho-narrative therefore unfolds in relation to the poem's Sanskrit. First there is the great fear of threeness on the Emmaus road, a fear that nonetheless marks the prospect of the healing or wholeness that comes with threeness. Then follows the carefully arranged Sanskrit commands with their mandalic threeness, marking moments that reach into the meaningful silence of emptiness mimed by blank space. Subsequently the speaker finds himself/ herself/ itself on the shore at last, with the "arid plain" (wastelands) behind, at last, calmly involved in the act of fishing, at a meeting point of the spiritual (in reference to the Fisher King that crops up repeatedly in the poem) and the concrete (plainly sitting and fishing)—

> I sat upon the shore
> Fishing, with the arid plain behind me

—while this peaceful moment gets dashed instantly, however, when the speaker asks

> Shall I at least set my lands in order?[34]

—thus inflating himself/ herself/ itself with an attempt at sounding exactly like gods from the past, therefore identifying with them excessively since, as the poem well knows, in modern time such direct identity is no longer sanely possible. We can see the wholeness of experience as in the Sanskrit mandala, but we can hardly directly adopt the voices of former gods as if we were still identical with them. And this leads into the collapsing passage that has been described above. It involves, once more, a very necessary deflation and admission of human shortcoming. In this sense the passage is at once the most human and inhuman moment in the poem's story. It is as though the entire lesson to be learned by the twentieth century (remarkably, then still to come for the most part) sits in this passage: the lesson that relatively unconstrained freedom from certain earthly and mythical parameters requires enormous wisdom if it is not to destroy humanity, including above all humanity's essential links with Earth. As Eliot says in his prose, we "have yet to learn that it is only through an effort and a discipline, greater than society has yet seen the need of imposing upon itself, that material knowledge and power is gained without loss of spiritual knowledge and power."[35] The loss of wisdom in the face of modern gains goes along with titanic new cultural control over Earth, and this poses a real threat to the well-being of the opposite pairing of humanity and Earth. Regaining wisdom entails re-unification of the opposites.

A crucial aspect of Eliot's skeptical stretching is therefore his emphasis on opposites, and how it leads to religion, wholeness. If existence begins with an utter unity in which even all "somethingness" and all "nothingness" are one, it soon differentiates into opposite worlds in a relational, linguistic sphere. For Eliot the story does not end there. He insists that the ground of one's experience, the originary unity and immediacy, remains part of grown-up, relational experience. One is able to *access* the originary experience of unity in grown-up life, when opposites such as feeling and thought combine again. He refers to this as transcendental experience, after the philosopher F. H. Bradley on whose work he wrote his PhD dissertation.[36]

This third position enjoys clear resonances with mystical notions such as the *coniunction oppositorum*, and the kind of symbolic arithmetic that goes on in the axiom of Maria the Jewess. It is prevalent in all kinds of modern poetry. And it is also related to what I have been terming *a la* Steiner real presence: actual recognition of and participation in the meaningfulness of one's more-than-ego in connecting with the immediacy of the other, as well as that ultimate and most self-evident other, Earth. In threeness, reality comes to one in its fullness.

Earth is masterful when it comes to continuing unity. It enjoys immense integrity, being the actual ground of seamless continuation, mysterious and yet unmistakable, always *there* in one's here-ness. To realize its mastery of unity, one has to remind oneself only of the endless space, the endless cold and heat, solidity and fluidity that it effortlessly "handles," transforming these opposite energies continuously into every new now-moment of *being*. To be a living, conscious, reflecting part of this makes this knowledge all the more clearly mysterious and elevating, as I have been indicating here, and *The Waste Land* is nothing less than a stark reminder of this.

What, then, separates humans from "living in" the presence of the now-moment? At least in part, it is the distance brought about by thought and its language. On the one hand, such distance involves necessary forms of maturation, respect, and empathy, also for Earth's otherness. It further involves necessary and painful differentiation on the road of maturation. On yet another hand, if life is reduced to linguistic categories, language turns into the torture of the trap that *The Waste Land* describes, embodies, and dissolves. In surpassing the trap, a vital part of the oriental tradition that Eliot evokes is not only the transcendent-participatory sense of between-ness, fullness, full-emptiness, mindfulness, or integrity and calm that I name threeness (once more, because it moves through and beyond duality or twoness, back to oneness),[37] but also the very important poetic maneuver, on the economical scale of the printed page, of the printed characters presenting being, and blank space non-being,[38] as indicated.

This now-here-nowhere form of threeness is a prevalent modern poetic phenomenon induced by Buddhist and Taoist traditions,[39] and modern poets have different devices available to them when it comes to emphasizing the interplay of oppositional energies to the reader. In modern poetry, the fragmentary procedure that characterizes the work of exponents like E. E. Cummings and William Carlos Williams serves excellently for this purpose, as we see here in the case of Eliot, too. One may go as far as to speak of "shades" and "colors" of blank space in modern poetry, and in his oeuvre. A black-white dialectic is at work, for instance, in "The Hollow Men," resulting in blank space that plays not only the fairly familiar and important role of inducing pauses, but also the role of indicating the intrusion of a nihilistic shadow drenched in impotence.[40] It could not be said that the blank space there enjoys the meaning of vibrant emptiness, but its opposite. There it signifies a sterile vacuum or void. (Similarly, there are at least two different kinds of darkness in *Four Quartets*: that of salvation, and that of despair.)

However, there is little doubt that in the carefully rendered Buddhist context created at the conclusion of *The Waste Land*, the poet signals vibrant emptiness by means of a formal aesthetic, as shown. That there is no full stop to the poem after the last *shantih* then has the meaning not of giving up on the affair, but of allowing the signs openly to swim into benedictory emptiness. The mandalic sense of a unifying structure emerging as if from nowhere to point into cosmic wholeness therefore begins not purely in *Four Quartets*, but in the compelling Sanskrit moments of *The Waste Land*. The gift half understood (as *Four Quartets* states)[41]—Incarnation—therefore involves a solution to Prufrock's mermaid-dilemma. Threeness is encompassing, actively combining the animal world and the human, the god-world and flesh, the (empty) still point and the (full) dance, hence nothing and something; all of this on the level of grown-up perception of these childlike truths. One concludes that Eliot's dislocating sensibility is committed to re-location. The image springs to mind of a rescuer who removes healthy soil from a toxic environment to restore growth elsewhere. The poet's role in the linguistic community is in this exact sense unique. "The Metaphysical Poets," in which he talks about the necessity of dislocating language, balances itself by demonstrating the singularity of the poet's place in society as he or she pursues (renewed) wholeness. "When a poet's mind is perfectly equipped for its work," he says there,

> it is constantly amalgamating disparate experience; the ordinary man's experience is chaotic, irregular, fragmentary. The latter falls in love, or reads Spinoza, and these two experiences have nothing to do with each other, or with the noise of the typewriter or the smell of cooking; in the mind of the poet these experiences are always forming new wholes.[42]

The poet finds himself or herself at the relative fringe of society where one's job is to look for the unity of apparently disparate things. He or she is paradoxically more on the outside of social life in order to get closer to its inside, its full meaning, not unlike a modern shaman of sorts.[43] Eliot's difficulty is therefore to make such wholeness by using the fractured language of his day, language severed from the wholeness of corporeal belief,[44] differentiating to the point of fragmentation. Despite this, the *kind of place* that he seeks as a poet is one of wholeness. At this place things come together, and this is the place from which they (continue to) emanate. And as has been indicated here, that religious sense of wholeness includes the crucial fabric of connections between oneself, one's culture, and being on Earth. The connections between the human and concrete worlds are vital. There can be no integrity without them. It is therefore interesting that the image of wholeness in the passage above has to do with a concrete sense of place. Someone is reading and someone is typing in a homely space filled by the smell of cooking. Intimate turning of pages prior to dinner comes to mind. As if to underscore the awareness of emplacement, the author mentioned is Baruch Spinoza, who does not see much difference between one's earthly place and the wholeness of eternity.[45]

In his poetry—Eliot's most important and significant space after all these years of critical deliberation, culture studies exhumation and forensics of his "personality," and even the production of his plays—his sense of wholeness and emplacement find their most experientially alive form. Mandalic structure and Sanskrit threeness should therefore be allowed their historical significance. The poet has achieved radical techniques of fragmentation and dislocation in order actively to *locate* language. Now, new materialism opens the prospect of restoring healthy awareness of Earth's vibrancy after a long period of materialist-scientific reductionism and semiotic-referential "infinite semiosis," the latter which for the most part unnecessarily complicates the relations between signs and Earth. An important part of this new material emphasis is on the recognition of "vibrant matter," that is, the critically important acknowledgement that not only humans or projected gods enjoy agency, or the ability to change things, as mentioned in the present book's introduction. Matter enjoys agency, inducing responses, for example, and matter (also) *makes culture*,[46] since the patterns that clouds assume steer the projections of human shapes into them as much as the act of projecting human interpretations onto them does. There can be no projection without the cloud shape. But this is only the bland way of saying that a certain magic of threeness permeates existence—to which Eliot gives poetic shape. In his eco-*logos* this is taken a crucial and radical fraction further, in that matter *responds to inner human states* by reflecting them. Wastelands within cause wastelands in real life, as indicated. In its turn Earth without has effects on humanity within. Violence to women and Earth come back to haunt patriarchy, making the experience of maleness thin and dry, as is the case for prudent Prufrock the matchstick glutton, or for the graysuit husband of the nineteen fifties.

Moreover, the poems are acutely aware that Earth continues in motion, inducing long term and short term changes. For instance, houses crumble (they "live and die" in Eliot's words), and a trotting field-mouse returns to the lost wainscot.[47] The reciprocal creativities and sympathies between humanity and Earth are remarkably strong in Eliot's poetry. Jane Bennett, arguably the mother of the new materialist burgeoning, is therefore entirely right to suggest that the field will find intriguing insights in the aesthetic world.[48] There is a "vitality intrinsic"[49] to modern art as it mixes itself into and from its dynamic earthly embedding. We see here in *The Waste Land* that modern art does not simply tell about or explain that embedding. The reader has to get involved "inside" the poem's world to see or follow the unfolding of those mandalic structures and their considerable significance. He or she gets invited or steered into the process of recombining disparate fragments into new wholes. It amounts to a new way of "seeing" meaning. Vitally, again, this involves a view of Earth *not* as a set of removed, static objects "out there." Neither does it involve the notion that such "objects" are brought to life or movement simply by an intervening hand, whether deistic or human or both.

The poem is a becoming. The reader is the co-creator as it comes to life. This is the way in which it has been composed, and in which it is meant to be read. A certain surrendering occurs as he or she actualizes the material into the recognition of earthly being-and-non-being, and the enormous meaningfulness of that recognition, which recognition is not an arrival but a process. The poem is verbal rather than explanatory. Through this verbality new materialism finds in Eliot's poetry and modern poetry in general an ally. When, as all ecopoetic writers do at some stage, Bennett doubts the ability of everyday grammar to follow creative materiality (one wants to add in terms of oneself: especially in academic prose), modern poetry springs to mind as an alternative of note. Especially in "trying to choose the appropriate verbs," admits Bennett, "I have come to see how radical a project it is to think vital materiality. It seems necessary and impossible to rewrite the default grammar of agency, a grammar that assigns activity to people and passivity to things."[50] Such a grammar denies much, including the sensuality of experience as inner and outer worlds rub against and flow into one another. It is a relief to know that a poem such as *The Waste Land*, among a wealth of modern poems, acts as a huge verb—the whole thing is dynamic.

Eliot carries this dynamism further in *Four Quartets*. The occult challenge for him is to compose poetry that does not stall into stasis, because that would be to undercut the very nature of his project, which is exactly to reconnect signs and the interwoven dynamism of existence. And he succeeds to a remarkable degree.[51] In recognizing this, one comes to the sensuousness of Eliot's poetry (!), its supreme ability to act as a form of embodiment, as part of its locating achievement. For, language, too, wants to be embodied. It is not satisfied, as poets know, with the epistemologies of semantics and lexicons, it wants to enter ontological worlds of verbality.[52] With its roots in earthly, concrete, and bodily phenomena such as rhythm, contrast, dreaming (seeing existence in pictures), sound, gesture, and so forth, poetry's embodiment connects with matter and matter's motion.

This sensuousness of modern poetry, as embodied in Eliot's compositions, includes a crucial break with everyday grammar, as has been demonstrated amply here. One of the most profound and ill-explored aspects of this sensuousness is that modern art, including Eliot's, enjoys turning oppositional expectations on their head, for instance when it comes to the supposed control of the "objective," "outside" world over the "subjective," "inner" world. In modern art, in fact, the world "outside" responds to subjective perception with a directness hitherto not acknowledged in full within the usual "objective" framework. In Virginia Woolf's novel *Jacob's Room*, people on the embankment and the embankment itself wobble and stretch as the perceiver wobbles in his boat.[53] It is as though the piano key responds to the pressing finger, pressing back, as in E. M. Forster's Edwardian-modern novel *A Room with a View*.[54] Equally, in *The Waste Land*, it is not simply that one's heart controls one's blood circulation as the objective view would want. No, it is blood that shakes one's heart! One does not simply look at the flower. Roses respond to seeing, they have "the look of flowers that are looked at,"[55] as *Four Quartets* further advocates.

One sees that one important example of how new materialism may find affirmation of and in great literature, is the way in which Eliot's dislocating procedure locates signs toward the real presence and wholeness of Earth's reciprocal *continuation*. Poetic emplacement in the mystery of matter would be to acknowledge the presence of that continuation, that impossible going-on amidst a world charged with change and opposites in conflict. That is, his poetry enlivens the mytho-poetic sensibility of participation in that continuation in modern days, where such enlivening is direly necessary. This is what his radically modern dramatization of the onomatopoeic *Da* within accentuated blank space and a context of renewed unity through and beyond mature opposites enlivens. The *Da* mandala points into this. The economical further mirroring of the *Da* mandala by three instances of *shantih*, again within accentuated blank space resonating with that sense of non-being that is the silent source of active meaning, the source "beyond understanding," is a return precisely, after the collapse of all fragments of power, to threeness again. So to speak, one has the pattern of *Four Quartets* in highly economical form here already. A Buddhist divine comedy finds its way into the open, non-full-stopped conclusion of *The Waste Land*, and it continues in *Four Quartets*, as will be shown in chapter 5.

Underlying this is the age-old recognition, made modern by *The Waste Land*, that it is doubtful that respect for and living with nature is possible without some sense of its holiness, as William Blake has indicated centuries ago.[56] A secular sacredness is necessary, one that finds its path between the immature need for vitalism on the one hand and the immature reduction of matter and signs on the other. A position is necessary that is able to continue to move among, between, and through the reduction of Earth to a mere deistic clockwork on the one hand and the reduction of matter to muteness and signs to omnipotent cultural status on the other.

For instance, central aesthetic values of Eliot's poetry, such as confirmation of existence in its fullness and emptiness, connect with the absence and presence of religious values such as a Christian and/ or Buddhist sensibility of heaven and nowhere. To deny the latter in his case would be to destroy the former. Here the reader needs the wisdom neither to view art as the clumsy "replacement" of religious loss, nor to lose the real presence by which it is carried, and which it carries. Neither institutionalized belief *only*, nor disbelief *only*, Eliot's poetry points in this direction of maturation about Earth's holy, whole vibrancy.

Just one of the illuminating aspects of Eliot's project in the new material context of vibrant matter, as one continues to follow his poetry, is furthermore that it does not end by embodying the indubitable creative reciprocity between agentic humanity and agentic, process predominant Earth. Eliot's sensibility goes further: it craves *immersion* in this reciprocity. Location is not a static destination. It needs the further intensity of complete, utter participation. He foresees a level of authenticity in human existence akin to the authenticity of the immersed jellyfish, immersed in its element to the point of complete integrity. In fact, as the next chapter shows, creatures and motifs of immersion permeate his thought and poems.

Thus one begins to recognize that a less cynical literary view influenced by new materialism, one that strives for a more mature view achieved by greater, active balance between theoretical skepticism and artistic affirmation, has the very real potential of moving the field to—or following it into—greater depths, heights, play, and illumination. One foresees a new materialism skeptically *and* affirmatively immersed in poetry, life, process, matter, and real presence. Again, real presence should not be misunderstood as a positioning aloof to and disconnected from ordinary being. Again and again Eliot makes this clear. As the next chapter shows, a celestial totem of how one should see the holiness of matter is none other than the hippopotamus, he of flesh and blood frailty, he who makes hoarse and odd sounds in sex, being in complete harmony with his own existence, therefore leading a life of the greatest possible material substance.

NOTES

1. Jewel Spears Brooker, *Mastery and Escape: T. S. Eliot and the Dialectic of Modernism* (Amherst: University of Massachusetts Press, 1994), 240.
2. Brooker, *Mastery and Escape*, 88.
3. T. S. Eliot, *The Waste Land* (Norton Critical Edition), ed. Michael North (New York: W. W. Norton, 2001), 18.
4. A similar mandala emanating from or pointing into the sign "Death" at its center occurs in Eliot's poem that perhaps longs for a daughter of his own, "Marina," as found in T. S. Eliot, *Collected Poems 1909-1962* (New York: Harcourt Brace, 1991), 105. The return to the sign "Death" in this poem was mentioned by Robert Crawford at a question session of the First International T. S. Eliot Summer School.
5. Gary Snyder, *The Real Work: Interviews and Talks 1964-1979* (New York: New Directions, 1980), 57.
6. P. S. Sri, *T. S. Eliot, Vedanta and Buddhism* (Vancouver: University of British Columbia Press, 1985), 104; Northrop Frye, *Northrop Frye on Twentieth Century Literature* (Collected Works of Northrop Frye, Volume 29), ed. Glen Robert Gill (Toronto: University of Toronto Press, 2010), 233.
7. Michael Edwards, *Towards a Christian Poetics* (Grand Rapids, Mich.: Eerdmans, 1984), 113.
8. Murray Stein, *Jung's Map of the Soul: An Introduction* (Chicago: Open Court, 2001), 152–154, 158.
9. John Elder, *Imagining the Earth: Poetry and the Vision of Nature* (Urbana: The University of Illinois Press, 1985), 21.
10. T. S. Eliot, *Selected Prose*, ed. Frank Kermode (London: Faber & Faber, 1980), 236.
11. M. E. Grenander and K. S. Narayana Rao, "The Waste Land and the Upanishads: What Does the Thunder Say?" *Indian Literature* 14.1 (March 1971), 88.
12. A. K. Sharma, "The Relation between Buddhism and the *Upanishads*," *The Monist* 38.3 (July 1928), 447.
13. *Oxford English Dictionary*, http://www.oed.com.nwulib.nwu.ac.za, retrieved 5 February 2015.
14. See Norman Friedman, *(Re)Valuing Cummings: Further Essays on the Poet 1962-1993* (Gainesville: University Press of Florida, 1996), 112.
15. Eliot, *Poems*, 177.
16. Eliot, *The Waste Land*, 21.
17. Brooker, *Mastery and Escape*, 117–118.
18. Eliot, *Prose*, 177–178.
19. Eliot, *The Waste Land*, 19.
20. William Shakespeare, *The Globe Illustrated Shakespeare*, ed. Howard Staunton (New York: Gramercy, 1979), 1711.
21. Eliot, *The Waste Land*, 26.
22. Donald Kalsched, *Trauma and the Soul: A Psycho-Spiritual Approach to Human Development and its Interruption* (London: Routledge, 2013), 171–179.
23. Matthew K. Gold, "The Expert Hand and the Obedient Heart: Dr. Vittoz, T. S. Eliot, and the Therapeutic Possibilities of *The Waste Land*," *Journal of Modern Literature* 23.3–4 (Summer 2000), 519.
24. Jewel Spears Brooker and Joseph Bentley, *Reading* The Waste Land: *Modernism and the Limits of Interpretation* (Amherst: University of Massachusetts Press, 1990), 138.
25. Eliot, *The Waste Land*, 17.
26. Eliot, *The Waste Land*, 26.
27. Carl Gustav Jung, *The Archetypes and the Collective Unconscious*, trans. R. F. C. Hull (Princeton: Princeton University Press, 1990), 170.
28. Eliot, *Prose*, 291.
29. Eliot, *The Waste Land*, 19.
30. See Friedrich Nietzsche, *The Antichrist*, trans. H. L. Mencken (New York: Knopf, 1924), 38, 43–44.

31. Eliot, *Poems*, 81.
32. *See* Michael North's notes (numbers 1–5) in Eliot, *The Waste Land*, 19–20.
33. Eliot, *The Waste Land*, 19.
34. Eliot, *The Waste Land*, 19.
35. Eliot, *Prose*, 291.
36. Brooker, *Mastery and Escape*, 186–187.
37. Etienne Terblanche, *E. E. Cummings: Poetry and Ecology* (Amsterdam: Rodopi, 2012), 15.
38. *See* Nina Hellerstein, "Calligraphy, Identity: Scriptural Exploration as Cultural Adventure," *Symposium* 45.1 (Spring 1991): 329–344.
39. Terblanche, *Cummings*, 230.
40. Eliot, *Poems*, 82.
41. Eliot, *Poems*, 199.
42. Eliot, *Prose*, 64.
43. *See* David Abram, *The Spell of the Sensuous: Perception and Language in a More-Than-Human World* (New York: Vintage, 1997), 6.
44. *See* Gabriel Josipovici, *What Ever Happened to Modernism?* (New Haven: Yale University Press, 2010), 3, 14.
45. Harold Bloom, "Deciphering Spinoza, the Great Original," review of *Betraying Spinoza: The Renegade Jew Who Gave Us Modernity* by Rebecca Goldstein, *New York Times*, 16 June 2006, http://www.nytimes.com/2006/06/16/arts/16iht-idside17.1986759.html?pagewanted=all&_r=0, retrieved 10 December 2013; Sharman Apt Russell, *Standing in the Light: My Life as a Pantheist* (New York: Basic Books, 2009), 125.
46. Jane Bennett, *Vibrant Matter: A Political Ecology of Things* (Durham: Duke University Press, 2010), 115.
47. Eliot, *Poems*, 182.
48. Jane Bennett, "Artistry and Agency in a World of Vibrant Matter," YouTube video, https://www.youtube.com/watch?v=q607Ni23QjA, retrieved 5 February 2015.
49. Bennett, *Vibrant Matter*, xiii.
50. Bennett, *Vibrant Matter*, 119.
51. *See* Brooker, *Mastery and Escape*, 147, 163.
52. *See* Aaron Moe, *Zoopoetics: Animals and the Making of Poetry* (Lanham: Lexington Books, 2014), 23.
53. Virginia Woolf, *Jacob's Room* (London: Penguin, 1992), 29.
54. E. M. Forster, *A Room with a View* (London: Penguin, 1990), 29.
55. Eliot, *Poems*, 176.
56. William Blake, Letter to the Revd. Dr. Tusler, 23 August 1799, http://www.unc.edu/~kastone/pagelinkletter.html, retrieved 5 February 2015.

Chapter Four

Immersion

The Authentic Jellyfish, the True Church, and the Hippopotamus

In Eliot's world, the vital connection with matter, crucially missing in Prufrock and grippingly present in the Sanskrit pattern of *The Waste Land*, is possible to the point of immersion. This is important for new material and ecocritical perception, because on the mytho-poetic level, relatively abstract terms such as "enmeshment" and "entanglement" finally find their deeper significance of utter oneness with being in view of poetic immersion in being. At some level of being, differences cease to exist. The boundaries set up by semiotic doing dissolve, and one paradoxically enters a world that is utterly meaningful and authentic, *because* it precedes linguistic construction. This is the world of immersion in one's actual being, and the jellyfish enjoys it according to the poet.[1] Its existence is particularly authentic, because it is as submersed in that existence as it is part of the ocean, with the result that it *lives* its earthly wholeness. This has radical implications for one's view of language and its potentials, as maintained in brief further detail in the next chapter, chapter 5.

As we have seen, wholeness is a key element of Eliot's religious imagination, not least because in wholeness opposites continue to dissolve into the integrity of Earth's remarkable continuation. He certainly does not deny the importance of differences, once more, but he equally certainly does not deny the importance of unity. And when it comes to the latter, he brings the poetic insight that creatures of immersion enjoy singular integrity. His bestiary of very different and very unified, immersed creatures includes not only the jellyfish, polyps, and anemones, but also a crustacean or tortoise scuttling across the floors of silent seas with a pair of ragged claws (as mentioned), an old crab grabbing a stick held out to it in an urban pool (also mentioned), and that unlikely beast of immersion—despite its humungous terrestrial appearance—the river horse or hippopotamus. On the human level, it includes the drowning Prufrock and Phlebas. And the mermaids (who will not sing to Prufrock) of course inhabit the level in between humanity, animality, Terra, and the ocean.[2]

These creatures attract him, because their experience drowns, so to speak, in their existence. That is, there is no difference between their inner and outer worlds of being. This is what makes their being so authentic, whereas in the human realm there is always the possibility of a certain inauthenticity. As Daniel Albright says in his book *Quantum Poetics: Yeats, Pound, Eliot, and the Science of Modernism*, all our human "specifying, this making-exact, is somewhat artificial and deceptive. The more minutely I articulate my world and myself, the more it and I assume a specious solidity, intelligibility." As a consequence one's sense of being becomes "derivative, second-hand, artificial." In contrast, "the jellyfish's touch is crude, but it is authentic."[3] As we have seen, Prufrock's ultra-refined experience is so inauthentic as to be barbaric. Perhaps Albright therefore attributes the word "crude" too readily to Eliot's jellyfish. He is right, though, to assert that for Eliot there is a modern need to return to "urgency, to human life" concomitant with the recognition that our "mentality has failed: we need to learn to be jellyfish once more, swimming in ourselves. The thirsty man must drown."[4] This sheds new light on Prufrock's drowning at the end of his love song—I return to the point.

The inauthenticity of modern material existence finds perhaps its most immediately visible critique in Eliot's minor 1920 poem that focuses on the hippo who dwells for long periods of time on the bottom of aquatic bodies such as rivers or dams:

The Hippopotamus

Similiter et omnes revereantur Diaconos, ut mandatum Jesu Christi; et Episcopum, et Jesum Christum, existentem filium Patris; Presbyteros autem, ut concilium Dei et conjunctionem Apostolorum. Sine his Ecclesia non vocature; de quibus suadeo vos sic habeo.

S. IGNATH AD TRALLIANOS.

And when this epistle is read among you, cause that it be read also in the church of the Laodiceans.

The broad-backed hippopotamus
Rests on his belly in the mud;
Although he seems so firm to us
He is merely flesh and blood.

Flesh and blood is weak and frail,
Susceptible to nervous shock;
While the True Church can never fail
For it is based upon a rock.

The hippo's feeble steps may err
In compassing material ends,
While the True Church need never stir
To gather in its dividends.

The 'potamus can never reach
The mango on the mango-tree;
But fruits of pomegranate and peach
Refresh the Church from over sea.

At mating time the hippo's voice
Betrays inflexions hoarse and odd,
But every week we hear rejoice
The Church, at being one with God.

The hippopotamus's day
Is passed in sleep; at night he hunts;
God works in a mysterious way—
The Church can sleep and feed at once.

I saw the 'potamus take wing
Ascending from the damp savannas,
And quiring angels round him sing
The praise of God, in loud hosannas.

Blood of the Lamb shall wash him clean
And him shall heavenly arms enfold,
Among the saints he shall be seen
Performing on a harp of gold.

He shall be washed as white as snow,
By all the martyr'd virgins kist,
While the True Church remains below
Wrapt in the old miasmal mist.[5]

Though this poem is a playful pun on Théophile Gautier's nineteenth-century poem "L'hippopotame," it has a serious side: its said critique of materialism. The True Church does not reach for food, appears not to utter inflexions hoarse and odd in sex (lines 13, 14, 17, 18), and so forth. It is out of touch with matter. Paradoxically, this is an indictment on its spirituality, which has become so esoteric as to be gray and meaningless. It will stay down below in the old miasmal mist (final line). The hippo will ascend to heaven (and even play a harp!) because it is true to its material existence, as the various stanzas vividly portray. Interesting are the quite serious citations that act as the poem's mottos. The first of these is a message about being worthy (or not) of being called a church, as contained in a message from an early church father, St. Ignatius of Antioch, to a congregation in Turkey.[6] It introduces the notion of a false church, which the poem ironically labels in the upper case as the True Church. More interesting is the second citation, from Revelations, since it suggests that the church is lukewarm, without zeal, like the church in the poem. Also like Christians in Eliot's time, as perceived by him, for in this view belief itself has turned into a form of neutral materialism. But since this kind of neutral materialism probably drenches all of enlightened society as a whole, it includes the poet as well as the reader. The poem therefore aims to show that one is complicit in that materialism and its corollary lack of significance and authenticity.

Although from an aesthetic viewpoint this may be the poem's weakest point, and the reason for its minor status, since it involves a tone of sermonizing, it is also its most vital point in terms of materialism, because it implies widespread disconnection from Earth. But exactly how does the poem achieve this "getting in under the skin" of the reader? One way of seeing how this is done is to consider the complex size-sound symbolism at work in it. Size-sound symbolism is the phenomenon in many languages that bigger or heavier animals will relatively consistently carry lower-frequency sounds in contrast to smaller or lighter ones carrying higher pitched ones[7]—not in isolation but in tandem (in terms of the relative contrast between them) and in terms of the semantic context at work in any given linguistic situation.

An obvious starting point to such symbolism in the poem is that, at least initially, the hippo carries rhyming sounds that are low in pitch when compared to the sounds allocated to the church. The [ʌ] sound dominates the first stanza in which we are introduced to the creature: "m$\underline{u}$d," "$\underline{u}$s," "bl$\underline{oo}$d." These iconic sounds suggest the size of the creature as well as, perhaps, a faint sense of disgust that some may feel in the face of its sheer concreteness, clumsiness, and closeness to dirt. As soon as stanza 2 introduces the church, however, sounds with a higher pitch enter the poem. The first line gives over from a last [ʌ] in "bl$\underline{oo}$d" to an [iː] and an [eɪ] in "w$\underline{ea}$k" and "fr$\underline{ai}$l," although these sounds and their semantics clearly still belong to the hippo, thus inverting, from the outset, the allocation of sound-symbols. The allocation roughly takes the shape of the heavy, down to Earth hippo associated with "heavier" vowels, as indicated, while higher frequencies such as the fruit of peach [piːtʃ] coming from over sea [siː] (stanza 4) accompany the church, which is light, ethereal, esoteric, out of touch. It is perhaps even somewhat hysterical or thinly present, despite all appearances of aloofness in the safe remove from touching the ugliness of organic interconnection.

As indicated, stanza 2 already turns the ironic tables: every second line returns to the heavier sound pattern with the [ɒ] sound in the cases of the rhyme words "sh_o_ck" and "r_o_ck." Given the reading made so far, this means that there is something heavy about the church, too. The context of the stanza shows that this heaviness is deeply ironic, because the church, unlike the hippo, is static and impervious to life, since it is not susceptible to nervous shock, it is not merely flesh and blood, it is not weak and frail, and in a sense it is not on Earth at all. As in Prufrock's case, the matter with the church is its misappropriation of its place on and within Earth, its misappropriation of matter.

The deepest irony, however, is that the poem itself suffers from size-sound symbolic confusion. This is the meaning of the fact that the high pitched sounds cannot be read as if they purely indicate a condemnation of the church. It should also be read as a poetic participation in it. From this perspective, the poetic speaker's voice condemns the church on the sonic level by means of church-like sounds, so to speak. It is an ambivalent speaker who must see, on the one hand, the hippo's concrete elevation and, on the other, his inevitable connection with a church hopelessly out of touch with concreteness: the speaker must see his ambivalence.

If we now follow this patterning through the poem as it unravels in our reading performance, we find scintillating further ironic moments. In stanza 5, "odd" rhymes with "God," subliminally (therefore all the more profoundly) suggesting that the church makes God odd in the wrong way by deracinating him from concrete existence. Simultaneously, it suggests that an odd God is necessary, a God who will be true to concreteness to the extent of leaving the church behind and embracing the hippo with its hoarse inflexions as it connects with its opposite other as well as its frailties, its inabilities, its imperfections, and its upside-down working life, which forces it to hunt for grass at night. Eliot's God is ecological, not patriarchal.

And the hippo will be kist by all the virgins, while the patriarchal church with its miasmic mist—that is, a polluting, toxic mist—wraps itself away from life even in the final moments of spiritual connection, when the end comes. The church's "integrity" or "unity" is false. At the exact moment in which it should be unified and connected, it prefers to "sleep and feed at once." The word "once" with its dormant suggestion of wholeness carries a dubious meaning, especially in contrast with its rhyming word "hunts," which entails action, search, connection, the continued attempt to survive, and the urgency that goes with this . . . an urgency that connects one to life in the downward, healthy direction of instinct and utter engrossment.

Of course, the final stanza appears to clinch and entrench an absolute opposition between the hippo and the church. Its first two lines celebrate the hippo, and the final two lines squarely denounce and even slam the church. (Underneath its playful surfaces this is a passionate poem.) Here it seems to split between righteousness and judgement in favor of the hippo and nature, and almost absolutely in disregard of the church and culture. But what about the fact that the church remains below? Is it not in remaining below that the hippo finds its elevating salvation? I think the poem leaves a door open for the church. If it can rid itself of the polluted aspect of its mist, or get rid of the mist, or perhaps see the real mystery in the mist—which is participation in concrete life—then it would find its way to the truly odd God: the mysterious, alive God-image as embodied in the mere hippo.

Again one senses that the poem expects of the church in particular to retain material clarity in a materialistic world. The virgins would also kiss the church—it would find its earthly and female connection at last again—if it could wake from its sleep and reach for the mango on the mango-tree. Interestingly, reaching for a fruit should therefore not be the sin that the cliché has made us to believe or accept on second nature, because participation and rootedness in Earth are the important matters.

Among other things, one is struck here by the fact that Eliot's sense of Christianity is very far removed from any textbook version in his time. Reaching for a fruit on a tree has those instant sexual connotations of a certain fall into sin from a textbook-Christian perspective, but this Eliot also turns upside-down. Reaching for the mango is a natural thing for a hungry and humble creature, and perhaps, like the hippo, one can learn from it that one simply cannot deny one's healthy instincts and failures.[8] Of course, this is very metaphorical, because the hippo can hardly literally reach for anything but grass, and not for a fruit in a tree. But the metaphor is a vehicle indicating the importance of earthly reaching as opposed to "spiritual" non-reaching, in any event.

The poem's penultimate stanza again fluctuates from higher pitch to the lower: [iː] to [əʊ] in "cl$\underline{ea}$n" to "enf$\underline{o}$ld" as well as "s$\underline{ee}$n" to "g$\underline{o}$ld." And the final one fluctuates from lower pitch to the higher: [əʊ] to [ɪ] in "sn$\underline{o}$w" and "k$\underline{i}$st" as well as "bel$\underline{o}$w" and "m$\underline{i}$st." Given the findings of this reading so far—that the distribution of frequencies implicates the speaker as a participant in the hierarchical corruption that the poem condemns and overturns—the inverse sound pattern of these final stanzas may be read as the necessary cross-stitching of the opposites contained in the hierarchy, that is, those of artificial pureness versus truthful impurity, absolute ability versus inability, remoteness versus humility, dissociation versus connection, and so on. This cross-stitching carries those opposites to a space beyond judgement so pure or harsh that it would have undercut the strategic warning that the poem instills for the Laodiceans, the materialist culture of which the speaker, and perhaps even the poetry, is at least a slightly corrupted part. From this perspective the poem is not a roundly guilty verdict, but rather a dramatization of an intrinsic and complex problematic centering on the values of matter.

The unity of Eliot's oeuvre comes to the fore also from this angle, for the truthful integrity between culture and nature that we have seen in the cases of other poems such as *The Waste Land* here find satirical castigation in terms of its absence in the modern church and (its) culture. The "savannas" and "hosannas" in "The Hippopotamus" comically anticipate the return to "significant soil," not "too far from the yew-tree," in *Four Quartets*.[9] But the early, minor poem with its hippo acts as a Trojan river horse who is able to enter one's semiotic nerve ends to bring home one or two disturbing aspects of the modern severance between deep cultural perception and natural existence on Earth. It shows that the loss of *significant* soil is a meaningful loss. Its persuasive sound patterns cause us to smile or laugh and worry a little about the integrity of that laughter, at once. Perhaps it also reminds us that, at least in some respects, the move away from a life that used to be closer to that of the hunting hippo entails the unsettling demise of our authenticity.

We have seen that Prufrock cannot overcome the dilemma of this demise. One is therefore not surprised to see that, in Eliot's poetic world, his lack of authenticity can only be restored by immersion. Even if, within the dramatic world of the poem, *he* is unable to drown or drench himself in the flow of existence—since his drowning brings an abrupt end to the existence of his persona in the poem—at least the poem and its reader succeed in drowning:

> We have lingered in the chambers of the sea
> By sea-girls wreathed with seaweed red and brown
> Till human voices wake us, and we drown.[10]

There is more than one way to attempt an interpretation of these layered lines. For instance, if Prufrock's voice is perhaps a little a-human as a consequence of its extreme dislocation and the concomitant solipsism that seals him off from his very existence, then the fact that he hears *human* voices at last (final line above) must mean the end of his world, as if that world finally breaks apart to become actual. In becoming actual, he comes to his end, then. This could be interpreted as something of a positive end, since at least the voices he hears *are* human, if only for a fateful instant.

The rich aquatic imagery in these lines prompts a slightly different angle of interpretation, perhaps in addition to the one above. Prufrock's world, including the external world, is so fluid as to enjoy intriguing agencies of its own, so that it may also appear as if the external world controls *him* as much as he believes that he controls it. One thinks of streets "that follow like a tedious argument," leading one "to an overwhelming question."[11] The wonderful jazz-like, feline image of the absolutely fluid yellow fog rubbing its back on window panes offers another example.[12] In "Preludes," one enjoys the further examples of a street that cannot understand one's vision of it, and that is impatient to assume the world. And there the worlds revolve like ancient women: they have weakened agency, but they do have agency.[13]

In short, the world is so fluid, also to Prufrock, as to have a veritable will of its own. Seen thus, Prufrock's drowning is as inevitable as the world is liquid. When the boundary of his enclosed self gives way, he must come to the full state of his being—which was his being all along—of immersion in life to the point of the complete loss of boundaries. It is not farfetched to say that in Eliot's view, this is the fate of all humans and all creatures, given that the original condition from which differences emanate according to him is one of complete continuity. "*We*"—Prufrock's persona, the reader, modern humanity, even—have lingered in the chambers of the sea (final line above), to drown.

As mentioned in an earlier chapter, the image that Prufrock has of himself as a pair of ragged claws down in the ocean—claws scuttling on the ocean floor without the center of a body of motion[14]—is either disturbing, or funnily clumsy, or both (the latter is, of course, even more uncanny). One now sees an additional reason for the disturbing effect. What *should* be an image of immersion in that instance has turned into one of utter isolation. The ragged claws have turned into their own textual objects, since they do not enjoy the center of a body. They "propel" themselves, but by what means? Therefore they do not enjoy the participation that would have gone along with actual immersion in existence.

An aquatic image and immersed creature in another poem, "Rhapsody on a Windy Night," finds its ability to embody a very moving moment of the oeuvre. As indicated in chapter 2, this poem arranges urban imagery to show a world of insignificance, and the poem's significance indeed arises from its brilliant portrayal of that meaninglessness. Consider the creature of immersion in the context of this stanza from the poem:

> Half-past two,
> The street-lamp said,
> 'Remark the cat which flattens itself in the gutter,
> Slips out its tongue
> And devours a morsel of rancid butter.'
> So the hand of the child, automatic,
> Slipped out and pocketed a toy that was running along the quay.
> I could see nothing behind that child's eye.
> I have seen eyes in the street
> Trying to peer through lighted shutters,
> *And a crab one afternoon in a pool,*
> *An old crab with barnacles on his back,*
> *Gripped the end of a stick which I held him.* (emphasis added)[15]

The poignancy of this moment resides in the contrast between the vacancy, the disconnection, in the child's eyes on the one hand (line 8) and on the other the actual moment of connection between the speaker and the barnacled old crab in the pool, characterized by the unlikelihood of the crab gripping the end of that stick, and the relief of the actual moment of contact. It brings location, the sense of being connected to the world around one, another important form of immersion. *The Waste Land* contains an equally striking passage related to immersion—the entire short Section IV titled "Death by Water:"

> Phlebas the Phoenician, a fortnight dead,
> Forgot the cry of gulls, and the deep sea swell
> And the profit and loss.
>   A current under sea
> Picked his bones in whispers. As he rose and fell
> He passed the stages of his age and youth
> Entering the whirlpool.
>   Gentile or Jew
> O you who turn the wheel and look to windward,
> Consider Phlebas, who was once handsome and tall as you.[16]

Immersion here takes the form of death and decay, something that everyone will experience in some way or another, like Phlebas. One becomes wholly part again of the Earth from which one comes. In Phlebas's case, this goes along with drowning, as predicted by the clairvoyant Madame Sosostris in an earlier part of the poem.[17] Participation in life in the end means complete immersion in it, an utter return to unity in death, and the re-integration of one's very cells and minerals back into Earth. And Eliot's evocation of Phlebas's drowning enjoys the real presence of impossible plainness mixed with (what should have been) grotesque details, as well as a very persuasive invitation to the reader to immerse himself or herself in the poetic moment on offer. To my mind, we have here one of the instances in which Eliot's poetic voice reaches the complexity and compelling nature of the most supreme artists in classical music—an instance of the reason why his poetic voice is particularly unforgettable. And as in the cases of the jellyfish and the crab, the instance again engages a mandala in motion, in this instance a vortex running to a center as Phlebas returns to the whirlpool. This anticipates the still point from which the dance of life emanates and to which it returns, which predominates the structure of his most flowing poem, *Four Quartets*. Here, flow and its concomitant sense of immersion find positive permeation. The poem is in fact drenched in images and patterns of flow. The imagery of flow begins in Section II of "Burnt Norton," although by then Eliot has established long since a circular formal pattern of fragments, words, and lines that, in themselves, flow:

> The circulation of the lymph
> Are figured in the drift of stars
> Ascend to summer in the tree
> We move above the moving tree
> In light upon the figured leaf
> And hear upon the sodden floor
> Below, the boarhound and the boar
> Pursue their pattern as before
> But reconciled among the stars.[18]

A major reciprocity moves in these lines, of images within images, spheres within spheres, and the stillness of dynamic harmony. Repetition and rhythm combine in them to evoke a sense of circular motion: "tree," "tree," "floor," "boar," "before" and, beautifully clinching the cycle, "stars" (line 2, final line) at the beginning and conclusion of the passage. Fluidity further allows satisfying metaphorical transgressions of the usual boundaries (though there is something wise or ancient about the language), between human and animal, animate and inanimate. What happens in the stars has to do with what happens for humans. These processes share important circulatory qualities. The stars drift, humans and animals drift, and all is flow, while all these processes find their equivalent in circulation of lymph. The sensibility of the lines partakes attractively in the dynamic openness carried along with this flow. They are definite, clear, and open-ended at once. Of course, in Eliot's time it also becomes apparent with renewed interest that humans emanate from universal matter, and that our lymph therefore indeed shares intimate makings with the stars.

A few lines further down in the same section of the poem, one reads of "a grace of sense, a white light still and moving."[19] This image involves poetic immersion into the aquatic sense of light. Water in a river, for example, moves, and yet the river remains there, stable between its embankments as one looks across it. It flows and is stable at once, and this is one of the miracles of being. One's cyclical participation in Earth's cyclical process indeed is such a plain miracle, and for once Eliot celebrates the unity between male and female, in Section I of the second poem in the *Four Quartets*, "East Coker":

> The association of man and woman
> In daunsinge, signifying matrimonie—
> [...]
> Rustically solemn or in rustic laughter
> Lifting heavy feet in clumsy shoes,
> Earth feet, loam feet, lifted in country mirth
> Mirth of those long since under Earth
> Nourishing the corn. Keeping time,
> Keeping the rhythm in their dancing
> As in their living the living seasons
> The time of the seasons and the constellations
> The time of milking and the time of harvest
> The time of coupling of man and woman
> And that of beasts. Dung and death.
>
> Dawn points, and another day
> Prepares for heat and silence. Out at sea the dawn wind
> Wrinkles and slides.[20]

These lines involve carefully, cyclically constructed poetic entrance, not only into the moving unity of man, woman, stars, and animals, but also into the movement of water and the movement of air (final three lines of the passage). As mentioned, as the ocean wrinkles and slides, to that degree does the wind become visible. For at least a moment, there is no difference or separation between the two elements, but active integrity in their movement. One experiences it again as one would as a child, before differences become so entrenched as to blind one to some extent to wholeness. One touches again immediate experience, the immersed sense of being, akin to the authentic experience of the jellyfish. And as is tellingly the case on more than one occasion of Eliot's poetry and prose, there is here immersion also in another earthly aspect, that of generation and generations. Acutely aware of the fact that one is here *or there*, here in one's own lifetime or (equally) *there in the lifetimes of the generations that make one's existence possible*, he persuades the reader to enter with him in the lines above the rustic past of English existence, his roots of which East Coker is the entrance. He gets entrance-d, so to speak, in those roots. If one were to come too close, one would not be able to enter that as-if and yet all too actual world, shattering it. Staying at just the right distance of imagination, one can feel it in one's veins again, veins that are as rustic as they are modern, again literally because without those earlier rustic veins, the modern ones would not exist. One is immersed also in one's generational being. As has been indicated, this goes right back to the Indo-European roots revived by fragments and recycling in *The Waste Land*.

At the conclusion of "East Coker" one finds another instance of immersion linked to cyclical returning:

> Old men ought to be explorers
> Here and there does not matter
> We must be still and still moving
> Into another intensity
> For a further union, a deeper communion
> Through the dark cold and the empty desolation,
> The wave cry, the wind cry, the vast waters
> Of the petrel and the porpoise. In my end is my beginning.[21]

Again oceanic creatures, immersed in their element, surface in Eliot's poetry. It is little wonder in one respect. He loved the ocean all his life, and, as indicated, spent real time at it, on it, and in it, especially when he was in need of healing.[22] "East Coker" begins with the sentence that reads, in "my beginning is my end," and it is fitting that the poem ends with the line stating that in "my end is my beginning."[23] One has come full circle in terms of an immersed life. In "The Dry Salvages," the only title to refer to Eliot's American roots, the sense of immersion reaches a climax:

> The river is within us, the sea is all about us;
> The sea is the land's edge also, the granite
> Into which it reaches, the beaches where it tosses
> Its hints of earlier and other creation:
> The starfish, the horseshoe crab, the whale's backbone;
> The pools where it offers to our curiosity
> The more delicate algae and the sea anemone.[24]

These lines connect a full circle in Eliot's oeuvre that begins with polyps and other creatures of immersion, as indicated. One is oneself such a creature, filled with water inside and outside, the river within, the sea all around. In this sense, there is no barrier between oneself and one's existence. One has come to recognize the actuality of one's being in the real presence of flowing time. It is being that belongs wholly to or within Earth: its elements and processes, its ocean and circles. One cannot do else but to be moved by Earth, since, after all, one is a radical part of it. The mandalic motif is present again, now residing in the shapes of the creatures referred to such as the starfish, the horseshoe crab with its round body, and the sea anemone with its flowery shape and centered mouth. By mentioning an "earlier and other creation," somewhat reluctantly perhaps, Eliot (again) nods in the direction of the evolutionary process, for the signs here are not embedded only in metaphor, but also in physical actuality. But how can a poem so immersed in immersion, and so aware of flow and openness, be brought to an end? For, would ending it not formally obliterate its very aim of demonstrating and expressing the said immersion and flow? It is here that we find a striking passage in the oeuvre overall, at the conclusion of *Four Quartets*:

> We shall not cease from exploration
> And the end of all our exploring
> Will be to arrive where we started
> And know the place for the first time.
> [...]
> At the source of the longest river
> The voice of the hidden waterfall
> And the children in the apple-tree
> Not known, because not looked for
> But heard, half-heard, in the stillness
> Between two waves of the sea.
> Quick now, here now, always—
> A condition of complete simplicity
> (Costing not less than everything)
> And all shall be well and
> All manner of things shall be well
> When the tongues of flame are in-folded
> Into the crowned knot of fire
> And the fire and the rose are one.[25]

One lives a lifetime to know where it is that one finds oneself: this Earth with its timeless waterfalls, rivers, waves, and the stillness between. In the concluding image, which indeed concludes the entire *Four Quartets*, Eliot merges the rose with its petals and the fire with its flames. For a moment, aesthetically pleasantly, flames are petals, and petals flames; the rose is a fire, and fire is a flower. The image is drenched in a virtually complete fluidity between classes and categories of things and processes. The material pattern, the image, appears to dissolve. And the dissolving, as is clear enough by now, is the point: immersion in life.

From Prufrock to the fiery, liquid rose, then, Eliot's poetry signals in absence and in affirmation that an authentic, mature existence cannot rely purely on skepticism, infinite distance, differentiation, solipsism, epistemology, and so on. It also needs a sense of location in wholeness and immersion, that is, affirmative connection with one's lifetime on the planet with its many lifetimes. From this perspective, one of the most important passages in *Four Quartets* states that

> The stillness, as a Chinese jar is still
> Moves perpetually in its stillness.
> Not the stillness of the violin, while the note lasts,
> Not that only, but the co-existence,
> Or say that the end precedes the beginning,
> And the end and the beginning were always there
> Before the beginning and after the end.
> And all is always now. [26]

It is from the all-encompassing now that everything continues to flow, has flowed in the past, will flow in the future. Now is not encapsulated by past and future as a linear progression might want one to believe. It is not a static point in a series of points. Now continues to open out into the future from the past. The "co-existence" in Eliot's view therefore enjoys a very profound sense of continuity, active continuity, continuity carried by and within the present. To be present is therefore the ultimate gift, and not simply to be present in some esoteric stream, but rather to be present within Earth's very process. And to exist is to coexist. There can be no other meaningful position.

This is to find the peace that passeth (the language of) understanding: the Chinese jar that moves (first line above), moving the eye along the lines of its profound stability, with the result that a satisfying aesthetic experience occurs when movement and stillness combine. The passage asks one to measure the authenticity of one's humanity in terms of one's immersion in that jar, that still motion, or moving stillness, seeing one's participation in the coexistence of opposites in concrete actuality, that is, open-ended earthly unfolding or continuation. This is to honor one's coexistence with the charged awareness that one's being is as important as the existence of the anemone, the jellyfish, and the authentic "jellyfish" within.

If we were to move on a fraction further from within immersion with its equality of inside and outside in earthly being, we would find that boundaries between inside and outside appear to dissolve, disappearing altogether, thus to reach an utter unity of being-and-non-being. This is when one reaches the recognition that *all is always now* (see the final line above) where time and timelessness meet seamlessly in the meaningful miracle of being, or IS. And this formulation brings into early focus the next chapter of the present book (chapter 5), and an appreciation of Eliot's Buddhist and ever-incarnating Tao—the unfolding rose or way of nature in each now-moment, as embodied in his poetry.

The focus here on immersion as a condition of existence and poetic experience leads to further new material considerations, in resonance with the various conclusions of preceding chapters. The stock verbal nouns of new materialism are enmeshment, entanglement, and so forth. They play an important role, because they allow the discussion of culture-nature connection in theorizing language. These terms drift, at once sufficiently specific in their relative novelty within the discourse and sufficiently vague to include various kinds of the said connection. They have about them also a necessary caution: they sound, for lack of a word, "abstract," including in their mood the kind of skepticism and reticence required from their discursive context.

But it is to poetry that one needs to turn to meet with a stronger from of "enmeshment"—immersion. One meets it there even on the textual level, immersed in the concreteness of being by way of paradox, resonance, sound pattern, tone, visceral response, and so forth. Here one encounters at last that it is possible to say that the jellyfish is "fully alive," realizing that there is nothing as filled to the brim with jellyfishness as the living jellyfish. How often it is poetry that comes closest to keeping natural aliveness alive in the domains of semiosis, as in the case of Marianne Moore's 1959 poem "A Jelly-Fish." In this poem the speaker wants to catch the beautiful jewel-like creature. But he or she realizes that it contains a deeper magic: the complete otherness of being a living phenomenon in its own right. The entire poem actualizes this sense of being-alive in contact with an-other. The speaker expands and contracts a hand and an arm to catch the creature, miming its movement, to withdraw it instantly as the full awareness of *its* ability to expand, contract, and quiver comes home. The instant withdrawal of the (perhaps little) hand, probably saves the speaker from a dangerous sting. Simultaneous with this recognition comes the visceral thrill of Moore's ability to give her striking abruptness of form to the instantaneous movement, by virtue of brevity of line and sudden closure as well as an aesthetically attractive clinching of thought by means of rhyme. Besides this quality of the role played by the rhyme scheme and other embodying (formal) aspects of the poem, it mimes the animal's movement on the page, with lines that weave down to mime rhythmic motion. This is no little part of its ability to connect reader and creature.

Eliot has the highest regard for Moore's poetry,[27] and consciously or unconsciously they share their modern awareness of that living mandala, the jellyfish. For them there is about it still the actual sense of complete aliveness, and the magical congruence between jellyfish-being and human, poetic, mandalic being. This sense of immersion is, of course, not carried entirely by new material verbs such as "enmesh" and "entangle." One has to follow the reciprocities of so-called subjectivity and so-called objectivity down into the poetic level to find enmeshment intensifying into immersion. The qualitative difference between the two kinds of verb and their sensibilities perhaps does not matter from a "purely" theoretical perspective. But if we talk of *literary* theory, they matter. Here is an example of how new materialism can expand its project by paying close attention to poetry. As indicated earlier in this book, this entails greater balance between skepticism about great literature and its affirmation. As for the latter, it will perhaps never be possible to do justice to the real presence of poetry by means of a response written in academic prose. Describing the immediacy of music gives rise to a similar problematic.[28] However, the responsiveness of the response to great literature is perhaps as important as breathing. And allowing and steering radical semiotic entry into the poems by way of close reading is one way of being less skeptical about literature. At least, it prevents wild prosaic statements about it to a more satisfactory degree; a point to which I also return in chapter 6. To cite excellent poems and integrate them into one's discussion results in the poet's voice speaking for itself, with one's (skeptical) academic voice alongside it, influenced by it. This procedure *is* sufficiently skeptical, since it amounts to the literary form of the broader scientific imperative of evidence management toward relative truthfulness and generalization, as well as a critical form of the literary democratic and three-dimensional Bakhtinian imperatives of dialogics and heteroglossia.[29]

But it is striking how rare such citation and integration have become in general within theorizing discourse, in particular in the case of ecocriticism. This belies the fact of just how important poetry is to our perception of nature—and I have in mind all kinds of poetry from all kinds of eras and geographies. Perhaps the fear of what amounts to "fair use" plays into this, along with many other factors, such as the need for prose so clean that everyone's prose begins to look like everyone else's, about which, ironically, some natural-scientific scholars are concerned.[30] There is also the concern of being caught committing the supposed sin of submitting to the complex actuality, even mystery, of referentiality, that is, the entertaining of the sign's magnanimous capacities to link up with worlds outside itself. In any event, it is intensely ironic that a discipline so wary of homogeneity should sound less and less heterogeneous in its collective style. In the green writer and herpetologist Richard Kerridge's words, it is "alarming how standard a certain method of putting together an essay has become."[31] One way of actively working against this is (again) to allow the poet's voice into one's textual doing, because the latter will no doubt be persuaded by the former into new, sometimes difficult and even knotty, responses and formulations.

For decades now the claim has been that such literary doing is narrow, whereas theorizing is liberating. It is now emergent, however, that theorizing can be equally narrow, precisely to the extent that it strategically or bluntly ignores great poems, while these poems no doubt have considerable capacity to open minds. Lawrence Buell has called upon ecocritics and literary scholars in general to delve into canonical texts from an Earth-slanted perspective.[32] Rightfully so: and we will not make them present as if they were in need of resuscitation; as if we were trying to rescue a corpse. As Eliot has long since shown, past texts are what make us present, and our presence alters the past.[33] We will therefore rediscover their presence on a green level.

The urgency of the maturation envisaged here comes (as indicated in the introduction) in the face of global literary and natural skepticism, bordering on cynicism inflated with secondariness. Pockets in which "wilderness"—the sheer presence and aliveness of mytho-poetic connections with Earth—thrive, have become rare, marginalized, isolated. Being South African, I am struck by the fact that local poetry in English and Afrikaans relish in global trends of professionalized poetry, the abuse of classics and "big names," and lack of poetic form. Poor works put themselves on the same scale as the best works of the past by means of easy adoption of intertextual references, while those past works sometimes enjoy more presence than the new ones; excellent writers dilute their poetic form to the point where a volume of poetry becomes so much additional theorizing without daring to give poetic shape to the affair; and a professionalized poetic world indulges in back-patting mediocrity.[34]

Surely these trends call upon, not further classics-bashing or classics-elision, but skepticism turned inward, into the discipline itself. What is the nature and status of our theorizing and culture studies? Trailblazing books have appeared in this regard: Valentine Cunningham's as well as Terry Eagleton's different books titled *After Theory*, Raymond Tallis's *Not Saussure*, Umberto Eco's *The Limits of Interpretation*, and Steiner's *Real Presences*. To my mind, the new material turn is itself an important marker of some sense of discomfort with the directions that theorizing have taken. Lest I be misunderstood, I do not in the least make another plea for "the end of deconstruction" or the end of this or that. It would be immature simply to go ahead as if theory is not still happening. Nor do I have anything against interdisciplinarity, inherent to literary study by virtue of artistic literature's age-old tendencies to combine all kinds of fields of human endeavor, ranging from the psychological to the philosophical, and more. Even the focus on secondary matters and affairs strictly outside concerns about literary art cannot and should not be avoided in ecocritical studies. Instead, what I am calling for is a moment's pausing and reflection on whether the balance between focusing on secondary affairs and primary canonical literature is still intact, including the question as to whether the balance between arrogant skepticism about primary literature and even nature itself on the one hand, and *critical* affirmation on the other, is still a dynamic reality within literary studies. No empirical study is necessary to confirm that this balance is at the moment probably skewed in favor of the cynical and the secondary, for the levels of the intensity of those attitudes presently are not helpful.

My call is for renewed willingness to grant mytho-poetic content and form as expressed by great literary artists their place in the larger scheme of things. This proposed balance has to do with David Abram's notion of the spell of the sensuous: patiently returning to kinds of language activity that know the magic that relates humanity and the more-than-human world.[35] The spell of the sensuous, as I hope to be showing in the present argument, prevails in Eliot's poetry. Among other things, his manner of poetically embodying Earth-experience is striking. Getting immersed in poetry is a way of rubbing experience back into its earthliness, and Eliot's project is imperative for the modern way of getting around to such immersion.

Greg Garrard's important reminder further springs to mind that the mytho-poetic (his term is "mystico-phenomenological") dimension should not be left behind in ecocriticism concerned too much with its anxiety about its status in terms of "hard," biological disciplines.[36] This would be part of nature skepticism running awry. Again poetry's voice can be healthy in this respect. We have seen how Eliot's skepticism finds its way into affirmation, by continuing to find semiotic connections with Earth even in modern time. To bring his poetry into the discussion therefore has the capacity to work against the grain of the form and style of theoretical prose itself, which form is, of course, problematic from the outset in terms of relating thought and discussion to something as sensuous as Earth. "I am not looking to dust off the old antitheory position," writes Kerridge in this regard, "but they did know one big thing about theory, those early ecocritics. They saw theory's difficulty in finding a form other than abstract argument: its tendency to crowd out the personal and experiential." He further has the courage to admit that in theory, "sometimes there is an anti-climax. The theoretical argument doesn't connect with enough in the text for the theory to come to life, yet the particularity of focus shuts out other possibilities of the text. We get neither the elucidation of the theory nor the surprises of the text." In the case of new material theory, which "insists upon the mesh and flow of things, their indivisibility and interdependence, the predicament of being confined to the medium of technical, abstract argument is a particularly ironical one."[37]

We may be splitting off the world of culture and the world of Earth more severely by means of the differentiating and narrowing style of our discourse, one infers. We may be losing sight of the supreme intelligence of the authentic jellyfish, which instinctive intelligence we share with it, especially in the visceral language of poetic worlds when it comes to the level of language actions. It is not for nothing that Eliot makes the vital remark that genuine poetry can communicate before it is understood,[38] for an important part of its communication resonates on the visceral, instinctive, and intuitive levels. "Small" visceral changes such as the recognition of sound patterns combining with images and noticeable or less noticeable emotive and bodily responses (such as shivering down the spine), may ultimately have large impacts, since large energies may hinge on them, and their initial energies may have unforeseen effects as they get amplified over time, for instance among generations. It is against this backdrop that I emphasize the embodiment of the poem and its radical inclusion in new material discourse by way of citation and resonance.

Kerridge continues to suggest that "more ecocritical formalism and close reading would help—more willingness to see the literary text's methods *and linger in its moments*" (emphasis added).[39] Such lingering and reflection upon the immediacy of a poetic voice as compelling as Eliot's indeed holds satisfaction and illumination of its own, related here to Earth-matters. Another way of posing this problem is perhaps to insist that art does not belong wholly to the left-brain domain of abstract objective relations. Art is in the nature of meeting another living person, as Steiner's real presence certainly intimates, and as has been shown even in research.[40] But there may be a tendency to confine it to the kind of specifying attention that the left brain brings about, given that the left brain dominates the professional and increasingly the academic world of activity, while the current entwinement of making art such as poetry on the one hand and professionalized academia on the other, is unprecedented. No doubt the left brain offers its thrills: readers of modern poetry in particular know the thrills of ambiguity, of difference as difference—difference as an end, not a means; though as an end it offers new prospects of exploration, for instance in Wallace Stevens's poetry. Again, however, this thrill belongs relatively to the left brain with its emphasis on specifying that comes with distance and rational relations between objects, as recent research increasingly indicates.[41] But would we be acknowledging art as art if we get stuck in the left brain thrill (and it is imperative, to be sure), ignoring or reducing Eliot's poetic insistence on Spinoza? Or is this exactly where literary studies and ecocriticism should have the increasing nerve to be skeptical about its skepticism?

Perhaps to acknowledge art as art (not to be confused with art for art's sake) even within our critical doing, a return is necessary to the connections of the left brain with the right brain, where even the ambiguous wavelength becomes part of affirmation—threeness. I do not wish to elevate the brain lobes into a reified position of be-all and end-all, but wish to indicate simply that the balance I seek has physical, embodied proportions connected to its other proportions of thought, emotion, and spirit.

A lesson from the hippo is at stake. It is centered in its being, being entirely hippo absolutely within its environment even when, sometimes sadly, the environment has been changed and confined radically by human intervention; though such intervention certainly does not make the world of nature as "hyperreal" as some American criticism would want us to believe, at least, not from an African perspective. The hippo, then, is *transcendent*. This puts the matter of transcendence in a wholly new light, by virtue of Eliot's poetry. For, transcendence then comes to mean simply the real presence of radical participation in earthly being. And the implications of immersion for language are radical, as has been hinted at here in the preceding pages. When left and right brain co-operate in understanding to the point of transcendence, one enters the domain of a kind of linguistic "dissolving." Signs, thought-patterns, completely imperative left-brain "objects," actively return to their limitations, and transgress those by "losing" themselves within a larger, ecological context that *knows* meaningful wholeness, whether that wholeness be in cultural artistic form, natural form, or both. In E. E. Cummings's imagery, this is to move on from a two-dimensional, flat, separating, and one-sided view into a vibrant three-dimensional world of seeing all the way around a tree trunk.[42] It is toward exactly this kind of dissolving into threeness that Eliot's poetry and modern poems in general frequently persuade one, as we have seen in the case of the mandalic Sanskrit in *The Waste Land*. His poetry does not halt at the point where it recognizes severe modern severance from earthly connection in Prufrock. Nor does it refrain from indicating and participating in renewed modern relevance of ancient Sanskrit location, or even the submersion in being that polyps and hippos enjoy. For, all of these degrees of intensity in his working toward culture-nature integrity, always already anticipate a still deeper resonance, a level at which the culture-nature boundary dissolves.

NOTES

1. Daniel Albright, *Quantum Poetics: Yeats, Pound, Eliot, and the Science of Modernism* (Cambridge: Cambridge University Press, 1997), 226.
2. T. S. Eliot, *Collected Poems 1909-1962* (New York: Harcourt Brace, 1991), 7.
3. Albright, *Quantum Poetics*, 226.
4. Albright, *Quantum Poetics*, 241.
5. Eliot, *Poems*, 41.
6. University of Toronto Representative Poetry Online, http://rpo.library.utoronto.ca/, retrieved 18 December 2013.

7. Brent Berlin, "Tapir and Squirrel: Further Nomenclatural Meanderings towards a Universal Sound-Symbolic Bestiary," *Nature Knowledge: Ethnoscience, Cognition, and Utility*, eds. Glauco Sanga and Gerhardo Ortalli (Oxford: Berghahn, 2003), 120.

8. *See* Wendell Berry, *Life Is a Miracle: An Essay against Modern Superstition* (Berkeley: Counterpoint, 2001), 139, 149, 31.

9. Eliot, *Poems*, 199.

10. Eliot, *Poems*, 7.

11. Eliot, *Poems*, 3.

12. Eliot, *Poems*, 3.

13. Eliot, *Poems*, 14, 15.

14. Eliot, *Poems*, 5.

15. Eliot, *Poems*, 17.

16. T. S. Eliot, *The Waste Land* (Norton Critical Edition), ed. Michael North (New York: W. W. Norton, 2001), 16.

17. Eliot, *The Waste Land*, 7.

18. Eliot, *Poems*, 177.

19. Eliot, *Poems*, 177.

20. Eliot, *Poems*, 183.

21. Eliot, *Poems*, 189.

22. Peter Ackroyd, *T. S. Eliot: A Life* (London: Hamish Hamilton, 1984), 114, 314.

23. Eliot, *Poems*, 182, 190.

24. Eliot, *Poems*, 191.

25. Eliot, *Poems*, 208.

26. Eliot, *Poems*, 180.

27. Celeste Goodrich, *Hints and Disguises: Marianne Moore and Her Contemporaries* (Iowa: University of Iowa Press, 1989), 106.

28. George Steiner, *Real Presences* (Chicago: University of Chicago Press, 1991), 16.

29. Mikhail Bakhtin, "Heteroglossia in the Novel," *Bakhtinian Thought: An Introductory Reader*, ed. Simon Dentith (London: Routledge, 1995), 208 209.

30. Japie van Zyl, "Curiosity Mission to Mars," lecture given at the Brain Bag event on 14 June 2013, Potchefstroom Campus of the North West University, South Africa. Attended by the author. Professor Van Zyl expressed concern about homogeneity in the humanities during question time.

31. Richard Kerridge, Review of *Ecocritical Theory: New European Approaches*, eds. Axel Goodbody and Kate Rigby; *Environmental Criticism for the Twenty-First Century*, eds. Stephanie LeMenager et al, *ISLE: Interdisciplinary Studies in Literature and Environment* 19.3 (Summer 2012), 597.

32. Lawrence Buell, "The Ecocritical Insurgency," *New Literary History* 30.3 (Summer 1999), 709.

33. Eliot, *Prose*, 38, 40.

34. Rustum Kozain, "Review: *Bodyhood* by Leon de Kock," https://groundwork.wordpress.com/2010/10/19/review-bodyhood-leon-de-kock, retrieved 11 February 2015; Kelwyn Sole, "Our Literature Needs Incisive Criticism, Yes, But on Exactly Whose Values Will It Be Based?" http://www.mg.co.za/article/2011-03-04-our-literature-needs-incisive-criticism-yes-but-on-exactly-whose-values-will-it-be-based, retrieved 11 February 2015; Dana Gioia, "Can Poetry Matter?" http://www.theatlantic.com/past/docs/unbound/ poetry/gioia.htm, retrieved 11 February 2015.

35. David Abram, *The Spell of the Sensuous: Perception and Language in a More-Than-Human World* (New York: Vintage, 1997), 273.

36. Greg Garrard, "Nature Cures? Or How to Police Analogies of Personal and Ecological Health," *ISLE: Interdisciplinary Studies in Literature and Environment* 19.3 (Summer 2012), 512.

37. Kerridge, [Review], 598.

38. Eliot, *Prose*, 206.

39. Kerridge, [Review], 597, 598.

40. Iain McGilchrist, *The Master and His Emissary: The Divided Brain and the Making of the Western World* (New Haven: Yale University Press, 2012), 96.

41. Donald Kalsched, *Trauma and the Soul: A Psycho-Spiritual Approach to Human Development and Its Interruption* (London: Routledge, 2013), 171–175.

42. E. E. Cummings, *A Miscellany Revised*, ed. George James Firmage (London: Peter Owen, 1966), 66–67.

Chapter Five

Dissolving

The Name of the Lotos Rose

A major and even unsettling implication of being immersed in one's existence is that language dissolves along with numerous egoic constructs that on occasion clutter and confine one's perceptions of being alive. These constructs and language come to vibrant nothing in moments of immersion. Being a masterful poet, Eliot is somehow able to mediate this dissolving that comes with immersion, through language. He exploits the boundaries and limits through which language mediates experience, bringing it to meaningful nothing. Those boundaries (such as automated grammatical categories) become permeable in his poetry again, with the result that opposite categories such as culture (language) and nature (outside-language) find their renewed saturation. And when the saturation is actively complete, the very boundaries appear to dissolve and, ultimately, language-as-boundary appears to dissolve. It appears to become natural again, in the strict sense that it seems to re-enter the presence of its origins. It participates in presence, and as such loses the dominance of its differentiating capacities. In short, it creates again a context of presencing, rather than getting stuck in a "context" of re-presented categories.

By means of fragmentation and recombination modern poets and Eliot increase the likelihood of such osmotic events between poem and reader. The poem offers more holes, so to speak, more porousness, through which original sensibilities of language-nature wholeness can occur. Such holes in other words offer more potentials for the poetic experiencing of being and no-thing or emptiness, or a vibrant hole or whole. As will be demonstrated in this chapter, Eliot carefully positions oxymoron and word order to create such porous effects of dissolving, for instance when he places the word "rose" in such a way that it becomes a noun *and* a verb. In that moment, the verbal and nominal boundaries of English, so meticulously erected, maintained, and entrenched over time, dissolve again, to return one to an original sense of the wisdom that comes from knowing that the relatively static rose object (presented by the noun) and change (presented by the verb) are one and the same in overall being: *things change*, they continue to unfold, and one unfolds with them. This is part of the thrilling mystery of a lifetime on the planet. Moreover, the merging of the nominal and the verbal suggests something like: *change is IT!* Or, IT IS. Or, to be alive is to (be a radical part of cosmological) change, right down to the minutiae of physical and wise growth. A radical shattering occurs of the neat world in which the object is a static backdrop for the actions of the verbal subject. And these descriptions fit the case of *Four Quartets* overall.

This is not to doubt that language is critically important to being human. At its best, poetic language *forms part of the acknowledgement* that language can also act as a trap, as has been determined in the present book. Eliot's poetic language goes one step further by achieving the singular event of language escaping from its own ensnarement into a sense of its dissolving. The paradox then becomes that language is able to find that which moves outside it, and of which it is a movement, after all; that is, language comes to nothing in a positive sense. It manages to mingle with that vibrant nowhere from whence the "ten thousand things," *including language*, continue to emerge.

The notion of nothing in literature has not always been received in this way, though. Reading modern poetic criticism soon reveals that critics tend to think of "nothing" mainly in terms of nihilism and annihilation.[1] Given that the modern poets were born into an era that was jadedly conscious of nihilism, the critics' insistence on it appears to make immediate sense. That they further tend to be indignant about moments of nothing-as-nihilism in modern poetry seems equally sensible: a world, culture, poetic project, or long poem that "comes to nothing" is not a pleasant thought. Sinking into the vast malaise of an empty sensibility appears weak, as if poetry withdraws from vitality.

There can be little doubt that these problems centering on nihilism were pertinent for modern artists in their time, and that they had to find ways to grapple with and reflect it. A "pretty" art that would have denied nihilism by glossing it over with "positive" contents would have amounted to an artistic crime. It would have meant that no artistic commitment or integrity existed among the artists of those days, and that they were in denial of the very nature of their milieu. Viewed in this light, the enormous artistic commitment and courage of those artists that we now honor, such as Franz Kafka, Vasily Kandinsky, W. B. Yeats, and Eliot, virtually speaks for itself. And we forget all too readily that Eliot risked his career and even his well-being for the sake of reflecting the less attractive actualities of his time in his art.[2]

However, the commitment of Eliot and modern poets includes another sense of nothing altogether, one that is neither nihilistic nor annihilating, but elevating and vibrant. One way of describing this vital (and overlooked) *kind* of nothing in modern poetry, is to insist on the existence in their poetry of childlike, meditative perception of being in vibrant relation to non-being.[3] The poems return their readers to the "first ground" of being, uncluttered by preconceptions and a maze of linguistic relations, to the recognition that the existence of (any) something is a miracle. The life-giving no-specific-thing from which that something comes, equally is a miracle.

In the case of modern poets such as E. E. Cummings and William Carlos Williams this childlike celebration of being within non-being is fairly directly clear. In Eliot's case, one finds greater emphasis on the world-weariness of a "mature" civilization, but this does not prohibit his own, singular sense of childlike joy, and of the primal love embodied in being-and-non-being, as has been demonstrated in chapter 3. In fact, this situation makes his singular poetic expression of such phenomena all the more compelling, because they stand in greater contrast with the nihilism that his poetry reflects, thus gaining in affirmative outline. And his sense of Buddhist skepticism takes this form, to which I return.

On the broadly meaningful level propounded here—the level of real presence or numinous, spacious nowness—the question is not whether we know what *The Waste Land* means, or not. The question that the poem poses is far more akin to the theologian Thomas Küng's question, rightfully posed to doubtful Thomases of the doctrine of inert materialism: why is there something, and not nothing? The question was posed initially, in 1714, by Gottfried Leibniz.[4] To this *The Waste Land* adds: why is there nothing from which something comes, and not simply logical absence? It is important that there is nothing, because in day-to-day experience, and especially in meditative moments of experience—*not* restricted only to special persons, just as dreaming is not restricted to shamans[5]—it is clear that things emerge from/return to a miraculous nowhere. This is so even if only on the level of the bare recognition that we cannot restrict such emergence or returning to (say) the world of a particular tree or a particular object of possession. In this way all is very much related to nothing, and precisely not only on the epistemological level.

Here Eliot shares a modern poetic sensibility with Wallace Stevens when the latter famously composes the nothing that *is*, Cummings when his entire oeuvre is soaked in the now-here-nowhere, Marianne Moore when she profoundly wishes to be invisible like the (Taoist) dragon of heaven, which gives shape to the ten thousand things, and Williams when bloom and butterfly merge into utter one-ness within accentuated silence and blank space.[6]

The importance of this kind of nothing is the fact that a certain openness continues to become or come-into existence from which all that is possible and actual continues to emerge. Continuation is the point, and emptiness is essential to it: death and rebirth enter a cycle of openings and newly emerging forms. The connection with the miraculous nothing is therefore vital. Equally vital is the accent on blank space in modern poetry albeit that, in true Taoist manner, once the awareness of nowhere is grasped, the signs leading to the awareness are not of too much further consequence, or, rather, the signs show their remarkable ability to become part of something greater than themselves. Again, they dissolve, so to speak.

How does this dissolving work? Consider again the syllable *Da* in *The Waste Land*. Since at least for a moment the natural event and the onomatopoeic syllable are able to suggest that they are one, it follows that the boundary between signs and nature has dissolved. Since language, signs, is that which marks the limits of the human boundary between the semiosphere and Earth, it follows that this is the exact boundary that has dissolved, at least momentarily becoming part of something much larger than itself (natural event, thunder) which includes it (the Earth-process). Given this, the story of *The Waste Land* can in summation (again) be told as one of holding down the tension between opposites until it becomes unbearable, leading into the relief of signs dissolving into threeness at their limit, followed by a collapse of terrible fragments and the subsequent heightened return to dissolving, the vibrantly full-empty immersion in being-and-nothing, as signaled on the poetic page. Dissolving then entails that words come to interface with (or enter) the nothing beyond them (again) in a positive sense. *Four Quartets* throughout strikes one as a poem composed with an eye on dissolving of this nature. It is Eliot's most overt Buddhist poem (even as it is also as overtly Christian as "Ash-Wednesday," of course), and the reader who is willing to see semiotic dissolving in action, does well to examine it anew. It uses its paradoxical cycles and oxymorons persistently to point into that very place where language ends, and nothing begins:

> At the still point of the turning world. Neither flesh nor fleshless;
> Neither from nor towards; at the still point, there the dance is,
> But neither arrest nor movement. And do not call it fixity,
> Where past and future are gathered. Neither movement from, nor towards,
> Neither ascent nor decline. Except for the point, the still point,
> There would be no dance, and there is only the dance.
> I can only say, *there* we have been: but I cannot say where.
> And I cannot say, how long, for that is to place it in time.
>
> The inner freedom from the practical desire,
> The release from action and suffering, release from the inner
> And the outer compulsion, yet surrounded
> By a grace of sense, a white light still and moving.[7]

Dissolving 117

These questions and images, unusually similar (among other texts) to the *Tao Te Ching*, as will presently be shown, persistently open and return to nothing. What can be neither flesh nor fleshless? Nothing. What kind of movement in space can occur neither from nor toward anything? *The movement of nothing*. And so on and so forth: again and again Eliot uses familiar opposites (movement and stillness, forwards and backwards, animate and inanimate) to point beyond them into the unity of being-and-nothing. The unity of being-and-nothing, that "place" where opposites continue to dissolve, is the way of nature; it is the place from which the natural dance continues to emerge as if by magic, out of the blue, becoming yew tree, figured leaf, (significant) soil, joy, tears, love. And yet the becoming and the open-ended nothing are one: in the original pattern, very much the one that occurs now, there is no difference between stillness and movement. To sense the root of movement is to sense its stillness in nature, like the active, open space within which and through which trees grow. The lotos rose symbolizes no less than this, just as it symbolizes the integrity in Eliot's poetic sensibility between orient (lotos) and occident (rose). The stillness of the Chinese jar as it moves is therefore, like so many other images in the poem, a metaphor that resonates throughout the whole poem.

Again, Earth is the first master at dissolving opposites—immense ones such as impossible heat and cold in the Cosmos and on Earth, for example—thus to continue into its seamless and almost unnoticed becoming. The "grace of sense" (final line above) is to recognize this (again) in all its full-emptiness (Afrikaans *volledig*, complete), its completeness that somehow remains active. Release from the inner and outer compulsion ties in radically with this, since it amounts to the Buddhist notion of accepting somethingness in combination with nothingness, so to be free from the desires that sometimes constrain one's view of (and peaceful elation in) being. It is also to accept the process-nature of earthly existence in its fullness, which is mindfully empty enough to allow all that continues. On contemplation this is a staggering thought full of peace. To know, unlike the case of the superstitious aspect of our pagan forefathers, though, that sacredness does not reside in this particular tree or that particular stone, just once again. For, being cannot be reduced to one given thing. Being consists of no-thing that continues to shape into this or that, or the "ten thousand things" in all their suchness: the still point, an empty point since it is also a deeply spiritual point, permeates the whole dance!

Four Quartets is a modern poetic statement of these baffling and joy-giving truths. If nothing remains, it can be as much a Buddhist and Christian phenomenon as a nihilistic one, and the poem chooses to affirm the former in the face of the latter, given that Eliot composes the poem in the very face of the Second World War. How far removed from that reality is the Chinese jar in its fragile, affirming stillness, moving perpetually in that stillness:[8] the perfect stability and flow as the eye traces the shape of such an aesthetic object made from this Earth! In the same way does Earth's encompassing, elusive Tao (natural way that never gets stuck in what it produces) retain its stability of changes, and one enters a wholly different space in connection with place and emplacement. Acknowledgement of that elusiveness is what makes Earth's seamlessness of changing clear, as found in Lao Tzu's ancient *Tao Te Ching*, now more part of modern Buddhism than was the case already even in Eliot's day:

> *One looks for it and does not see it:*
> its name is 'seed.'
> *One listens for it and does not hear it:*
> its name is 'subtle.'
> One reaches for it and does not feel it:
> its name is 'small.'
> [. . .]
> Its highest is not light,
> its lowest is not dark.
> Welling up without interruption,
> one cannot name it.
> *It returns again to non-existence.*
> *This is called the formless form,*
> *the objectless image.*
> [. . .]
> *Walking towards it one does not see its face;*
> *following it one does not see its back.*
> If one holds fast to the DAO of antiquity
> in order to master today's existence
> one may know the ancient beginning.
> This means: DAO's continuous thread. (emphasis added)[9]

The passage bears intriguingly close correspondence to Eliot's notions of that space in which the still point becomes visible: neither high nor low (but both), neither from nor toward (and both), neither light nor dark (and both), Tao is all movement and all stillness at once. One moves toward it without seeing its face: it is neither from nor toward, and so forth. As indicated in the introduction of the present argument, Buddhism is now a hybrid that includes the broad (and hence also Taoist) notion of being emanating from nothing, while Eliot has a singular hybrid Buddhism of his own, focusing in modern poetic fashion on blank space and the still point. The Tao is the vibrant unity of vibrant matter (or Earth) and vibrant emptiness (or heaven), and therefore it eludes the differentiation concomitant with naming it:

> The DAO that can be expressed
> is not the eternal DAO.
> The name that can be named
> is not the eternal name.
> 'Non-existence' I call the beginning of Heaven and Earth.
> 'Existence' I call the mother of individual beings.
> Therefore does the direction towards non-existence
> lead to the sight of the miraculous essence,
> the direction towards existence
> to the sight of spatial limitations.[10]

This passage formulates in its way one of Eliot's central concerns in the poem: that naming the moving, dancing pattern emanating from stillness is in a certain sense to stall it, and to make it impossible. It is to stall its movement, because naming—such as grown-up grappling with relations between re-presented objects—introduces the distances, distortions, and differences between humans being and the authentic immediacy of jellyfish experience, ultimately cancelling the aliveness of phenomena if it becomes too insistent on being the "only" reality. (Such naming has in fact been denying, increasingly, the experience of beauty in the arts.)[11] And this denies the ongoing unity that he wishes to express, because it turns that prospect into a set of mental spatial confinements, Lao Tzu's "spatial limitations" that may strangle one. This difference between *saying* and the *said* is the ancient dilemma of all mystics, of course. They want to point into the continuous way, while they know full well that followers may get stuck at the road sign, and even argue about it. This is very common knowledge, but its truth has not evaporated. Eliot (though perhaps not a mystic in any strict sense, just as Taoism is experiential rather than mystical) grapples with it anew in this poem. At its height of depths, or depths of height, the poem succeeds in entering (the reader) into that dynamic thread where the way up and the way down continue to meet, becoming natural being on planet Earth. The signs dissolve into their now-here-nowhere earthly origins.

This profoundly simple and useful phrase, "now-here-nowhere," has been coined by Norman Friedman in relation to E. E. Cummings's poetry,[12] and at least by implication to modern poetry on the whole. It means that one is never as aware of the crisp outlines of now-and-here as when one sees it in terms of nowhere, that is, non-interference by preconceived or hardened notions that distort one's perception. Simultaneously, one is never more aware of the nowhere from which everything emanates as when one is utterly immersed in now-and-here. One is "in" the "now-moment," perceiving clearly at last. One's being-in-tune with the still point makes one dance with all the dancing of coexistence. Here silence sings, and singing finds its unity with silence. Here the Chinese jar is at once in motion and in stillness. Words dissolve into their now-here-nowhere origin, and all is always now. The note reaches into its silence, formulates the silence by which it is formulated. In short, the now-here-nowhere describes precisely the intersection of time and timelessness, place and placelessness, that is at the heart of the pattern that Eliot actively embodies in *Four Quartets*. Paradoxically, in Taoist manner of now-here-nowhere again, this is to name it and not to name it.

This importantly includes failure, which should not be understood blandly in relation to this poem. In much-discussed passages of the poem Eliot goes to great lengths to show that the attempt to encapsulate in time and in language this holy nowness of being, must fail. It is only by failing to encapsulate it, given careful use of bright oxymorons that open out into recognitions of nowness "outside" language, that language is able to participate in it. Of course, this involves a strategic and not an outright failure. This may be the poem's central paradox: that "all is always now," even though (or because) words "strain, / Crack, and sometimes break / Will not stay still."[13]

At the intersection between "England and nowhere,"[14] then, all is always now, and the chain of being comes into its own also in terms of the Incarnation. The latter is from a Christian perspective the instance of the intersection between time and timelessness, flesh and holiness, changing history. It also embodies the still point. Perhaps for this reason Gary Snyder makes the important and intriguing remark that what is "really fun about Eliot is his intelligence and his highly selective and charming use of Occidental symbols which point you in a certain direction."[15] The Incarnation points into and is the still point, as embodied again in the still motion of the Chinese jar. And so Eliot rubs Buddhist sensibilities into the Earth-sense of *Four Quartets*. The rubbing ranges from minute and thrilling moments of recognition to the overall dynamic pattern of nowness and wholeness that the poem seeks and, let it be said for once, achieves in its moving way. Eliot is very distinct about the nature of this magic of Earth's continuation; *Four Quartets*, though skeptical and even too philosophical on occasion, wants to be taken seriously on the matter. It instructs that harmony on Earth is not "sympathetic" in some fictional manner, but rather that its very actuality affirms its magically still unfolding. Plants will not bend down to us in sympathy, but the kingfisher's flight answers "light to light":

> Will the sunflower turn to us, will the clematis
> Stray down, bend to us; tendril and spray
> Clutch and cling?
> Chill fingers of yew be curled
> Down on us? After the kingfisher's wing
> Has answered light to light, and is silent, the light is still
> At the still point of the turning world.[16]

The first lines pose a question about the nature of the relationship between Earth and humans. They ask whether the relationship is magical and sympathetic in an artificial way. The last lines should be read, among other things, as the response to this question. It refutes artificial magic by replacing it with actual sacredness: the most ordinary reciprocity between creatures and elements. The light reflecting from the kingfisher's wing is an answer to the light that falls on it, including the reciprocal light between human observer, kingfisher, and sun. This kingfisher, moreover, refers to an actual bird witnessed by the poet as part of his personal history, and the personal unfolding of his life as a radical part of the dance emanating from the still point thus enters the poem. He exclaimed joy and surprise upon seeing a kingfisher at Kelham.[17] The quest for the fisher king legend in *The Waste Land* at last comes to a most ordinary point of acceptance and reality here. The magic of the dance—light bouncing toward light—is real; Eliot has not strayed from threeness and its actuality, that is, its open-ended combination of opposites such as the holy and the real. Of course, the fulfillment tasted here in the kingfisher image is anticipated already by one of the most poignant and plain moments in *The Waste Land*, when Eliot refers to the song of the hermit thrush, which he also witnessed with deep appreciation in his actual life.[18]

The most ordinary is the most extraordinary. The light is still as it moves, and moving in its stillness: it continues to be just what it is. A moment of seeing *tzu jan* occurs, that is, seeing the suchness of things, their IS-ness, so to speak.[19] That the kingfisher's wings turn as they row or propel the creature through the air is part of the point, since that is how it is able to answer the light, it reflects off that moving wing. The light is what it is by virtue of the kingfisher being what it is, and vice versa. This very plainness—so-ness—of earthly being is its *way*, its continuing unfolding. By way of hermeneutic trust, the reader knows that Eliot is after the moving stillness of nature, also known in hybrid modern Buddhism as its Tao. For the willing reader, hermeneutic trust here leads into an actual moment of stillness in recognizing nature's moving stillness. And this trust includes the notion that the words do and do not matter.

This brings into focus the centrality of the word "rose" in *Four Quartets*. It is a richly layered symbolic word, as is commonly accepted in literary studies, and in the context of this poem may well refer to all of the following: England, poetry, W. B. Yeats (perhaps therefore also Ireland), Christ, femininity, sex, blood, war, and more. In terms that are particular to the poem, it refers to the lotos, as intimated: "And the lotos rose, quietly, quietly, / The surface glittered out of heart of light."[20] *Four Quartets* thus invokes the lotus flower, that ancient symbol of now-arising in the quickening becoming of / from nowhere. He plays with the nominal and verbal uncertainty created through placement of the word "rose." It becomes a hybrid word that plays on our deep-seated expectation that "rose" is a noun, a kind of flower, in a context of flowers (evoked by "lotos"). But his placement grammatically reads that the lotos *rose* quietly, and a verb takes the place of a noun. A radical transfusion of categories occurs, a shimmering saturation point combining action and object at last. In the process, the usual grammatical barriers between verb and noun dissolve. We have in *Four Quartets* at its center a *dissolving grammar*. The poem is an open (dissolving) journey into the heart of that flower that we call existence, where it meets the fire, the inhalation and exhalation, the in-venting, of that existence:

> Quick now, here, now, always—
> A condition of complete simplicity
> (Costing no less than everything)
> And all shall be well and
> All manner of things shall be well
> When the tongues of flame are in-folded
> Into the crowned knot of fire
> And the fire and the rose are one.[21]

Fire and flower arise as one, as if from nowhere. (Consider that "nowhere" is carefully suggested by the first line in the passage, "now, here, now, always," just as silence, quietness, and emptiness are suggested as meaningful states throughout the poem.) "Fire" is one of those nouns that, especially from an "ungrammatical," maturely childlike perspective, slips almost instantly into the verbal world, because it denotes an "entity" alive with the motion of its leaping orange flames, not unlike a dancing creature— or, perhaps, a very wild flower. If we now take Eliot's formal recommendation seriously, that nouns should also be read as verbs, then it comes across as aesthetically satisfying that the nouns "fire" and "rose" would verbally *merge*, actively come together. The poet exquisitely skillfully "helps" the reader to follow the merging by visually showing how it could come to pass that a fire will become a rose. The tongues of flame, hence the leaf-like flames, are "in-folded," like the tongues of a rose. Again the resonances of Christianity and Buddhism remain intact, since the Christian aspect would be the tongues of flame at Pentecost, as well as the continuing grace of Incarnation, and the Buddhist the extinguishing of flaming desire into the moving stillness of the (lotos) rose. Eliot's entire project comes to moving stillness in every sense, given his struggles with the fires of desire in *The Waste Land*, which relates it to Prufrock, and so forth. The melting device he employs throughout his poetry, of which one example is Cleopatra melting into Philomela melting into an affluent modern woman,[22] here finds its full meaning. And the terror of flaming airplanes of *blitzkriegs* in the World War that the poet witnessed and feared at the very moments of composing this poem, dissolves into affirmation. The fact that both fire and flower literally or in "everyday" life do seem to spring forth from or return to a center makes the metaphor all the more believable, of course. The numinous, illuminating image brings the nowness of mergence and emergence into the mind's eye. We have here another living mandala in his poetic oeuvre, and this is the high note on which his major poetry concludes in all open-endedness. These things are not esoteric, though. The magnanimity of the poem is considerable. It includes the muddiest and most excremental realities of being under its Christian and Buddhist umbrella, showing that our "common *dhaatus* and efforts" (Eliot's phrase)[23] is part of sacred essence. Sex, too: is it worth revisiting briefly that place where man and woman find themselves to be

> Rustically solemn or in rustic laughter
> Lifting heavy feet in clumsy shoes,
> Earth feet, loam feet, lifted in country mirth
> Mirth of those long since under Earth
> Nourishing the corn. Keeping time,
> Keeping the rhythm in their dancing
> As in their living the living seasons
> The time of the seasons and the constellations
> The time of milking and the time of harvest
> The time of coupling of man and woman
> And that of beasts. Dung and death.
>
> Dawn points, and another day
> Prepares for heat and silence. Out at sea the dawn wind
> Wrinkles and slides.[24]

"Dung and death" reconcile and appease Eliot's rightful fear of "dearth and desert."[25] They are a concrete part of Earth's cycles and the truthfulness of rustic life, and those aspects of rustic being that continue to survive in modern lifestyles, despite all appearances to the contrary. It is therefore a flaw in Cleo McNelly Kearns's useful Indic survey of Eliot's project when she insists that oriental scholarship would want to deny the inclusion of the phrase under the rubric of reconciliation.[26] She further finds that "a less reassuring sea 'Wrinkles and slides'" outside the serenity of fixed land suggested by the rustic scene.[27] Such reading makes sense, but another reading is possible: that the passage, like the others in the poem, is not after the supposed serenity of fixed land. It is after change, and catching up with the way of earthly changes in a poetic way. That the wind wrinkles and slides on the water makes visible their elusive, changing unity.

All is part of existence, its purity includes all experience. One's own experience indeed occurs only because of other experiences. "I am here / Or there, or elsewhere. In my beginning" makes sense. One exists now only because of all those coexistences of the past that have made one's now-existence possible. The peasant's past is what makes modern being possible. One's existence here is therefore as much the peasant's existence there, just as the existence of English is impossible without the existence of Sanskrit. Equally, it is one's coexistence here with beasts there that literally makes one's life possible. One is (in) one's beginning. The passage brims with generational reverence of the kind underpinning the juxtaposition of Sanskrit and English in *The Waste Land*.

In this reading, meaningfulness enters concrete life to the hilt. One is reminded of Father Zosimo, the beloved orthodox monk in Fyodor Dostoevsky's novel *The Brothers Karamazov*, who has to pass the "test," after his death, of not decaying on his table in a room in the monastery for a number of days to be ordained a saint. He fails. But it is the very human odor that ranks from the room after only a day that confirms the immensely saintly life of this man, who connected with his most "common" fellows while on Earth, in the most extraordinarily ordinary way of love: love that comes precisely from the wisdom of knowing one's humanity, the very concreteness of one's existence, and that of others.[28]

Eliot's *Four Quartets* similarly embodies the renewed recognition among a modern audience that it is the concrete nowness of our moments on the planet that matters. One way of expressing this spiritual paradox, as Dostoyevsky and Eliot do in their different ways, is to give artistic response to the Christian Incarnation. For Eliot an equally important way is to see the sheer continuation of matter and emptiness in their elusive pattern or way. Hence it happens that words, after speech, reach into the silence of *Four Quartets*.[29] Such reaching embodies the ultimate "shape" that dissolving signs take.

And importantly perhaps for new materialism, this silence, this nothing, is vibrant. It sings. It sings silently that all is always now, as I have indicated here and there in the present argument. His poetry thus comes to its full connection with Earth, after Prufrock and all the other personas unable to reach it. The reaching of it in poetic language is of course, paradoxically again, also to know exactly how poetic language is unable to reach it. Hence the paradox that poetic language establishes the connection by strategically "giving up" on it. Already Prufrock gives up on it, but not in the full-empty affirmative manner of *Four Quartets*.

Is it not so that this is a key aspect of Eliot's sensibility of the *absolute*? Jane Bennett beautifully etymologizes that word: "absolute" consists of *ab* (off) and *solver* (to loosen). "The absolute is that which is *loosened off* and on the loose." Speaking with the political theologian Hent de Vries she says that the absolute is therefore "a some-thing that is not an object of knowledge, that is detached or radically free from representation, and thus no-thing at all."[30] This is *not* the absolute in Idealized terms, since it is in the nature of things that they are able to "loosen off" from our perception into no-thing-ness. That is, our perception of them is absolved in dissolving. That is part of the freedom of real presence; things are not merely re-presentational! In Eliot's poetry, this setting free of culture into renewed forms of being over which we have no final say, and into which we are immersed is also, paradoxically and attractively, one way of rediscovering, refreshing, re-collecting, and re-membering cultural activity. The now-here-nowhere in which all is always now comes into its own also on the level of the *praxis* of *poiesis*; the seeming self-making or spontaneous emergence and return to more-than-words of or in poetry.

In the process, Eliot strikingly combines two aspects of semiosis referred to in George Steiner's work: real presence (as mentioned) and hermeneutic trust. The subtle references to oriental meanings pointing into vibrant nothing convey the presence of the ancient wisdom of ongoing, unfolding and infolding integrity between being, non-being, Earth, and humanity. The enormous freedom of Earth to be, and the concomitant freedom of humans being, is communicated to the English audience by way of Sino-English,[31] that is, the celebrated ideogrammatic method of modern poetry influenced by Chinese.

This involves no less than a form of English quite prevalent in modern poetry, as indicated, so that the hermeneutic trust underpinning it is not only general, but specific to the reader of modern poetry. In his way, Eliot is saying-showing the real presence of nature through the real presence of his poetry, made possible in this instance by Sino-English trust: paradoxical, importantly "ignorant" use of vivid images and a sense of vibrant emptiness *into which signs ultimately dissolve*, or by virtue of which silence acquires its singing. The Sino-English impetus is crucial to Ezra Pound and modern poetry on the whole, as Steiner indicates, among other scholars. He wonders how Pound's translucencies (Eliot's word) occur.[32]

Pound's amazing ability to penetrate to the original spirit of the Chinese poems without knowing the language is indeed a near-magical puzzle. Using only Ernest Fenollosa's notes, he somehow restored the poems to their original sensibility, even while making technical mistakes in translation. One important reason for the achievement, as Steiner indicates by following the thought of Eliot and Ford Madox Ford, is that "Pound can imitate and persuade with utmost economy not because he or the reader knows so much but because both concur in knowing so little" (!).[33] Part of this contract of profound ignorance that makes trust and the transfusion of Chinese and English possible by now involves the concurrence on a vivid image-per-line style that goes along with, and/ or invokes a certain natural stillness, as we see also in *Four Quartets*. In his way, Eliot participates poetically in a version of Sino-English natural trust. He does not mention the Chinese jar as an aside. From this angle, not only does Eliot's project again appear much closer to Gary Snyder's than has been recognized, but his oeuvre seems to combine most saliently in the lotos rose of *Four Quartets* and the significant blank space in *The Waste Land*. However, the relative critical reluctance to see this in its fullness (full-emptiness), especially among Eliot's first critical receivers, the New Critics, has ironically been perpetuated by Edward Said's mammoth, impacting work on orientalism, the topic of the subsequent chapter. No small part of the achievement in *Four Quartets* is therefore that words enact their dissolving, thus pushing immersion into its ultimate "form." They break up, accentuating silence, and then they reach into the silence, as though disappearing there, not without considerable resonance, like the butterfly disappears into the blossom and the blossom into the butterfly in Ezra Pound's creative translation of a short Moritake poem:

> The fallen blossom flies back to its branch:
> A butterfly.[34]

The crucial moment of the poem is when the recognition comes that dynamic unity continues between opposite fields such as the animal and plant kingdoms. Similar dissolving of categories and boundaries occurs in Eliot's "rose," as demonstrated. At least for a moment, it is at once a noun and a verb, melting those opposite grammatical (pre)conditions. On a larger scale, as demonstrated further, *Four Quartets* continues to dissolve the categories of stillness and motion, the sound of words and (their) silence, or the silence that makes them possible in the first place, and so forth. The exercise is not purely philosophical or even metaphysical, though. It is ontological in the sense that recognition of the deep pattern comes with clarity about how earthly existence again and again unfolds into and out of that place where time and timelessness continue to meet. As in E. E. Cummings's imagery, poetry offers its reader the silence of singing and the singing of silence[35] in that "three-dimensional" place where opposite categories (an important limit of language) dissolve. I would insist further only once more that this is an actual reality in wilderness. The music of silence in a forest or grassland can be at first deafening (especially upon exiting the chaotic world of the modern lifestyle), and then actively peace-giving, so that one sees with brighter eyes where the inner and outer worlds meet.

On the level of orientalism and the occidental, a final important blending occurs in *Four Quartets* as much as in *The Waste Land* in terms of the relocation of vibrant existence within vibrant non-existence—Eliot calls it "unbeing and being" between which one continues to exist.[36] In his way, by means of the directness, indirectness, dislocation, location, and modern Buddhism that have been discussed in preceding pages here, Eliot is able to achieve an oriental-occidental welding of a kin with Pound's. About the latter, Steiner says that its "insinuation of self into otherness is the final secret of the translator's craft."[37] Though not in translation, and though not *as* Imagist and ideogrammatic, Eliot's use of oriental influences amounts to a similar ability to enter into the spirit of Buddhist skepticism/ ignorance and the resultant affirmation of earthly continuation and wisdom. After all, the poem advocates ignorance as the way to understanding. For, that wisdom is the taken-for-granted, but actually astonishing (and potentially peace-giving) truth that the ground of one's being rests and continues to move in that Being that radically comes from Non-being. One's particular personality, ego, body, and so forth, come and go along with all other things. They are not here forever. Accepting this coming-and-going (certainly with a loss of inflated ego, that is, ego that might think of itself as infinite) is the beginning of wisdom in this perspective. Beautiful is how the Christian and Buddhist notions, different as they are, of self-loss in coming to actual understanding thus coincide as an expression in Eliot's world.

This means, among other things, that one's life is a miraculous gift of individuality that *participates*, and participates only, in Being. This kind of humility is therefore indeed eternal in nature. On another occasion, perhaps, one may consider whether Eliot's impersonal theory of individual poetry is not therefore substantially informed by his Buddhist sensibilities. He formulated this theory during and fairly shortly after his soaking up of orientalism at Harvard. In any event, Eliot's own achievement—despite his reluctances and/ or confirmations about this professed in public (that is, outside the immediate actuality of his actual poetry)—of blending being-and-non-being in modern combination of orient and occident deserves its own historical acknowledgement.

What can new materialism make of such dissolving of signs, and the numinous world into which such dissolving enters? That is, how can it acknowledge and explore, as well as skeptically peruse, the numinous without turning into a religion? First, let it be said that the linguistic turn to which new materialism is a responsive response, and for which it wants to take responsibility, has had an effect opposite to the dissolving of language into the poetic mystery of Earth. In the linguistic turn, it is the Earth-mystery that disappears in the sense that it is forced into a re-presented world that gets rid of its real presence, while signs appear to take on an objectivity of their own. As for Prufrock, the sign becomes the thing. Among myriad examples of this overall and quaint disappearing act, one may name the postmodern notions that nature poetry has disappeared; that nature is unnecessary; that nature itself has disappeared; that seasonal cycles do not exist; that only darkly cynical views of nature are intelligent and welcome in our time; and more.[38] In contrast, new materialism is correct to remind us that we do not simply inhabit a world of signs at an infinite distance from seasons and nature. The linguistic turn is not the final word on concrete existence. It is not even the final word on anything, despite the baffling comprehensiveness of its ambiguity sustained into the supposed infinities of "infinite semiosis." We become enmeshed in concrete being, and signs are able to convey the notion, else new materialism would have been unable to say so. Signs weave themselves into concrete actuality. And new materialism offers the renewed prospect that the sign's connecting functions do not have to be made suspect to the degree that poststructuralism does, as if we constantly need to take the pulse again and again of the sign's referential abilities.

Another important way in which new materialism might find an avenue into discussion of the numinous without pretending to be a new religion, is to follow the modern poets down the mytho-poetic avenue not only of vibrant matter, but also vibrant emptiness, where signs and blank space reverberate with their peculiar knowing of profound being and nowhere. With reference to Bernard Stiegler's work, in a striking passage of her book *Vibrant Matter*, Bennett describes how proto-humans linked the past usefulness of a stone tool with its materiality, "archiving" its function. The tool's texture, color, and weight, "in calling attention to its projected and recollected use, produced *the first hollow of reflection*. Humanity and nonhumanity have always performed an intricate dance with each other" (emphasis added).[39] And so has concrete being, "somethingness," been performing a dance with non-being, "nothingness": the hollow is as important as the substance.

But these terms are not as abstract as they seem. Poetry reveals that their dance enjoys embodied meaningfulness in the human realm. In moments of mytho-poetic actuality, which again I do not deem to be esoteric or exotic, but as much part of being human as dreaming, the awe-inspiring realization may come of the significance of something in terms of nothing, and vice versa. At the plainest (but not less important) level, this is simply a form of deeply knowing that life is a considerable gift. Eliot's poetry and that of the moderns simply show the ability to relate charged poetic awareness of this gift. With poetry, new materialism can reach into that place where words, after speech, reach into silence: the life of significant soil and the vibrant emptiness from which that soil comes. For, it is in this silence, or with it, that objects may be said to "come to" one, as Bennett suggests in view of the thought of Baruch Spinoza and Henry David Thoreau,[40] relieving the indefinite effort or belief of one's "going to" them, and perhaps relieving the progressive tendency excessively to interfere with nature's flow.

All in all, from a new material perspective, Eliot's poetry works in three or four relative, interrelated stages, beginning with the disturbing and necessary reflection on and incorporation (into poetic form and formlessness) of dislocation, then to move on to location, immersion, and dissolving. These stages in one sense mark degrees of intensity, because immersion and dissolving are more intense aspects of location. In another sense they are elements of his poetic sensibility of wholeness and culture-Earth integrity, enabling the poems to participate in and/ or mediate for the reader the Earth-process as a holy, secular actuality. In terms of Eliot's development as a poet, this brings affirmation in *Four Quartets* closer to *The Waste Land*: his affirmation is not an afterthought. In terms of his skepticism, it reminds one that his Buddhist and secular sensibility uses skepticism in a way that is different in crucial respects from occidental epistemologies. In fact, Eliot uses skepticism to rub his thought, feeling, religious view, and poetry more deeply into everyday reality, including, at bottom, the being-and-nothing that continues to change (on) Earth. This oriental rubbing of signs back into everyday actuality has frequently been misunderstood, especially in the critical disdain for his orientalism, to which the book subsequently turns its focus as part of a survey of the new material field in its culture studies aspect.

NOTES

1. William W. Bevis, *Mind of Winter: Wallace Stevens, Meditation, and Literature* (Pittsburgh: Pittsburgh University Press, 1988), 25–26.
2. Frank Kermode, "Why Didn't He Commit Suicide?" review of *T. S. Eliot: The Contemporary Reviews* by Jewel Spears Brooker, *London Review of Books*, November 4, 2004, http://www.lrb.co.uk/v26/n21/frank-kermode/why-didnt-he-commit-suicide.
3. Bevis, *Mind of Winter*, 34.
4. *See* Edward O. Wilson, *On Human Nature* (Cambridge: Harvard University Press, 2004), ix; Gottfried Leibniz, *The Philosophical Works of Leibniz*, ed. George Martin Duncan (New Haven: Tuttle, Morehouse & Taylor, 1890), 213.
5. Bevis, *Mind of Winter*, 7.
6. Wallace Stevens, *Collected Poems* (London: Faber & Faber, 1990), 9.
7. T. S. Eliot, *Collected Poems 1909-1962* (New York: Harcourt Brace, 1991), 177.
8. Eliot, *Poems*, 180.
9. Lao Tzu, *Tao Te Ching: The Richard Wilhelm Edition*, trans. H. G. Ostwald (London: Arkana, 1987), 32.
10. Lao Tzu, *Tao Te Ching*, 27.
11. Iain McGilchrist, *The Master and His Emissary: The Divided Brain and the Making of the Western World* (New Haven: Yale University Press, 2012), 443.
12. Norman Friedman, *(Re)Valuing Cummings: Further Essays on the Poet 1962-1993* (Gainesville: University Press of Florida, 1996), 112.
13. Eliot, *Poems*, 199, 180.
14. Eliot, *Poems*, 201.
15. Gary Snyder, *The Real Work: Interviews and Talks 1964-1979* (New York: New Directions, 1980), 56.
16. Eliot, *Poems*, 179.
17. Helen Gardner, *The Composition of* Four Quartets (New York: Oxford University Press, 1978), vii, 38.
18. T. S. Eliot, *The Waste Land* (Norton Critical Edition), ed. Michael North (New York: W. W. Norton, 2001), 25.
19. *See* David Hinton, *Mountain Home: The Wilderness Poetry of Ancient China* (New York: New Directions, 2005), xiv.
20. Eliot, *Poems*, 176.
21. Eliot, *Poems*, 209.
22. Eliot, *The Waste Land*, 8.
23. Jeffrey M. Perl and Andrew P. Tuck, "The Hidden Advantage of Tradition: On the Significance of T. S. Eliot's Indic Studies," *Philosophy East & West* 35.2 (April 1985), 117.
24. Eliot, *Poems*, 183.
25. T. S. Eliot, *Selected Prose*, ed. Frank Kermode (London: Faber & Faber, 1980), 290.
26. Cleo McNelly Kearns, *T. S. Eliot and Indic Traditions: A Study in Poetry and Belief* (Cambridge: Cambridge University Press, 2008), 243.
27. Kearns, *Indic Traditions*, 244.
28. Fyodor Dostoevsky, *The Brothers Karamazov*, trans. Richard Pevear and Larissa Volokhonsky (New York: Farrar, Straus and Giroux, 2002), 331.
29. Eliot, *Poems*, 180.
30. Jane Bennett, *Vibrant Matter: A Political Ecology of Things* (Durham: Duke University Press, 2010), 3.

31. Robert Kern, *Orientalism, Modernism, and the American Poem* (Cambridge: Cambridge University Press, 1996), 191.

32. George Steiner, *After Babel: Aspects of Language and Translation* (London: Oxford University Press, 1975), 359.

33. Steiner, *After Babel*, 359.

34. Earl Miner, "Pound, Haiku, and the Image," *Ezra Pound: A Collection of Critical Essays*, ed. Walter Sutton (Eaglewood Cliffs: Prentice-Hall, 1963), 119.

35. E. E. Cummings, *Complete Poems 1904-1962* (New York: Liveright, 1994), 804, 839.

36. Eliot, *Poems*, 181.

37. Steiner, *After Babel*, 359.

38. Robert Langbaum, *The Modern Spirit: Essays on the Continuity of Nineteenth and Twentieth Century Literature* (London: Chatto & Windus, 1970), 101; Dana Phillips, "Is Nature Necessary?" *The Ecocriticism Reader: Landmarks in Literary Ecology*, eds. Cheryl Glotfelty and Harold Fromm (Athens: University of Georgia Press, 1996), 206; Fredric Jameson, *The Prison-house of Language: A Critical Account of Structuralism and Russian Formalism* (Princeton: Princeton University Press, 1972), ix; Slavoj Zizek, "Nature Does Not Exist," https://www.youtube.com/watch?v=DIGeDAZ6-q4, retrieved 15 February 2015; Helen Vendler, [Review of E. E. Cummings's *Complete Poems 1913-1962*] *Critical Essays on E. E. Cummings*, ed. Guy Rotella (Boston: Hall, 1984), 102.

39. Bennett, *Vibrant Matter*, 31.

40. Bennett, *Vibrant Matter*, xxiv.

Chapter Six

Bad Orientalism

Eliot, Edward Said, and the Moha

It seems as if Eliot's orientalism has rarely been appreciated for its full meaning, partly because it has not been linked to his eco-*logos*, or the way in which his poetic signs orient themselves to and within nature. On a broader scale, it is as though the discussion of modern ecopoetic orientalism occurs in a vacuum, while this vacuum has also swallowed Eliot's oriental eco-*logos* to a damaging extent. As has been shown, this has not always been the case, especially among those critics who took the trouble, albeit in brief, seriously to consider his ecocritical aspect, such as John Elder and Gary Snyder.

Still, the influence of orientalism on the earthly engagement of this poet "has been underemphasized," as Zhaoming Qian writes in terms of the neglect of the oriental influence on modern poetry as a whole in his book *Orientalism and Modernism: The Legacy of China in Pound and Williams.*[1] Much of modernist poetry's actuality, zest, energy, excitement, attractive dialectical puzzlement, and affirmative peace dynamically resides, or continues to resonate, within its oriental sensibility and *poiesis*. Now, no little part of the reason for the neglect of these oriental ecologisms in modern poetry has been the mammoth influence of Edward Said, who dismisses modern orientalism outright as so much historical fodder while, on a broader front, his work has tended to make critics apprehensive about discussing orientalism, even poetic orientalism, with open appreciation of its achievements. (One did not want to be the critic caught in a web of culture studies incorrectness.) And though Said's global influence on orientalism may have been exemplary, his good influence on the discussion of modern poetry is doubtful.

Reading Eliot's poetic orientalism shows up the weaknesses in Said's culture studies orientalist critique. In this, to my mind, resides an additional caveat for the burgeoning of new materialism within its overall culture studies context. I hope that bringing the caveat so relatively early in new materialism's development will have nourishing consequences. The danger to be outlined in context of Eliot and Said is that culture studies has a propensity to elide primary texts when it makes value judgements about authors, while the results of such a method will more often than not be predictably poor. An ultimate form of what I speak of would have been for future generations not to read our current production of ecocriticism for the reason that we knowingly flew around to conferences in planes pumping millions of tons of toxic material into the air that those future generations will be breathing. In a similar way, though attacking an all too human artist for his individual participation in the flaws of his day is not improbable or always to be condemned, attacking his legacy as if his art presents his flaws—without proof from the art itself—is not a fruitful avenue to adopt.

Where does this happen? For the most part, it happens in a subversive manner within current culture studies trends with such a persistent attacking of the artist as person that it comes to marginalize or replace discussion of his or her art. Add to this the postmodern tendency deliberately to focus on trash art, as well as the new material fixation on waste, departing from Bennett's initial aesthetic, sensitive, and illuminating presentation of it, and one has a veritable wave of interest within the world of literary studies on everything but great literature. The pressure of this amounts to a situation, by analogy, in which we were forced to spend our lives contemplating, say, the latest Christmas jingle in the jungle of Times Square, instead of listening to and trying to talk about Beethoven's incredibly moving music—a point that Said makes in his way, as I will show toward the conclusion of this chapter. Or, worse, as if one were always to discuss the implications of bacteria found on the composer's exhumed hairs and bits of skull,[2] instead of immersing oneself in his music, seeking for a worthy responsiveness and response to it as a critical listener. For, in many ways, the only real Beethoven we can meet is the one found in his music. Just one consideration in this regard is that we all hope that those who come after us will not assume that our photo albums, vegetal or digital, actually embody what our full life on the planet *was like* for the person living it, since there are too many gaps among the pictures, and who knows what may have happened inside a person in the periods of those gaps? To then "read" the person from what has remained of him or her and apply this unscrupulously to his or her life is at least discourteous, and at most dubious. Similarly, to "read" the life of an artist and apply that to his or her art without serious reference to the art itself, is equally dubious, while the elision of or scoffing at that artistic legacy based on what we supposedly "know" about the artist is perhaps the worst culture studies legacy of all.

Such elision and scoffing cannot be done too openly, of course: it sits within an insinuated, ironic, but persistent "thumbs-down" toward the legacy, often damaging the art, and equally often simply ignoring it.

Consider that in the case of literature, the critical doing that I propose here, of looking at lives and art with courtesy and responsiveness, is easier than in the case of music, since music is notoriously difficult to respond to in words. Yet such critical alertness, of giving evidence from the artistic text in response to literary art, is not sought frequently enough in current critical praxis, while new materialism may bring about greater emphasis on the primary classical artistic text, as I hope to be demonstrating here. Not for a moment do I mean that an art work should not be "hooked" back into the public eye by way of media or culture studies highlighting of this or that interesting find about the artist, provided it is done courteously. The position I try to take is more complex. It is that in such culture studies, postmodern doing should be balanced with the real work of responding to the art from within the perspective of one's individuality and one's generation. This would be to respond to its real presence. But this balance probably implies less work of the culture studies kind than is currently the case, and more (ecocritical) close response that is willing to linger in the moment of the primary text. At least, it implies bringing evidence from the art works to the table in reaching a critical verdict about the value of the artist's legacy.

For these reasons the *forms* of great poetry take on extra significance for the larger, ecocritical, and new material study of the relationship between literature and the physical world. Poetry, on the level of language and signs, is where language approaches anew its embodiment. Just one example, discussed in chapter 3, is Eliot's creative, modern-Buddhist arrangement of Sanskrit fragments within accentuated, active blank space in *The Waste Land*. Even in "ordinary" criticism (not ecocriticism as such) formal arrangements such as these have somehow been overlooked, including the overlooking of the vibrant nothing that comes with the arrangements. The Sanskrit fragments have been treated as so many obsolete lexicons. In a sense, this is too thought-ful, since it is easy for the intellect to overlook the fact that thought changes when it becomes formally poetic. In poetry, thought enjoys a different quality informed by form. Here a thought enjoys the sharp freshness of the odor of a rose, as Eliot advocates.[3] Playing on his blue guitar, the poet changes things as they are according to Wallace Stevens.[4] Experience itself changes as it becomes poetic. Poetry renders a different *kind* of experience. In this vein, as has been indicated, Sanskrit fragments take charged form in *The Waste Land*.

Poetry is in other words a special manner of communication whose forms can shape experience in the direction of renewed engagement with one's Earth-being; this is true in particular of occidental poetry that uses what it deems to be oriental forms. At its extreme, poetry can engage not merely one's own Earth-being, but Earth-being itself. This involves the connection between one's idiolectic Earth-being and the being of Earth that dynamically contains and resonates with that idiolectic being—there can be no infinite barrier between one's individual experience of Earth, and Earth as an experience. How frequently *poetry* is the vehicle that knows this, because its forms resonate with visceral experiences such as the rhythm that ultimately stems from a beating heart and circulating lymph.

At least, this is one of the very necessary extremities of poetic interaction, as has been acknowledged in various cultures over various periods, and recently by John Felstiner who suggests that many a poem offers a kind of field guide and wake-up call into connection with nature.[5] Poems of E. E. Cummings and William Carlos Williams open exactly into the earthly adventure carried by emergence as if from nowhere. In Cummings's words, written in his inimitable prose style with its tellingly unique omissions and additions of blank spaces,

> "I write"(whence our word "graphic")but originally "I make lines"—cf the Poet-Painter of China)and the *paperspace around each poem is a where in which it heres or a surface in which it floats* (emphasis added).[6]

Pictorially and otherwise, the modern poem is a phenomenon of emerging, the emplacement of emerging, the actively-becoming-place where emerging finds open presence, to phrase it clumsily out of prose necessity (unlike the freshness of a Cummings or an Eliot). The blank page is a "where" in which the poem takes place, but the place-taking is not static, it is a kind of floating. As a place, it enjoys stability, but as a taking-place, it is fluid. In this way, it is at once stable and fluid, which amounts to one of a considerable number of bafflingly informative modern dialectics: informative, because these dialectics celebrate the nature of life itself, which is not confined to this or that side of a set of opposites. In Williams's poems, paradox frequently points beyond the linguistic limit into the emergent nothingness of its origin—when the speaker for instance ascends and descends at once—and it is part of his particular poetic gift that he is able to depict the remarkableness of the apparently most ordinary solidity of things that have turned into supposed clichés in poems, such as a rose petal.[7] As we have seen, Eliot revitalizes the (lotos) rose as a phenomenon at once stable, peaceful, resonant, and dynamic. He uses oxymoron and paradox in his singular way to achieve the recognition of somethingness within nothingness and vice versa. One moves, though moving neither from nor toward anything[8]—one is within the movement of Earth, which on its large and fragile scale *simultaneously encompasses movement from and toward* with its seamless effortlessness of actually continuing amidst enormous and conflicting sets of opposite energies, as mentioned. Literally thousands of creatures move from and toward on the planet in any given moment. This is part of the miracle of being. Eliot brings simultaneity, co-incidence, into focus in these ways. Again, what appears impossible from the viewpoint of a moving individual's conception continues to happen effortlessly on the scale of Earth. A striking poem by Wallace Stevens, "The Glass of Water," formulates this insight with greater effect than academic prose can muster:

> That the glass of water would melt in heat,
> That the water would freeze in cold,
> Shows that this object is merely a state,
> One of many, between two poles. So,
> In the metaphysical, there are these poles.
>
> Here in the centre stands the glass. Light
> Is the lion that comes down to drink. There
> And in that state, the glass is a pool.[9]

The first stanza suggests that the (mere) standing of the glass of water is a miracle. It achieves a supreme moment of the sheer suchness of that glass and water. In the imagination, light becomes a lion drinking from the pool of water in the glass (second stanza). This is an additional miracle, another way of seeing the suchness of a glass of water, heightening the real presence of its poetic perception. All of this, in the plainest possible sense, Earth continues to make possible. The oriental perception of this brings to our attention acute, quicksilver, meditative ways of perceiving this, as mentioned—again, in terms of being and nothing. In seeing "through" nothing (and not via preconceptions or restrictions to a single idea), one sees with great clarity. This is how Stevens's speaker sees the glass of water, given that in his oeuvre overall, the nothing that IS plays a very profound role in seeing not ideas about things, but the thing itself, in this case the glass of water, so tellingly plainly there in the line "[h]ere in the centre stands the glass," emergent and utterly itself within a context of impossible opposites.

In his singular way, informed by his particular modernist encounter with oriental seeing of this nature, Eliot again achieves similar clarities. Perhaps no other poem makes this clearer than *The Waste Land*, while the critical overlooking and vacuum that I speak of, occur most drastically in its case. Important critics ignore that the poem arrives at a critical moment not of nihilism, but charged nothing—the kind of nothing that brings clarity. As indicated, this has to do with reducing the poetic form of the Sanskrit elements supposedly to Sanskrit semantics. Seminal Eliot critics such as F. R. Leavis and A. D. Moody[10] do reduce Eliot's Sanskrit (it is a unique Sanskrit, part of his formal idiolectical eco-*logos*!) to semantics. The tendency to ignore the Sanskrit forms further includes a penchant among Eliot critics to bounce off the Sanskrit elements into theories of meaninglessness. The complaints offered usually include that Sanskrit has to be looked up in scholarly books, and therefore means little, or that the note to them in the facsimile of the poem somehow means that they are feeble in meaning, and so forth. Of course, other critics attribute them with great significance, as in the case of Michael Edwards, as indicated in chapter 3. But he, too, makes an about turn after having confirmed that Sanskrit in the poem is a metaphor for wise and single speech, by following this assertion with a question posed in blunt conclusion: is *shantih* meant to be "darkly sinister"?[11] This insertion is telling, because, as has been demonstrated in terms of Eliot's dislocation, location, immersion, and dissolving, his skepticism works the other way around. It entertains the doubt of indirectness to the greatest degree so that affirmation and/ or the enormous significance of *being* may become apparent. Its sequencing is not one that *appears* to affirm wisdom only to splash it with darkly sinister cold water.

In fact, it is in the combination of their semantics and their form in *The Waste Land* that the Sanskrit elements show—with the narrative exception of their inclusion in the penultimate stanza, as discussed in chapter 3—radical affirmation of existence, while, in the dialectic, even the exclusion ultimately serves to underscore the importance of the affirmation. The embodiment of that meaningfulness in or by the poetry is as important as the message conveyed, that existence is itself meaningful in concreteness. Denial of the everyday experience of concreteness can therefore not lead to any truthfulness in Eliot's world, hence his discomfort with the epistemology of his day, as indicated. And hence his preference for Buddhism which, as philosophical and skeptical as it is, does not lose sight of everyday concrete existence, the physical limits of one's being, and their meaning. Once this vital aspect of Eliot's skepticism dawns on one it brings about a change in one's perception of his poetry on almost every level. It is not often recognized, for instance, just how Buddhist one of the much-cited and indeed satisfactory passages in *Four Quartets* happens to be:

> We shall not cease from exploration
> And the end of all our exploring
> Will be to arrive where we started
> And know the place for the first time[12]

These words, in their prosaic manner arranged with easy authority into poetic lines, embody the experiential truth of familiarity and unfamiliarity. The fact that it is true that scholarly oriental knowledge is not necessary for one's interpretation of these lines—while the lines enjoy clear Buddhist origins, as I will immediately show—is a token of how seamlessly Eliot is able to incorporate, by virtue of an effort taking many years, his oriental sensibility into his writing. This is the extent to which it (his orientalism) has become part of him and, above all, his poetry. The Buddhist aspect in these lines comes into view on recognizing that the passage as a whole sees life as a journey, a series of changes. Similarly, the second-century Indian Buddhist philosopher Naagaarjuna, a formative influence on Eliot in his Harvard years (as indicated), sees life not as a logically demonstrated theoretical position, but as "a complex of subtle and dramatic psychological changes, changes that result in seeing the world fresh. The end of the journey finds one either in a familiar landscape that appears to be utterly new, or in a foreign landscape that seems strangely familiar."[13] In his student essay "Degrees of Reality," Eliot writes that "the token that a philosophy is true is, I think, the fact that it brings us to the exact point from which we started."[14] As a student of Buddhism at Harvard, he therefore directly begins to formulate the memorable passage of *Four Quartets* cited above! The real presence of his oriental shorthand in this instance approaches a point of near transparency. But the transparency does not have the purpose of overcoming the link between literature and life, the *numen* of illumination and the *moha* of cloudy or messy or bodily knowing and healthy, instinctive uncertainties. Instead, it shows the extraordinary in the ordinary, the profound in the plain, the familiar in the unfamiliar, the known in the unknown, and so on.

About this journey that brings us to understanding the same place for the first time, the young Eliot further writes that "the wisdom which we shall have acquired will not be part of the argument which brings us to the conclusion; it is not part of the book, but is written in pencil on the fly-leaf." He adds that we will bring no objects, no treasures, through the customs house of our journey.[15] From the beginning, he does not seek the apparent solidity of treasures gained or "monuments" of wisdom gathered, removed, and isolated from life (this angle on the matter shows that the reification of his poems into cultural monuments is also ironic). Moreover, we borrow a lifetime from life, just as we make provisional notes in pencil in the fly-leaf within the covers of the life-book, on blank space. This paradoxically means that one's experience is in every sense part of life. It partakes in it by being only a part of it. It is not the theory that one gains that will seal a lifetime, but the life lived, of which one's theories are part.

In his dissertation on Bradley he further writes that any theoretical statement is "thoroughly relative." It "exists only in a context of experience, of experience with which it is continuous."[16] Among other things, this means that only the lived aspect of a theory, actual ideas emanating from or rooted in real experience, has value. It in fact has very authentic value in terms of its being-lived, and relative value to the alive theory of another. One's theory will be part of one's participation in life. This is very much part of the oriental understanding that flourishes in Eliot's poetry. As Carl Gustav Jung says about the oriental influence in the occident in general, it gives us no less than "another, wider, more profound, and higher understanding, that is, *understanding through life*" (emphasis added).[17]

These matters bring into focus Said's puzzling take on Eliot's poetic orientalism, for Said somehow feels that it distances Eliot from life. This puts the culture studies critic at considerable odds not only with the poet's oriental aims and values as briefly outlined above, but especially with the orientalisms at work within the poems. Like Eliot, Said in general emphasizes the participation of literature and literary figures in the concreteness of ordinary life. It runs like a golden thread through his work. Yet he insists that Eliot is deliberately out of touch with everyday reality, while orientalism is a key sin in this regard as far as he can see. Consider that this culture critic's much-cited, mammoth *Orientalism* has changed oriental discussion not only in anthropological studies, but also in literary criticism. However, though post-Said work by foremost scholars of modern poetic orientalism ranging from Robert Kern to Eric Hayot, Cynthia Stamy, and others, may show the obligatory politically correct nod in Said's direction to acknowledge his condemnations of modern poetic orientalism, it is not done to any striking critical effect. Simultaneously, the discussion of modern poetic orientalism has become too self-conscious and cautious about the real successes at stake, probably as a result of Said relegating modern poetry to the realms of banned, "bad" orientalism. He is entirely *not* positive about modern poetic orientalism. And he employs his usual measuring rod—participation in life—to castigate it. He in fact has a penchant for championing or castigating cultural figures and movements, and though this goes along with admirable passion and refinement, it does not always yield convincing results.

It is worth providing glimpses of the said golden thread in his work, while keeping in mind—given Eliot's choosing of orientalism *because* it puts one in touch with life according to the poet—that Eliot all along *confirms* Said's insistence on such connection, while Said simply does not see it. Said wants, for example, that a given sentence in given discourse will not be just another modicum of communication with another philosopher. It should instead reflect the "sometimes horrific pressures that render even the most humdrum and ordinary of sentences both threatening and full of dislocating force."[18] We have seen ample evidence in Eliot's poetry of such sentences and fragments. Lil's bar scene in *The Waste Land* teems with these utterances. "Now Albert's coming back, make yourself a bit smart," "get yourself some teeth," "He said, I swear, I can't bear to look at you," "HURRY UP PLEASE ITS TIME," "goonight ladies," are only some examples.[19] And they are all dreadfully full of dislocating force, once more describing her entrapment in modern biology, and her suicide under the weight of male domination; in the same poem in which Eliot rubs his writing further into a world of everyday being, linking Lil to Philomela and the typist and the clerk . . . the inclusion of such characters and prosaic lines was unheard of in serious English poetry before Eliot's.[20] The point is simple enough: Eliot belongs squarely under

Said's rubric of insistence on "ordinary sentences" that are "full of dislocating force."

Championing the philosopher Maurice Merleau-Ponty in a full-length essay, Said highlights how he emphasizes the "essential human difficulty" of "living at and acknowledging the point where so many opposites converge, where the meaning of our reality is at once threatened and asserted: Now."[21] Need one indicate again how well Eliot is able to stay with the dynamism of the now-moment in that moving place where enormously conflicting opposites such as culture and Earth continue to converge into contexts larger than themselves? If this makes Eliot mystical, it brings him into further alignment with the figure that Said prefers to champion. Merleau-Ponty has been "accused" of entertaining a mystical view of history, against which Said defends the philosopher.[22] Again, although Said will do the opposite, he should have included Eliot in this "circle" of those who stay with the golden thread of thought and writing connected to life. He further clarifies that for Merleau-Ponty theoretical experience resonates within a larger context of experience. Experience cannot be limited to the mind only.[23] We "are in the world before we can think about it." Therefore, Merleau-Ponty's "aim is to rediscover experience at the 'naive' level of its origin, beneath and before the sophisticated encroachments of science."[24] Perception (Merleau-Ponty's central term), adds Said, "is an activity that clarifies a primordial way of being, a being that lies beneath the level of intelligible discourse. Perception, quite literally, is the way human existence comes into being."[25]

Though there are differences between Merleau-Ponty and Eliot, these understandings about the meaning of existence correspond remarkably closely with Eliot's at one or two of the important nodes. He uses the linguistics of "relational experience" in his poetry to steer the reader into a jolt of recognizing "immediate," original experience under the surface. Closer to modern literature, Said composes a full-length essay in praise of the critic R. P. Blackmur, spearhead of New Criticism in America and ardent advocate of Eliot's poetry and his objective correlative.[26] Said, however, presents him as a phenomenon that is qualitatively, almost absolutely, different from Eliot. Though Said focuses almost exclusively on Eliot as critic, cynically eliding the poet, and though he relies heavily on the often simplistic postcolonial impression of what Eliot does and does not do as a critic—even in this narrow critical corridor, then—the question begs already as to whether Eliot can be condemned and Blackmur championed if the works of these two figures are historically interdependent, at least when it comes to Blackmur's championing of Eliot's poetry and thought.

In any event, the reason why Said praises Blackmur remains the same as in the case of Merleau-Ponty. He sees Blackmur as the critic who is most aware that literature must enmesh itself in life and history. He in fact makes of Blackmur virtually a culture studies critic. For Blackmur, Said says, literature persistently contains a "touch of the actual." Major artists use this touch of the actual, Blackmur says (again as stressed by Said), to put in and leave out just enough of instincts to occasion a back-and-forth "oscillating and shuttling" between "text and reality." Blackmur calls text and reality the *numen* and the *moha*.[27] Of course, Said does not mention that the struggle between meaningful illumination and ordinary life is a hallmark of Eliot's poetry. For him, again, the poet does not belong to the paradoxical elite of those literati who understand the connections between literature and life, *numen* and *moha*. Ultimately, he views the group that he elevates, including not only Merleau-Ponty and Blackmur, but also Joseph Conrad, as consisting of "untimely, anxious witnesses to the dominant currents of their own time."[28] The result of the anxiousness is a view of writing, entertained by this elite group, that holds it to be "less a delivery of a finished product than a series of moments fully embodied in experience."[29] Again the obvious truth has to be stated that these words relate distinctly to Eliot, perhaps *the* exponent in modern textuality of an anxious witness who reflects the dominant currents of his time in a poetic series of moments fully embodied in experience, to the point of concretely fragmenting the language that presents the fractured ontology that he perceives and experiences in his environment. This was in fact the reason why his work caught attention, having to overcome enormous critical and public resistance and ridicule in the process. His project touched a real nerve end in the collective psychological reality of his day, in the extreme. It is part of why we still remember and honor his project, not to mention that it is part of why we continue to find resonance in those poems, for they *still* touch that collective nerve end.

Given this intensity with which Eliot clearly prefers thought in relation to life above thought alone, and given the broad spectrum and passion with which Said contends for participation in life as the bottom criterion of good literature and criticism, one is truly surprised about how vehement, dismissive, and acidic the writing of Said becomes when he turns to the modernist trio of Eliot, Yeats, and Pound—and Eliot especially. On more than one occasion, with amazing abruptness, he scourges Eliot (and Pound and Yeats),[30] singling them out as the very avatars of stagnant, non-alive, aloof— in short, *bad*—cultural practice. Moreover, for Said that bad practice is a direct result of their corrupt orientalism. He contends that in 1934, at last, Raymond Schwab put orientalism "in its proper cultural context," in "stark contrast to his fellow artists and intellectuals for whom Orient and Occident" remained "secondhand abstractions." That "Pound, Eliot, Yeats" did not ignore at that critical stage the "'wisdom of the East,' as Max Müller had called it a few generations earlier," according to him put them in an even more backward category.[31] "Yeats, Eliot, and Pound," he says in a different text, "regarded with nostalgia a lost age of integrated life, thereby condemning themselves in the present to overcoming what Eliot called 'the immense panorama of futility and anarchy which is contemporary history.'"[32] The irony seems to slip by Said that this view of history enmeshes these poets in the concerns of their day and age. As indicated, it is part of their commitment to history *not* to gloss over the broken history—the fractured ontological story—of the Europe in which they lived their lives. It slips by that Eliot's embodiment of the Prajapati story at the conclusion of *The Waste Land* is dramatic and alive compared to the pedestrian scholarliness and stuffiness of Max Müller's admittedly important version.[33] And that these poets spiral back into the past in order to carry the present into the future.[34] Instead of admitting something in this vein, Said advocates that "Eliot is unintelligible without [his] emphasis on art opposed, in some way, to life, to the historical experience of the middle class, and to the disorder and dislocation of urban existence." The poet's "extraordinary powers of codification and influence produced the almost too familiar canonized critical practices and touchstones associated with the New Criticism along with its rejection of biography, history, and pathos in the form of various fallacies."[35] This belies the considerable discomfort with which Eliot's poetry actually sits in the New Critical sphere,[36] while Eliot is so readily assumed to be himself a comfortable New Critic, especially among culture critics such as Said. That Eliot, according to Said, was "rejecting the pain of experience in favour of poetry"[37] does not make sense. The pain of experience finds embodiment in his poetry.

Said contrasts the avoidance of experience that he sees in Eliot with "a strikingly different approach emerging in the study of literature." Most prominent in this emerging is "the new voice of feminist writers," exemplified in the modern work of Sandra Gilbert and Susan Gubar.[38] There is no doubt that Said is right about the healthy emergence of feminist writing, that it is necessary, and that it shows the promise of critiquing patriarchy in the direction of correcting its distortions and violence. There is equally little doubt that in Eliot's excellent poetry, the works by which we estimate him, sexism is transcended and patriarchy incisively critiqued, as I have demonstrated. These poems in fact *remarkably* transcend sexism—the sexism entrenched in his era. Now, in the case of the enmity with which Said's championed figures of Gilbert and Gubar "take down" the "huge" figure of Eliot in terms of the war-like landscape that they project onto literature, their blatant disregard for how dialectics work in his mind and poems is as violent as any patriarchal action. They simply misread his poetry, reducing it in the most one-sided fashion for the sake of their argument, as has been expounded fully by Jewel Spears Brooker.[39] In Said's case, he does not take the trouble of *mentioning* a line from the poetry. This action (for it is an action) opens into the abyss of a considerable problematic that continues to arise from culture studies, of which Said's is rightfully a prime example. When culture studies focuses on literature, there is always the convenience of ignoring the literature as the conversation unfolds.

Said should have seen in Eliot an ally instead of an enemy. The poet is not the foil for disdain with orientalism stuck in past "histories" that he makes him out to be. The final irony in this regard, once more, is that Eliot's orientalism is an important component of his life-long striving to rub his work into the *moha*. To be sure, Eliot does not lose sight of the *numen* in the process: it is the intersection between *numen* and *moha* that painstakingly receives his complete attention. The sacred awareness of Earth (*numen*) and its connection with concrete existence (*moha*), demonstrated here to be a very serious concern for the poet, is just one important example of this. The Western philosopher's "chief mistake," Eliot says, "is that, after abstracting the terms for his discussion from experiences shared with everyman, he takes his simplistic verbal substitutes to be the reality."[40] This error leads the theoretician to forget and consequently to distort the origins of his theory in commonplace experience. Eliot therefore writes that the "true reason, I think, for the failure of all philosophic flights, is not that they venture too far, but that they venture alone. The eye of the *honnête homme* on the ground does not follow them."[41] One cannot help but say (without any disrespect, and peculiar to the context of this argument) that this sounds exactly like words that could have come from Said, who insists, as we have seen, on the everyday experience of the middle class as that to which thought should attach itself.

Eliot finds in certain Buddhist schools, as he is finding in Bradley, an option that he believes to be unavailable in the range of previous European philosophy. He writes that the "world in which we live *lokadhaatu* is the result of our common *dhaatus* and efforts. (This is neglected in Western philosophy.)" He is saying that the world is the sum of its common parts, and he believes this is worth saying, because so much of occidental philosophy has been dedicated to demonstrating the opposite: that the "Real World" is something utterly apart from the shared world of human experience. What Eliot feels is lacking in the occident is the appreciation of experience, social convention, common sense, including an appreciation for "the *honnête homme* on the ground," as Perl and Tuck repeat.[42] Here it is pertinent to reiterate that Eliot suggests that the cultivated person of the world *keeps an eye on the ground.* He or she enjoys the humility of staying in radical connection with ground, whether it be the ground within or without, or both. And this intersection of *numen* within and *moha* without is what makes the experience of such a person actual, instead of either "philosophical" or "realistic." Again one sees that his orientalism is a major part of what makes the vitality of this actual, lived intersection clear to Eliot, and in his poems that actuality becomes clear to anyone who is willing to find this clarity.

The influence on Eliot's oriental formation at Harvard comes via his teachers there mainly from the thought of Naagaarjuna. The latter's aim is to show that nothing positive or negative can be asserted of reality. It is therefore *suunya*: vacuity and emptiness. Even to think of it as *suunya* is a mistake, though, because the concepts "vacuity" and "emptiness" are understood with reference to fullness.[43] In such a case, instead of entering what Taoists call "no-mind" in order to see the *tzu jan* or sheer "suchness" of things, the oppositional concepts of emptiness versus fullness simply keep one incarcerated in the language trap in which, thinking of the key, each confirms a prison. In the same way reality is unique, but even the concept of uniqueness is therefore not applicable to it, because uniqueness can be understood only with reference to the non-unique. It is beyond concepts, and beyond speech also, if speech represents concepts.[44] One may say therefore that this kind of skepticism is meditative, that is, meaningfully empty. It is to see without preconceptions, and as I have been intimating, this meditative experience is not esoteric, but part of human life to the same degree that dreaming in images is part of the everyday experience that occurs mostly at night. Even salvation, *moksa* (Buddhist "release"), the young Eliot writes, is not "an escape from the world but an epistemic revolution": it "*is the freedom from presuppositions*" (emphasis added).[45] It is an intense form of skepticism that remains radically open to the affirmation of living one's life at the forefront of one's existence in perception, precisely because it goes without the supposed safety of preconceptions, prejudices, and so forth. Here is a prime reason for the conclusion of *The Waste Land* that reaches, in its formal way, "into the silence" that comes "after speech."[46] *Shantih* actually reaches into the silence embodied in blank space. The poetic embodiment of that instance, the very pattern and fiber of the text, must *show* on the micro-level of the page (in terms of what can be done there) the macro-recognition that reality is beyond words, while that reality may include words *in its beyond-ness*.

The phrase taken here from *Four Quartets*, "after speech, reach," contains two instances of the assonance and alliteration in the case of the sounds [iːtʃ] within the words "sp<u>eech</u>" and "<u>reach:</u>" there are in a manner of speaking two instances of "an each," a something, a little embodiment on the page—a concrete sign—and this emphasis on the "somethingness"-in-sound of the words, repeated twice, contrasts attractively with the "nothingness"-in-silence into which they resonate. Nothing *can* be said. Things do not matter so much, for they are always near to the vibrant relativity of nothingness in the circle of life, certainly also in the most positive sense. It is the divine comedy: things do not matter, since life itself (in which one participates) is not a problem to be solved, or a tragedy to be frowned about. Life is that which, in the face of all kinds of concerns and impossibilities, simply responds to all of these complications by continuing, establishing again and again something that comes from and returns to nothing, as if nothing has happened. *Shantih* in blank space thus moves beyond the complication of signs. That "all shall be well" therefore begins in *The Waste Land*. This means that when skepticism runs deep for whatever reason (most likely for the reason of having suffered), when life comes to nothing, at that tipping point where one perhaps cynically notices the vast panorama of despairing existence that may lie around one, one discovers the utter meaningfulness of existence itself, again, within a different *kind* of nothing: vibrant nothing. One sees clearly, because nothing interferes with what one perceives.

At Harvard the Japanese scholar Masaharu Anesaki is also one of Eliot's teachers. His fortunes in this regard are considerable. In his notes on these lectures, he underlines Anesaki's assertion that if one takes Naagaarjuna "as a philosopher alone," one "might take him as a pure nihilist," while Anesaki is careful to emphasize that Naagaarjuna's skepticism should not be mistaken for nihilism.[47] From this angle one may define nihilism as a response to nothingness that denies its vibrancy, and it should not be confused with the Buddhist sense of emptiness as found in modern poems by Eliot, Stevens, Cummings, Williams, and others. Alas, this kind of confusion has been fairly prevalent in literary criticism. Harold Bloom's and Helen Vendler's ironically ignorant insistence (in different texts) springs to mind, holding that Stevens's snow man, who is able to participate in the nothing that *is*, epitomizes a hopelessly weak response to the fact of existence. For them it is a moment of unfortunate annihilation in his oeuvre.[48] Similar notions underpin Leavis's and Moody's responses to Sanskrit in *The Waste Land*. (Incidentally, Said conveniently overlooks these New Critics' dismissive responses to Eliot's orientalism, which dismissals certainly at least *complicate* the culture critic's easy identification of the poet with the New Critical enterprise.) One may start with Leavis, too readily associated with Eliot, not least because the critic ultimately decides that "his" modernist is not the poet, but D. H. Lawrence.[49]

Interestingly, Leavis is rare among early critics in that he embarks on a prototypical "ecocriticism" of *The Waste Land*, rightly insisting that the poem focuses on a "breach of continuity" with "the immemorial ways of life, of life rooted in the soil." The poem "celebrates" (one is not sure whether Leavis gets the verb right in this instance) the "remoteness" of civilization from "the natural rhythms." The modern wasteland has no "sympathetic magic" or "harmony of human culture with the natural environment," and cannot express "an extreme sense of the unity of life."[50] Since the thunder is dry and sterile without rain, as line 342 of the poem in fact says, Leavis finds that "there is no resurrection or renewal,"[51] and in this part of the poem it is true that the skepticism is extreme. But when it comes to the poem's conclusion, the reading offered in this book differs substantially from Leavis's. The book's reading follows Leavis still when he consents that the "Sanscrit lends an appropriate portentousness, intimating that this is the sum of wisdom according to the great tradition;" although "portentousness" may have the meaning of "pompousness," which does not strike one as true of Eliot's use of Sanskrit, again because the patterning and tone are modern. The critic subsequently says about the poem's Sanskrit that the "irony, too, is radical," citing from the English glosses to prove the point.[52]

As has been argued here, such irony participates in keeping the Sanskrit elements alive by way of contrast and connection. Though he further feels that the poem does achieve *unity* of an inclusive consciousness, as well as a musical nature[53]—unlike many critics of his day such as John Crowe Ransom, who see in the poem only the whimpering inability to overcome discreetness[54]—he also feels that the poem lacks *direction*, especially since it is unable to make its oriental contents *present*. "We can only conclude," he says about the oriental-occidental gamble that the poem takes, "that Mr Eliot here has not done as much as he supposes." The Sanskrit words remain "mere pointers to something outside," and the "irony, too, of the   Shantih   shantih   shantih   that ends the poem is largely ineffective."[55]

Though he gives credence to the form of the Sanskrit materials as indicated by the blank spaces between the *shantih*s as he cites them, he remains blind to its implications. Surely the careful form given to these terms indicates at least that their meaning does not simply fall "outside" the poem, but instead that they are an inherent, formal part of it. If the poetic *experience* in other words has to do with formal arrangement, and not simply lexicality, then the Sanskrit elements are immanent. In any event, this is where the ecopoetic reading in this book takes a different path from Leavis's when it comes to the Sanskrit invitations of the poem. I would in other words propose that one see the poem's Sanskrit as an important part of Eliot's "compression approaching simultaneity—the co-presence in the mind of a number of different orientations, fundamental attitudes, orders of experience"—to which Leavis pays tribute.[56] Fundamental, indeed, is skepticism upheld to the point of again acknowledging, in a richly modern context, the miracle of the now-here-nowhere as acknowledged by our Indian forebears, and under more barren spiritual circumstances by us today. A. D. Moody is nonetheless even more perplexed by the poet's employment of the ancient language. *Shantih* "thrice repeated is a strange ending for a poem so ambitious to reform the mind in its own language. Whatever might be 'our equivalent,' those words to most of us must be quite meaningless." The "Sanskrit is not meant to be readily understood. Its plain meaning may be just that it does pass beyond what we are likely to think and say. Its deeper meaning may be set dead against our likely turn of mind." He feels that the poem has not been seen for what it is. It is "radically subversive. If it appears to confirm some of our ideas and emotions, it probably does so in a way we never meant."[57]

On the other hand, as held here, its deeper meaning *may* be quite meaningful and confirming. The difference between this reading and Moody's is emphasis on how the formal patterning points to earthly affirmation. The mandalic moments of threeness, the active way that combines opposites as it moves through and beyond them, are too clear to ignore. The crucial element of this transcendence into threeness is that the concreteness of experiencing Eliot's poem mimes the concreteness of experiencing existence on Earth. It is an experience to the brim with vibrant something-in-nothing. For Earth, too, does not offer explicating statements of personal belief or principle, just as the poem formally renders the *shantih*s in accentuated blank space, explaining only in the notes that it means the peace that goes beyond understanding, there emphasizing its positive meaning.

For, it has not been said enough that Earth continues without fuss. It does not ban clouds for the reason that it feels that mountains get away with their height, for example. Cummings strikingly illustrates this in his satirical sonnet "when serpents bargain for the right to squirm."[58] Eliot illustrates it in his manner by giving us the Sanskrit patterns as patterns, without explanation, and those patterns lead into recognition of concrete being on the planet. Meanwhile the planet sustains, somehow, a constantly shifting, developing web of relationships with an agency of its own, an agency that includes and influences human agencies such as the *praxis* of engaging Earth in poems.

Also from an ecopoetic standpoint, then, Eliot belongs among the rubric of the best poets. His work can be read as an ecocritical classic, over and above the many other ways in which it has been read. Speaking of classical art, Said, a concert pianist, laments the fact that "modern culture seems to have isolated music away from the other arts, with the result that most educated people are far more at ease talking about cinema, photography, art, dance, or architecture than they are with Bach or Schoenberg." This involves the further loss of discussion about the "wonderfully problematic cross-fertilization between the musical and the immediacies of ordinary experience."[59] I lament with him the absence of such musical awareness where it exists, but in this point lives another irony that undercuts his take on Eliot. My experience as a teacher of literature has shown that this poet has an unforgettable poetic voice that imprints itself on students' minds and memories with an immediacy reminiscent of music. As has been indicated in recent Eliot research focusing on his relations with Bradley, "immediate experience" is a key phrase of his poetic enterprise.[60] One of the most important utterances about poetry to which one has to return again and again—his observation that genuine poetry *communicates before it is understood*[61]—to my mind combines with his keen overall sense of immediacy to underscore the crucial musical element, the element of immediacy, in his (and other) poetry. In short, Eliot has an indelible poetic voice of art. As art, his voice is comparable to (say) the compositional "voice" of Gustav Mahler or the lyrical-dramatic singing voice of Luciano Pavarotti. I mention Pavarotti, because Eliot, too, has a remarkable ability to be at once lyrical and dramatic, thus surpassing one of the most entrenched generic differences in art—a rare gift. Said's argument for the continued *inclusion* of profound music in the humanities should also be an argument for the continued inclusion of Eliot's poetic voice in the world of artistic profundity in the study of literature, especially in culture studies of literature, where that voice can hardly be cited and discussed enough.

If the culture studies approach to which new materialism is a critical inheritor therefore evokes one or two caveats (as explicated) pertaining to the inclusion and exclusion of poetic voices, what about the broad world of critical activity known collectively as "theory"? Will the theoretical aspect of new materialism do justice or potential justice to reading Eliot's poetry? Here one may turn to another mammoth figure on the horizon of literary studies, one usually and unwillingly categorized under the rubric of "theoreticians." Perhaps surprisingly, as Robert Kern seems to have been the first to note,[62] it is Jacques Derrida who gives full credence to orientalism in modern poetics. *Of Grammatology* distinguishes between two kinds of orientalism in the West: Leibniz's notion of a transparent, universal language based on Chinese, which Derrida terms the European hallucination, and Pound's and Stéphane Mallarmé's modernist breakthrough, based also on Chinese, through and beyond Western logocentrism.[63] Derrida argues first that Chinese falls outside logocentrism altogether. Among other things, one understands, because it does not hierarchically determine breath and speech to be superior to semiotic materiality, vision, and script. Chinese remains "structurally dominated by the ideogram or algebra and we thus have the testimony of a powerful movement of civilization developing outside of all logocentrism." In Chinese, writing does not "reduce the voice to itself." Instead, it *incorporates* it "into a system,"[64] and that system retains a visual immediacy of connections between signifying and natural being, as Pound has shown so clearly in his careful analysis of Chinese signs such as "red," which combines elements of rose, cherry, rust, and flamingo, pointing into the dynamic relations between them.[65] Subsequently Derrida says that Pound's and Mallarmé's fascination with the Chinese ideogram "should be given all its historical significance."[66] The reason is that this fascination embodies a historical break with logocentrism from *within the West*. The myth of an origin based on breath and speech that is merely mirrored or recorded on a lower or further level in linear writing, finally begins to crumble. Pound's "irreducibly graphic poetics," Derrida asserts, is "the first break in the most entrenched Western tradition."[67] The literary critic simply adds that the poems embody this break.

We are used to an immensely ironic and strategic Derrida, one who never approaches things antithetically, but always strategically. The result is that when we read these announcements, their straightforwardness and simplicity are spell-binding. They are profound statements, marking direct affirmations of literary value in a sea of nihilism. But what do they have to do with Eliot? As the modern critic Norman Friedman has been early to state,[68] and as is becoming increasingly clear with a view to the work that I have mentioned of

Qian, Kern, and others, the orientalist graphic emphasis is far more prevalent in all kinds of modern poetry than has been acknowledged in criticism of the past. The case of Cummings springs to mind immediately. His poetry *is* a kind of graphic writing, to its core. On a far more general scale, poetry with its line-breaks has always tended to work against the linearities of thought presented in prose. Still, a modern poet such as Yeats is far less radical than Cummings, Pound, Mallarmé, or the Dutch poet Paul van Ostaijen when it comes to visual maneuvering against the main grain of Western discourse. This precisely brings Eliot into renewed focus. As is almost always true for him, he occupies a formal modern middle ground, which is perhaps the overarching reason why he is so often viewed as the most seminal of modern poets. In other words, not only does he actively occupy the modern poetic middle ground between (say) tradition and experimentation, fragmentation and recombination, and so forth, but also most pertinently the one between traditional visual presentation of poetry on the one hand and the radical, often ideogrammatically informed, Imagist, or modern Buddhist-Taoist-Zen experimentations and shorthand on the other.

As a consequence, his poetry forms a very important part of that ideogrammatic experiment, exactly because it shows its middle ground. I mean that Eliot's occasional employment of negative or affirmative blank space is simply his particular shorthand for ideogrammatic experience, and it is as unique to him as it is unique to every modern poet mentioned here. It forms part of his idiolect, while his ideogrammatics is his way of participating in a broader modern expression of the vibrant now-here-nowhere within a social context of nihilism, for instance again in the case of *Da* and *shantih* soaked in blank space, or the entirety of his composition for the singing still point, as the Chinese jar is still in its movement, *Four Quartets*.

Though championing these kinds of modern poetic development for their historical and disruptive "outside-ness" from centuries of violent hierarchy in Western culture, Derrida does not take it further. He does not say, for instance, that it presents real presence on the levels of poetic language and poetic experience *as part of experience as such*. One comes before a choice: will one allow the ideogrammatic maneuvering—fragment/ blank space in *The Waste Land*, oxymoron/ still point in *Four Quartets*—real presence, or not? Perhaps unlike Derrida, mainly for the reason that modern poetry is so persuasive in its incorporation of one's mind's eye into its worlds and worldliness, and its vibrantly reciprocal Earth-participation in particular, I opt for the latter actuality. Critical evidence exists for my position. In his biography of Eliot, Peter Ackroyd summarizes the dilemma faced by the modern poets. Both Pound and Eliot, he writes,

> sought for a tradition or order of their own. But they had to create it for themselves, going to sources as remote as Platonism, Buddhism or medieval

literature. Until they found some centre, some kind of coherence or wholeness, they would remain like the character in *The Education of Henry Adams*—the passive, cynical or merely sceptical observer of an environment which seems meaningless and of other lives which seem absurd.[69]

This profound choice that these poets *experience* in their time brings them to the nothing that is, *shantih* in significant blank space, the still point from which the dance emanates, while there is only the dance. Similarly, the reader who has relished and studied *The Waste Land* comes before a choice, as formulated in the moving words—moving in every dynamic sense—of Jewel Spears Brooker and Joseph Bentley. The reader "can suppose" that the poem is

> a simple set of variations on lost unity with no unifying perspective this side of a metaphysical absolute. Or he can suppose that it is a deep intuition of the alien patterns of perception that prevailed in his first world. We tend toward the second choice, in part because it associates the poem's overwhelming power and life with a primal source. *The Waste Land* evokes a perfect, wordless love that existed before all language and all meaning. That is the primary reason it is a great and lasting work of art.[70]

The "first world" of which they speak is that of one's earliest childlike experience which, clearly according to Eliot not only in terms of Bradley's philosophical layers of experience, but also in terms of Buddhism, remains with one as one matures. To continue to remain open to this intensity and aliveness of experience is everything but to deny, nostalgically, the connections between poetry, writing, thought, criticism, and the *moha*. From this perspective in fact, the insistence on certain ideological stances as prerequisites into experience may seem somewhat stale, sentimental, and nostalgic, mainly for the reason that they lack self-irony, while they continue to erect a barrier of linguistic complications between the participant in life, and actual participation. It is this vital recognition that Said surprisingly overlooks, because he does not take the poetry into account. He overlooks the parallel developments in Eliot's career of choosing poetry and not a promising epistemological career; the role of the bank clerk and not that of the bohemian, individualistic, "professional" poet; orientalism and not (as far as Eliot sees it) experience-denying Western philosophy; and so forth. Worse, though, Said overlooks the poetic reflection of these choices: fragmentation that refuses to gloss over modern difficulties with "neat, sense-making, pretty" (and familiar) forms; recombination that refuses to allow a one-sided sentimentality of purely lamenting a given, broken (fragmented) "Situation"; and a radical going-against-the-grain of historical metaphysics as uncovered by Derrida in terms of logocentrism.

The point is that one can write culturally as if the poems exist, and one can write culturally as if they do not; one can go further and write in ignorance of those values that are carried by and carry the poem, values that, to reiterate Brooker's and Bentley's words above, embody the primary reason why it is a great and lasting work of art. By eliding the poetry—as culture studies must frequently do if it is to remain intact, since the actual literary examples may disrupt or engulf its claims irrevocably, as in the case here—Said has managed to replace Eliot's character Eeldrop, found in his only published short story, with the character of one Appleplex. The latter insists on thought as the avenue into fuller understanding of life, and the former feels the avenue is ordinary life.[71] For, if messiness and worldliness (getting "mixed up" with ordinary life) is next to godliness, as Said claims along with the "mystical" Merleau-Ponty, there is nothing messier than Earth, while its messiness somehow gives rise to an enormous clarity of all that continues to be. In this exact vein, Eliot is that poet who prefers the dung and death of Earth to the dearth and desert of materialist aloofness from it. He always prefers connection to disconnection, even when he honors the respect that comes with distance. His supreme ability to dislocate in order to locate, and to be direct in indirect, Buddhist ways, offers his reader a singular poetic path into an utter form of connection, location, immersion, and dissolving.

For Said, unlike Derrida, then, the modern poets are the very epitome of the old orientalism that fails to be part of the "anti-Orientalist critique," Said's "good" orientalism. Of course, Said himself gives the ultimate impetus to that "good" orientalism, which he views as part of the burgeoning of contemporary and "ongoing disciplinary discourses where each of them posits nothing less than new objects of knowledge, new praxes of human activity, new theoretical models that upset or, at the very least, radically alter the prevailing paradigmatic forms."[72] To the extent that this is indeed the case, modern poetry should belong under this same rubric: it is a radical form of poetic writing. And to the extent that new materialism owes the potential of its existence not only to those liberations that the linguistic turn do bring about, but certainly also to the literary venturing into cultural domains outside the strict study of literary art only, it will do well, in this respect unlike Said, not to turn a cold shoulder to modern poetry and (its) orientalism. When new materialism studies literature, for instance, it might avoid the trap of talking about it without giving voice to it, that is, the Saidian pitfall of ignoring the embodied poetry in reaching conclusions about the cultural value or not of the poets, and, by thick implication or casual neglect, their poems.

The old-fashioned habit of having the critical courtesy to cite the poems that you critique, or even poems from poets that you condemn, here shows just how dangerous and extreme it has remained. It interrupts the easy, self-convincing flow of prosaic utterances rather effectively. We hear the poet's voice for a moment, even if it is decontextualized, and easy claims of stock disdain are no longer so readily forthcoming. It brings about nothing less than a new knowledge of (poetic) objects as a new generation practices and performs the poetic lines in the manner of responsive criticism. Also in this very pragmatic sense, I believe, one may find response to Bennett's call for the aesthetic discussion of new materialism.

But new materialism remains first a response, as said, to the linguistic turn with its emphasis on "infinite semiosis" and "no outside-text." Though these phrases relate to the individual work of Derrida and others, they are now part of everyday literary discussion along with other theorizing terms such as intertextuality, foregrounding, defamiliarization, and deconstruction. We have seen that Eliot's poetry, very much part of the modern beginning of subject-object volatility that makes poststructuralism and postmodernism possible (despite their occasional and incisive protestations to the contrary), shows important awareness of the fact that differentiation certainly is possibly infinite, *while the infinite potential is not always beneficial.* Prufrock suffers hilariously, but painfully, from the sheer weight of the weightlessness of his differentiating capacity. So sensitively does he slice up his connectivity with Cosmos that he becomes immune to experience. His sensitivity, very much akin to infinite semiosis, is in the nature of an incarcerating semiotic regime. It should be worth the attention of the brave new materialism to consider this potential of the theoretical tyrannies of differentiation, to which the argument subsequently turns.

NOTES

1. Zhaoming Qian, *Orientalism and Modernism: The Legacy of China in Pound and Williams* (Durham: Duke University Press, 1995), 2.

2. James Barron, "Beethoven May Not Have Died from Lead Poisoning, After All," *New York Times*, accessed 5 September 2015, http://www.nytimes.com/2010/05/29/arts/music/29skull.html?_r=0

3. T. S. Eliot, *Selected Prose*, ed. Frank Kermode (London: Faber & Faber, 1980), 64.

4. Wallace Stevens, *Collected Poems* (London: Faber & Faber, 1990), 165.

5. John Felstiner, *Can Poetry Save the Earth? A Field Guide to Nature Poems* (New Haven: Yale University Press, 2009), 15.

6. As found in the poet's notes kept at the Houghton Library of Harvard University, cited by Michael Webster, "'singing is silence:' Being and Nothing in the Visual Poetry of E. E. Cummings," *Form Miming Meaning: Iconicity in Language and Literature*, eds. Max Nänny & Olga Fischer (Amsterdam: John Benjamins, 1999), 202.

7. William Carlos Williams, *The Collected Poems* (Volume 1), eds. A. Walton Litz and Christopher MacGowan (New York: New Directions, 1986), 195.

8. T. S. Eliot, *Collected Poems 1909-1962* (New York: Harcourt Brace, 1991), 177.

9. Stevens, *Poems*, 197.

10. F. R. Leavis, "The Significance of the Modern Waste Land," *The Waste Land* (Norton Critical Edition), ed. Michael North (New York: Norton, 2001), 181; A. D. Moody, "A Cure for a Crisis of Civilization?" *The Waste Land* (Norton Critical Edition), ed. Michael North (New York: Norton, 2001), 240.

11. Michael Edwards, *Towards a Christian Poetics* (Grand Rapids, Mich.: Eerdmans, 1984), 113.
12. Eliot, *Poems*, 208.
13. Jeffrey M. Perl and Andrew P. Tuck, "The Hidden Advantage of Tradition: On the Significance of T. S. Eliot's Indic Studies," *Philosophy East & West* 35.2 (April 1985), 119.
14. Perl and Tuck, "Eliot's Indic Studies," 120.
15. Perl and Tuck, "Eliot's Indic Studies," 120.
16. Perl and Tuck, "Eliot's Indic Studies," 121.
17. Carl Gustav Jung, "Commentary on *The Golden Flower*," http://carljungdepthpsychology.blogspot.com, retrieved 19 February 2015.
18. Edward Said, *Reflections on Exile and Other Essays* (Cambridge: Harvard University Press, 2002), xxii.
19. Eliot, *The Waste Land*, 10.
20. Lawrence Rainey, *The Annotated* Waste Land *with Eliot's Contemporary Prose* (New Haven: Yale University Press, 2006), 10.
21. Said, *Reflections on Exile*, 14.
22. Said, *Reflections on Exile*, 6.
23. Said, *Reflections on Exile*, 7.
24. Said, *Reflections on Exile*, 3.
25. Said, *Reflections on Exile*, 8.
26. R. P. Blackmur, "Notes on E. E. Cummings's Language," *Critical Essays on E. E. Cummings*, ed. Guy Rotella (Boston: Hall, 1984), 109.
27. Said, *Reflections on Exile*, 252; R. P. Blackmur, "Between the *Numen* and the *Moha*: Notes towards a Theory of the Novel," *The Sewanee Review* 62.1 (Jan–Mar 1954), 6.
28. Said, *Reflections on Exile*, xxi.
29. Said, *Reflections on Exile*, 6.
30. Said, *Reflections on Exile*, 247; Edward Said, *Orientalism* (London: Penguin, 2003), 253.
31. Said, *Orientalism*, 253.
32. Said, *Reflections on Exile*, 247.
33. Max F. Müller, *The Upanishads* (Delhi: Motilal Banarsidass, 1969), 189.
34. Jewel Spears Brooker, *Mastery and Escape: T. S. Eliot and the Dialectic of Modernism* (Amherst: University of Massachusetts Press, 1994), 19.
35. Said, *Reflections on Exile*, xviii.
36. David E. Chinitz, *T. S. Eliot and the Cultural Divide* (Chicago: University of Chicago Press, 2005), 162.
37. Said, *Reflections on Exile*, xx.
38. Said, *Reflections on Exile*, xx.
39. Brooker, *Mastery and Escape*, 213.
40. Perl and Tuck, "Eliot's Indic Studies," 117.
41. Perl and Tuck, "Eliot's Indic Studies," 117–118.
42. Perl and Tuck, "Eliot's Indic Studies," 118.
43. Perl and Tuck, "Eliot's Indic Studies," 118.
44. Perl and Tuck, "Eliot's Indic Studies," 118.
45. Perl and Tuck, "Eliot's Indic Studies," 120.
46. Eliot, *Poems*, 180.
47. Perl and Tuck, "Eliot's Indic Studies, 121.
48. William W. Bevis, *Mind of Winter: Wallace Stevens, Meditation, and Literature* (Pittsburgh: University of Pittsburgh Press, 1988), 26.
49. A. D. Moody, Lecture Presented at the First International Eliot Summer School.
50. Leavis, "Modern Waste Land," 174.
51. Leavis, "Modern Waste Land," 177.
52. Leavis, "Modern Waste Land," 179.
53. Leavis, "Modern Waste Land," 179.
54. John Crowe Ransom, "Waste Lands," *The Waste Land* (Norton Critical Edition), ed. Michael North (New York: Norton, 2001), 167–168.

55. Leavis, "Modern Waste Land," 180–181.
56. Leavis, "Modern Waste Land," 181.
57. Moody, "Cure?" 240–241.
58. E. E. Cummings, *Complete Poems 1904-1962* (New York: Liveright, 1994), 620.
59. Said, *Reflections on Exile*, xxxii.
60. Brooker, *Mastery and Escape*, 185.
61. Eliot, *Prose*, 206.
62. Robert Kern, *Orientalism, Modernism, and the American Poem* (Cambridge: Cambridge University Press, 1996), 7.
63. Derrida, *Grammatology*, 80, 92.
64. Derrida, *Grammatology*, 90.
65. Ezra Pound, *ABC of Reading* (New York: New Directions, 1987), 22.
66. Derrida, *Grammatology*, 92.
67. Derrida, *Grammatology*, 92.
68. Norman Friedman, "Post Script" [to "E. E. Cummings and the Modernist Movement"], *Critical Essays on E. E. Cummings*, ed. Guy Rotella (Boston: Hall, 1984), 174.
69. Peter Ackroyd, *T. S. Eliot: A Life* (London: Hamish Hamilton, 1984), 25.
70. Jewel Spears Brooker and Joseph Bentley, *Reading* The Waste Land: *Modernism and the Limits of Interpretation* (Amherst: University of Massachusetts Press, 1990), 222.
71. Perl and Tuck, "Eliot's Indic Studies," 126–127.
72. Said, *Reflections on Exile*, 212.

Chapter Seven

The Tyrannies of Differentiation

Eliot, New Materialism, and "Infinite Semiosis"

In turning attention to theoretical discourse, the matter of how new materialism will choose its path ahead within ecocriticism, which at least entails some kind of literary focus, comes into the picture with even more intensity than in the case of culture studies discussed in the preceding chapter. The reason, as suggested, is that by virtue of its moment of emergence new materialism must act as a response to the linguistic turn of which it is a critical continuation, and from which it is a critical departure. It cannot assume radical, seamless continuation with that turn, because its conception stems from the recognition that infinite emphasis on signs probably distracts from humanity's connections with agentic Earth.

Taking a large view, this relative double bind at the heart of new materialism flows from the basic differences that are carried between poststructuralism-postmodernism on the one hand and ecocriticism on the other, two interrelated fields of focus arising more or less simultaneously within the history of literary studies in the 1960s, 1970s, and 1980s. One had, as it were, the emergence *within* culture of C. P. Snow's much-cited "two cultures," one drastically emphasizing culture in the form of the linguistic turn, and the other emphasizing nature in ecocriticism. This contradiction comes to a head in new materialism, a notion that this chapter and the subsequent conclusion will examine. As such, new materialism offers a more manageable (in terms of sheer bulk) and pertinent playing field on which to test ideas about the differences between poststructuralism-postmodernism and ecocriticism.

To begin somewhere in this labyrinth, "infinite semiosis," whether in its highly technical and slippery Derridian aspect (as opposed, though, to its more correct Peircian aspect),[1] or its ubiquitous aspect as a major episteme of current cultural praxis, has become a kind of literary datum of life, underlying and making possible much of the epistemological spirit within which current cultural doing takes place. In general it holds that signs continue to refer to other signs in difference and the concomitant deference of real presence. There is no "ground zero" where signs end and concrete reality begins. One lives in a world of signs and perceptions, and even the most basic concrete reality comes to us at least in some semiotic form. I focus pertinently on this generalized, sometimes nebulous form of the term ("infinite semiosis") that has become a stock part of the literary milieu, because its technical formulation and defense is too slippery to work with, while its "spirit" is the problem. Distrust of the sign's referential purpose that would link it with extra-semiotic worlds is its obvious corollary. That is, the general spirit of "infinite semiosis" will hold as impossible or unwanted any straightforward or affirmative attitude toward transcendent experience that reaches into realities or actualities beyond the scope of the infinite, always already complicating differences between signifiers. What I have been terming in extension of George Steiner's work *real presence* therefore enters the radar of this signifier-producing machine, "infinite semiosis," only on the most skeptical levels imaginable, if at all.

But perhaps the concept of "infinite semiosis" is beginning to lose some of its predominance on the literary map, especially compared to the late 1960s and early 1980s. New materialism probably announces its diminishment in the coming and going of literary emphases, in the sense that it wants to argue for agency outside purely human or subjective agency, which implies at least some sort of "ground zero" where reality is not humanly semiotic or significant in the narrow sense of how human language gives agency to things, or not.

However, new materialism at the moment appears uncertain about the place of "infinite semiosis" within its discourse. On the one hand, given that new materialism emphasizes the materiality of existence outside strict notions of reality limited to signs, as indicated, it surely must be the case that new materialism is a critique exactly of "infinite semiosis." It has to be a critique, one would expect, of the idea that worlds exist only in the manner in which signs can or cannot do things with them. On the other hand, in some instances new materialism seems to want to accommodate the patterns and values of "infinite semiosis" into its discourse in a sort of seamless fashion, as this chapter and the subsequent conclusion will be at pains to uncover.

Even in the heyday of "infinite semiosis," though, it is challenged, and the challenge is necessary. The idea that signs have purposes toward or referential capacities *into* worlds outside themselves, no matter how complex those purposes and referents are, is not that easy to dismiss.[2] Neither is the letting go of the referential purpose always desirable, as has been shown among others by the green critic Laurence Coupe.[3] Surely the living material world has meanings and being outside of signs to which signs may relate themselves in a kind of active humility, while the human experience of those meanings and being cannot be restricted to language systems of re-presentation. Surely this active humility furthermore affirms the interconnectedness between the world of human sign-making and the world of natural processes.

In this light it is worth exploring the limits of "infinite semiosis" as found in Eliot's poetry. In line with this position, I wish to start out with a humble, simple imagery of "infinite semiosis": the onion, which consists of houses within houses, as does Eliot's poem "Gerontion." For, the onion reminds of "infinite semiosis," but it enjoys limits, because everything on Earth is not an onion, even if onions have been reproducing themselves in various forms over millions of years in which not a single human signifier was yet in the air—although mind and agency may well have been in the air then. Nor is everything on Earth a house, though houses produce and reproduce themselves in a myriad of histories, cultures, and imaginations.

In what strikes one as perhaps the best extant reading of "Gerontion," Jewel Spears Brooker points out that its structure is that of houses within houses within houses.[4] (I must hasten to add that the onion I have in mind, is dry.) In these abodes Gerontion, Greek for "little old man," lives, wilts, or most probably shrivels into further aridity of soul, since he is one of the hollow men. The "infinite semiosis" he suffers from is neither exciting nor semiotically profitable, although, as usual in Eliot, on the level of the reader it is instructive. In this instance, its instructiveness has to do with a *critique* of the assumption that an infinity of signs related to signs, or sign-houses related to more sign-houses, is necessary, healthy, or relatively unavoidable. The poem exquisitely and even painfully shows not only that such proliferation of sign-worlds can be unhealthy, but that the proliferation is itself symptomatic of cultural corruption. I believe one should relate these considerations with that aspect of new materialism that desires a seamless continuum with "infinite semiosis." I wish to question the idea that differentiation itself, differentiation into infinity, differentiation that *should* always already be able to avoid the semiotic limit between signs and concrete realities, has to be incorporated without question in new materialism.

In this vein, then, "Gerontion" presents its dry onion structure of houses within houses, but the houses are "filled" with terrible emptiness, and the destructive limit of their infinitude is all too apparent. The poem begins with Gerontion's description of his literal house, but it soon becomes clear that another house is that of the reader's mind, within which Gerontion's body is "an old house with tenants, one of which, his brain, is again a house with tenants, his thoughts."[5] He inhabits, and is inhabited by, various houses, structurally erected in the poem through an array of allusive dwellings imposed on and extant within other allusive dwellings. These include various cultural houses: ancient Greece, modern Greece, Belgium, Christianity, Judaism, modern culture, Europe, religion, the economy, and so forth. All of these houses, as well as their literal and mental tenants, are in a state of virtually complete decay.[6] These striking descriptions of the corruption, materialism, rotting, and crumbling that characterize Gerontion's modern house within houses come to a kind of halt in the poem's second stanza, a halt that has become over time a much-discussed barrier where many readers have struggled to make the interpretative jump that the poem requires at that stage. But as Brooker points out, this halt is experienced as such only when one insists on reading the poem linearly.[7] The real, onion-like structure of the poem makes of the halt not a halt, but a more inclusive viewpoint:

> Signs are taken for wonders. 'We would see a sign!'
> The word within a word, unable to speak a word,
> Swaddled with darkness.[8]

The inclusive, onion-like viewpoint soon shows that these lines signify that the concrete mystery of Incarnation, of "God being immured in a house of flesh," is scorned in modern perception. The body as temple has gone amiss.[9] Only matter remains again, as in Prufrock's case. Disconnection occurs between real presence and its incarnated embodiment on the one hand, and (on the other) signs. The disconnection is caused by a "materialist," rationalist mindset for which "infinite semiosis" should supposedly compensate, while it actually results in the considerable spiritual dilemma that arises when the word within the word is lost. Conversely, once more, the loss of spirit is the cause of this uncanny disconnection. The word within the word would therefore be love, it would be connection (given that love is vibrant connection, as argued before, including awareness of vibrant emptiness). But this inner word is swaddled in the darkness that arises from the absence of meaningful connection with flesh and blood. Concreteness has as little meaning as signs. The tone of the exclamation "We would see a sign!" is cynical to the point of mockery.

These mocked and mocking houses within houses spawn from the infinitely rationalistic house-minds of the modern Pharisees who will not believe even when it is clear that belief is in order. Gerontion is the poem's type of the Pharisees, but as type he implicates modern humanity. And so we see the beginnings of "infinite semiosis." For it to be born, a severe level of one-sided cynicism about meaningful links between significance and concreteness is a prerequisite. To be sure, this is of particular importance to new materialism with its renewed emphasis on meaningful concreteness, as I will argue immediately. The curse on the house that has brought all these houses (Greek, Jewish, Christian, and so on) to ruin, is "a mentality that isolates intelligence from passion and from belief." The Pharisees view all the signs that Christ indeed gives with irony *in any event*. They refuse to see the miracles that Christ performs in their very presence as meaningful events, removing understanding from belief. This distancing from the miraculous lies at the root of "infinite semiosis." For, it is always possible to act differently, to insist on difference, or to "make a difference" when it is not difference that is called upon, but recognition and active acceptance of an unfathomable and present unity between spiritual meaning and concrete reality. Supposedly so open as an attitude, the insistence on differentiation in such instances closes down the situation, and one sits again in the prison house of language with its other one-sided energy, the biology trap, neatly in place. Where there should be integrity of opposites, there is the mere violence of two sets of one-sidedness.

This Pharisee attitude represents the way the modern church views miracles, too. The Church "is another of the poem's decaying, crumbling houses in dry and windy lands."[10] The True Church of "The Hippopotamus" therefore crops up again in "Gerontion." Unlike the hippo, Gerontion is incarcerated in a wasteland of ever-further, allusive differentiation represented by the infinite wall barriers between houses and their rooms. Immersion in actual existence is out of the question for him. There is exhaustion here, and despondency, bordering on the madness of disillusionment with the overwhelming riches of differential refinement that Western civilization is capable of offering, provided you are something of a Prufrock or a Pharisee, or someone on the Emmaus way toward impossible threeness that appears insane. Indeed, these concerns were shared by most of the sensitive artists and thinkers in Eliot's day.[11] Thus the wind blowing in Gerontion's infinite houses, as the wind in *The Waste Land*, is again "mere" wind, devoid of spiritual connection. Wind in these poems suggests infinite absence carried by infinite difference. The difference moreover carries or is carried by indifference. It paradoxically therefore acts as "a dynamic absence with enormous power to corrupt and destroy."[12] But the poem's imagining of this absence is dazzling, and directly relevant to the general deconstructive desire toward "infinite semiosis." Consider again this passage in the poem:

> Signs are taken for wonders. 'We would see a sign!'
> The word within a word, unable to speak a word,
> Swaddled with darkness. In the juvescence of the year
> Came Christ the tiger[13]

A terrible absence has been born. Mocking the miraculous nature of concrete being has given life to a frightening chimera. Christ comes now not as a savior, but as a tiger:

> The tiger springs in the new year. Us he devours. Think at last
> We have not reached conclusion, when I
> Stiffen in a rented house.[14]

The process of communion has been reversed. Instead of eating and being edified by spiritual truth, one is devoured by its absence. As a consequence, death and sex come to their exhaustion, their pointlessness of derivation and deprivation, their inability to come to conclusion. They are mere matters of difference, and Gerontion stiffens in a crumbling, false house. He also stiffens in Freudian manner within a vagina for rent. His only "love" is sex with a whore. And he is stiffening, of course, on the level of the Freudian twin to sex, death, but also in a rented place that offers neither rootedness nor active meaningfulness. That sex, long since viewed as a mystical "small death," becomes so dull and dead is therefore another characteristic of Western civilization according to this poem. The deathly inner mask of Freudianism becomes visible in the poem, adumbrating such literary developments as the insistence on infinite signifier-perversion in Roland Barthes's essay titled *The Pleasure of the Text*.

For this reason, too, the split of Carl Gustav Jung (whom I have cited in regard of the modern Prufrockian material dilemma) away from Freud marks, indeed, one of the most important events of the early twentieth century, for Jung embraces the colorful meaningfulness of myth, while Freud clings to dark materialism reduced to one or two forces of will, sex, and death.[15] It is little wonder that the Freudian house in this poem is part of the corruption in general, and interesting to think in this context of the fact that Freud is mentioned so frequently in literary studies of the second half of the twentieth century when compared with Jung. It is as though postmodern thought has a greater taste for the materialist Freud, discarding or ignoring the more spiritually meaningful, therefore materially more profound, Jung. Again "Gerontion" anticipated these events that were to come after its publication.

But, as deconstruction knows all too well, in this instance along with "Gerontion," the absence of meaningfulness somehow remains active, *de*(con)*structive*. As Brooker says, "the absence of god is not a simple absence, but an absence with claws and teeth"[16]—Christ the tiger. This is the horror at the bottom of this poem, mirroring the horror of Prufrock's auto-consumption at the bottom of his solipsistic world of endless differences. In contrast, consider once more that perception of wholeness is perception of connection, love, and hence that which is holy, and this colors difference differently. But what happens if we are imprisoned within differences that deny wholeness, again even on the most secular levels of holiness, that is, in a general sense that denies the deep human value bestowed on concrete being on the planet? "Gerontion" suggests that in this kind of dire situation, knowledge remains trapped in a wilderness of differences, differences that can only reflect their differentiation in unbearable sameness:

> These with a thousand small deliberations
> Protract the profit of their chilled delirium,
> Excite the membrane, when the sense has cooled,

> With pungent sauces, multiply variety
> In a wilderness of mirrors.[17]

How ironic that wilderness has become so civilized! Intriguingly, Eliot follows this directly with one of the most overlooked and moving little moments in the poem:

> What will the spider do,
> Suspend its operations, will the weevil
> Delay?[18]

In Gerontion's mind, this is part only of his despair. What, he seems to think, will nature continue indifferently, while I wither away bodily? This is the implied question characterized by sentimental misery about nature's very continuation in his old, dry mind. On the reader's level, though, who can help but feel a strange sympathy for these creatures, continuing in a way utterly true to themselves, albeit in a cultural world that, unbeknownst to them, has become completely barren by way of infinite differentiation, infinite distances? The weevil, if one may say so, is an amazing beetle with its snout and an herbivorous, slow nature, albeit that Eliot might consciously have had another creature in mind. The spider "operates" by making webs. At least for a moment, nature's continuing innocence is here suspended from Western doubts and "coils of disgust."[19] No, nature will not wait for a disconnected culture. It and its creatures will continue their minute and vast processes. Literally, Earth cannot "afford" to halt its processes for the sake of someone such as a Gerontion who must pass away. Nature's indifference to his condition is also a form of in-difference: continuing integrity. And like Gerontion, a civilization may mince away at further little differences, those Prufrockian decisions and revisions that a minute will reverse.[20] But such a civilization will do well to look anew at Earth, to re-spect it, as Eliot indeed advocates in *The Idea of a Christian Society* and elsewhere, as has been demonstrated here.

For, there is something in the continuation of the spider building its web that does *not* merely fit the sentimental notion of the horrors of death, that is, those horrible images of a room or house in which someone has died, resulting in the spiders taking over the place, of which we have cheap renditions in horror movies *ad nauseam*. Spiders as such are innocent: what else can they be? Will they suspend their operations, because culture is decaying? They do not intentionally bring the evil that a mind such as Gerontion's, all too conscious of death and imminent spider-webbed rooms, projects onto them. It is one's own evil that one sees when one sees the spider's web in this way. The spider patiently continuing to build its aesthetic web perhaps has more faith of the right, instinctual kind, indicating the creature's creative living out its life within its limits, than has Gerontion with his manifold houses of cultures and words and his manifold tastes of nuances and distinctions. So refined and overwhelming are the distinctions that instinct is lost in a world without any difference that matters.

At the reader's level, not strictly "within" Gerontion's world, the poem therefore calls upon a certain critical restlessness about the notion of infinite difference that would turn so bright in postmodernism. Gerontion's powdery, infinitely ironic world within worlds challenges cynicism. Instead of a kind of irony that reveals certain truths, one has in his case irony that veils only the fact that there is absence behind the veil, and more ironies to be had, while life dwindles into further pulverizing corners. Where Prufrock "enjoys" more teas and ices, albeit rather semiotic ones, Gerontion "enjoys" further words from a book read to him. One comes again to the blunt but actually bright point that an irony that is all-pervasive would no longer be an irony, because there would be no foil for it to be ironic against, just as Earth-denial cannot work without confirming Earth. The dialectic, the presupposition between these two vital opposite worlds—a dying Gerontion and a weaving spider, culture and nature, irony and non-irony—cannot be escaped from by creating more and more (poststructuralist, postmodern) differences. And so, for the reader, behind Gerontion's infinity of ironic veils there does lie the truth that existence is substantial. Even in the most one-sided position, Gerontion's, the culture-nature dialectic establishes itself. The reader knows there is more to life and spider's webs than the projection of infinite cultural house-signs.

The philosopher Kate Soper has done all the hard, excellent work of showing that postmodernism cannot escape from, but actually continues to confirm, this culture-nature dialectic, as argued throughout her book *What is Nature? Culture, Politics and the Non-Human.* With "dialectic" I mean here simply that culture presupposes nature, and vice versa, so that even the most "hyperreal" position that might want to argue that Earth is mostly or merely constructed by human differences, always already assumes the existence of an Earth *not* constructed thus. On the most "base" level of this truth, a million million slithers of the most differentiated, refined signs cannot replace the fact that humans are material creatures. Ironically, the fact that a word has sound and printed forms, or that a movie must be burnt into a disk, continues to confirm that there is no meaning without concreteness. One infers that it is not *whether the dialectic exists* that matters, but exactly *how* one works with it. Does one, for instance, subjugate the opposite conditions into the static, hierarchical, dichotomous "properties" that have rightfully been the target of postmodern modes of making differences? Is the view that holds opposites in violent hierarchy transcendent, or precisely not? If a world is trapped in two sets of one-sided conditions, as is Prufrock's and Gerontion's, what is the potential of an actual solution to the dilemma and, worse, what is the potential of actually enjoying the dilemma as dilemma? For, no dilemma can exist without its counterpart, the dissolving of opposite energies in the integrity of renewed life. Do forms of transcendence exist, in acknowledgement of secular earthly holiness, that are not hierarchical, but rather participatory, in the nature of the freedom that comes with real earthly presence?

As we have seen, these questions Eliot opens up widely in his poetic project. Their potential bearing on new materialism, which senses that its handling of opposites will be critical, will be examined in the conclusion to this book. Meanwhile, "Gerontion," of which the structure therefore marks a birth place of "infinite semiosis," at least intimates that skepticism about "infinite semiosis" is necessary. Gerontion's relative infinitude of houses within houses are not pleasant to live in. They lack almost all joy. One suffers the tyrannies of difference. At first glance, some kind of relief from these tyrannies for the blind little old man is brought about only by the boy reading to him, and the reading itself. However, it is clear that the boy is likely to turn into another Gerontion, perpetuating the onion-like structure of the dire situation.[21] The decaying aspect of the cycle therefore *appears* to promise relief from endless cycles as things at last fall apart in rotting, but this is merely part of infinite decay. That the relief is only apparent amounts to the final twist of the infinite semiotic knife within Gerontion's semiotically dominated life. His life is secondary, consisting only of semiotic replicas of what used to be meaningful words.

As shown in the preceding chapter, nonetheless, in Derrida's embracing of orientalism in modern poetry one finds at least one instance that causes optimism about affirmation of great literature beyond the infinite infatuation with secondariness. In one of those strangely cross-stitching twists that characterizes literary complexity, another cause for optimism is the fact that Said embraces deconstruction as belonging to his strategic cultural method, *but with serious provisions*. He clearly expresses his wariness about the deconstructive maneuver.[22] The wariness has to do with weariness: there is a cynical monotony to the broad deconstructive mood with its painstaking procedures of producing semiotic difference, not unlike Gerontion's weariness within his cultured, differentiating houses. I believe Said's (Gerontion's) weariness is one felt by more critics, and it is the result of an overdose of differentiation. We have nearly reached the point where difference is viewed as more important than, and preferable to, notions and actualities of unity. In the imagery of Iain McGilchrist's work, the emissary has turned into the master.[23] The "referential," "transcendental," and the notion of unity as "monolithic" and "homogenous" are the near pejoratives of our day. Worse, wholeness gets confused with being monolithic—as shown throughout this book, Eliot's wholeness is everything but monolithic. It is a radical form of participating in the agentic meaningfulness of concrete being.

It is worth taking a brief look at how differentiation is claiming the master position in current cultural activity. A kind of hysteria about difference is replacing the *cortesia* of balancing distance and integrity. Just one example of how difference is championed as the present-day position of choice is Derrida's insistence on the incorrectness of evolution on the basis that it is too unifying, too familiar or familial. With a surprising intensity of pertinence, Derrida does not critique so much the material reductionism that at once limits and makes possible evolutionary theory. Had this been his position, one could have joined the conversation. Instead, he is against one of evolution's more optimistic and poetic implications, the evolutionary family tree. He has it against this aspect of evolution "creating a single large set, a single great, fundamentally homogeneous and continuous family tree going from the *animot* to the *homo* (*faber, sapiens*, or whatever else)." To "admit to this would be an *asinanity*, even more so to suspect anyone here of doing just that. I won't therefore devote another second to the double stupidity of that suspicion, even if, alas, it is quite widespread."[24] The cleverness of this stream of thought cannot hide its plain implausibility, perhaps to the embarrassment of those who follow Derrida unconditionally. The word "*animot*" and the neologism "asinanity" certainly are clever in their context. By means of the former he keeps unconditionally open the prospect of an animal-word, the notion of animal-language,[25] punching through immediately with an example of such a word, "*asinanity*." The latter says that to take evolutionary classification of animal species into one family seriously would be to stoop down to the stupidity of an ass. One would be animal-stupid and inane at once, showing lack of substance, interest, or ideas. But this is a double stupidity according to Derrida's word play here, also because we are already an animal, and/ or the animals always already "speak" to or through us. Those who reduce matter to muteness, such as evolutionists, one supposes, he views as doubly stupid, because they have muted the animals in the same stroke of reductionism, *while* they always already are themselves animals (as evolution would claim). Those who philosophize, as does Derrida, according to this line of thought come closer to a lively interaction with asses and other animals.

This paradox seems bright and innocent enough. By making differences in following his thoughts, Derrida points at the double bind in which evolution finds itself, its inherent contradiction that holds that humans are materially one with animals, while we are on that very basis superior in terms of the ability to use words. The evolutionists' ass-stupidity is therefore an animal-word belonging in the category that Derrida emphatically sticks to in this essay, "The Animal That Therefore I Am (More to Follow)," when he says: "It is a question of words, therefore."[26] But is it not still a question of material origins? When Derrida grapples in this essay with origins in Genesis, one has to concede that it is a matter of words, although those words relate themselves to spiritual concreteness, which he denies. But in daring to tackle in the said essay the other source of origins, material evolution, it can no longer be a matter of words. Here his theory, which bases itself on the notion of an origin always under erasure, always under the supplementary division that comes with the signifier, that is, difference as such, comes to a halt that he refuses to acknowledge, a halt not of "ground zero," but a necessary pausing in sensing that material explanations of evolution are not simply matters of playing with words.

For, how will Derrida refute evolution, and the physical primacy of the fossils of living beings? How can he refute the originary existence of matter? He cannot, and therefore his insistence on difference and deferral—the neat little pun on the human ass as something bound infinitely to linguistic difference—appears forced. That he wishes to close the matter so suddenly by declaring his unwillingness to devote "another second to the double stupidity of that suspicion" is symptomatic. Why the hurry? Following the evolutionary argument with greater patience can be very revealing indeed. It means that, over millions of years, on the level of star dust, my perception of the powdery butterfly with its metallic glint and that butterfly are utterly one, not least because I come from the same star dust, and not least (as Derrida would be first to admit) because it sees me as much as I see it, in our variously combined terms. It goes further: it flies up from the *Ocimum* in the soil when I approach it, our actions are reciprocal, we dance the still point together. Evolution is therefore entirely right to have discovered, painstakingly and by way of a very strange philosophical viewpoint indeed, a viewpoint made possible only by the deliberate reduction of matter to something a-religious, that the butterfly is my brother, my sister, my fellow countryman, my cosmological fellow. This unity makes our difference remarkable. But for Derrida difference must work differently. It works only *as difference*. What guarantees the double stupidity of the evolutionary reality of a biological family tree for Derrida resides in infinite distances, that is, the insistence upon infinite differentiation. In "refuting" the evolutionary family tree, he again rather insistently speaks of

> the infinite space that separates the lizard from the dog, the protozoon from the dolphin, the shark from the lamb, the parrot from the chimpanzee, the camel from the eagle, the squirrel from the tiger or the elephant from the cat, the ant from the silkworm or the hedgehog from the echidna.[27]

In terms of celebrating the wonder of differences between individual creatures the passage holds true, and is even revelatory. But the slippery word "infinite" is in this context simply wrong, because it is given that all these enormously different animals are of a startling concrete similarity. To mention one thing of which the poetic meaning has not nearly been done justice to, we all consist of cells. The dolphin consists of cells retaining their nucleated form that is materially indubitably the same form that the protozoon enjoys as it swims in some instances free from a larger collective. Here even the Great Chain of Being comes closer to the truth of unity and difference than Derrida. As much as one is related to angels, so one must "say to Corruption, Thou art my Father, and to the worm, Thou art my sister."[28] One is a polycellular creature with other such creatures, and to my mind it is easier to agree with Immanuel Kant that what bees produce is "a work of art"[29] than it is to agree with Derrida about the nature of differentiation. After all, Derrida's use of a phrase such as "the shark" already implies that all individual sharks, not to mention the many species involved, form a single group that makes their differences all the more startling.

To deny the natural kinship to which evolution distinctly points, displacing it with infinite difference, is therefore another double stupidity. The notion that humans and all the animals share family traits varying from playfulness to osmotic cells is perhaps too much to bear for a French poststructuralist sensibility, given that French thought has been in denial of evolution for longer than most.[30] In fact, it appears that Derrida is still mainly in denial of evolution, an astoundingly irrational position! This double stupidity may have been quite harmless and playful, were it not for its narrowing of the human and animal kingdoms by denying the extent of their cross-stitched integrity, which in turn denies the wonder of their differences, despite one's appreciation, seemingly without Derrida (?), of problems surrounding material reductionism. But will one reductionism (parading as an infinite chimera) serve to put another in its place? Will the reduction of animality and materiality to their human linguistic point of delivery alleviate the matter? In this instance, is it not the evolutionary streak that offers the more affirmative position, the more meaningful one, despite or through its reductionist view, which reductionism, after all, is a limited but nonetheless sobering philosophical method of ensuring new insights into the nature of life?

In Eliot's world there is difference between the existence of Earth and the existence of human mirth, but he cross-stitches the two worlds to show the interconnected significance of their aspects. He has no need of stressing the infinite differences between species, including humans, as we have seen. If one furthermore "does not come too close," in an open field, one will witness the magic vision of one's forefathers' and foremothers' dancing around a fire, enjoying a life of utter closeness with earthly being. Coming "too close" would end the magic, because magic requires a singular act of distance, of disbelief suspended by the imagination to enter the realm of actuality instead of the realm of "realism" only, where actuality means precisely the connection between imagination and reality, the *numen* and the *moha*. By coming too close in its particular, systematic, nihilistic form of close reading, Derrida denies this magic, magic that does not exclude evolutionary familiality, the fact of generations. This magical space is surprisingly earthly, and besides reminding of evolution as accepted by Eliot who sees a valid, as well as a popular, invalid version of it,[31] the magical space reminds of our forebears who enjoyed rustic laughter and the lifting of "heavy feet in clumsy shoes,"

> Earth feet, loam feet, lifted in country mirth
> Mirth of those long since under earth
> Nourishing the corn. Keeping time,
> Keeping the rhythm in their dancing
> As in their living the living seasons[32]

The poem reminds one, as in the case of *The Waste Land*, of the continuity that is central to (even) modern existence. The simple truth, again, is that without all the lives of all our forebears, one would literally not be here now, and on the merest contemplation of the effort and events that have gone into this, the recognition is astonishing. In its way, evolution acknowledges this on a very profound scale, of which the poetic potentials have remained dormant so far. Without millions of animal lives leading up to it, humanity does not exist. This is how closely bound up humans are with asses, with no infinite distance in sight, but only the real presence of distributed eternity. Eliot is able to give particularly moving poetic expression to this, precisely by "keeping it simple," maintaining its plainness, in words that are plain and yet bafflingly poetic, hence striking. In other words, we may now think that we are separate from the material cycles that nourish a lifetime on the planet, but is this true? I have in mind such asinanities, made possible only by the poststructuralist play with infinite semiosis, as that there is no such thing as seasonal cycles, while the reality of matter (as opposed to charged, positive nothing) is stupid, this time in the mouth, however, of a rather exciting and passionate current philosopher.[33]

From the angle that considers the generations that have literally brought us here, the idea that we are separate from natural cycles dissipates. We are still part of nature's cycles, and the apparent obviousness of the fact still hides its profundity. The intellectually stimulating, postmodern distance we perceive between us and the cycles is in any event speculative and tenuous, even in the case of current generations. The more so for Derrida's insistence on infinite distances between evolutionary creatures. When it comes to evolution, Derrida is disrespectful, forcing his insistence on linguistic differences onto a theory that he does not really wish to entertain with any seriousness in its own terms, while making sweeping statements about it—an embarrassment of the trans-disciplinary drive of theoretical studies in this instance.

It is not only the "obviousness" of evolutionary theory that Derrida underestimates, but also the obviousness of expressing presence. Stating the obvious cultural and natural things of the now-moment unfolding, of the fact that one is here by virtue of all that has gone before and continues to continue, is not as humdrum as it appears. *Four Quartets* excels at expressing this; it is a considerable achievement, even more so compared to the deconstructive drive toward infinite difference. The specific (our dancing, in the broadest and most detailed sense of twirling through a lifetime as it takes us on its course) and the universal are completely entwined in the timeless pattern of the still point. Indeed, the lines cited show that time and timelessness form a mandala characterized by being on Earth in human mirth, adding to Eliot's gallery of mandalic structures:

> *Earth* feet, loam feet, lifted in country *mirth*
> *Mirth* of those long since under *earth*

Earth and mirth form a chiasmus where their diagonal cross-stitching meets, as presented in figure 7.1.

The poetic sensibility, as opposed perhaps to the linguistic, the philosophical, and certainly the deconstructive-theoretical, hardly needs explanation upon perceiving this mandalic effect in the context of *Four Quartets*. It signifies the wholeness of that still point where differences meet, and from which they continue to emanate. Such a sensibility instantly recognizes that this is not a matter of the signifiers "earth" and "mirth" referring to one another and to other signs on an infinite plane of subjective, internalizing sign-objects. It offers instead playful entry into transcendence, provided once more that one understands the latter not as subjugation, but participation in existence, that is, the mirthful real presence that comes from being on Earth.

The effect is very much one of focusing one's attention on language as a sign-system, because the lines foreground repetition and sound. However, the words dissolve. At the meeting of the chiasmus, at the point where the

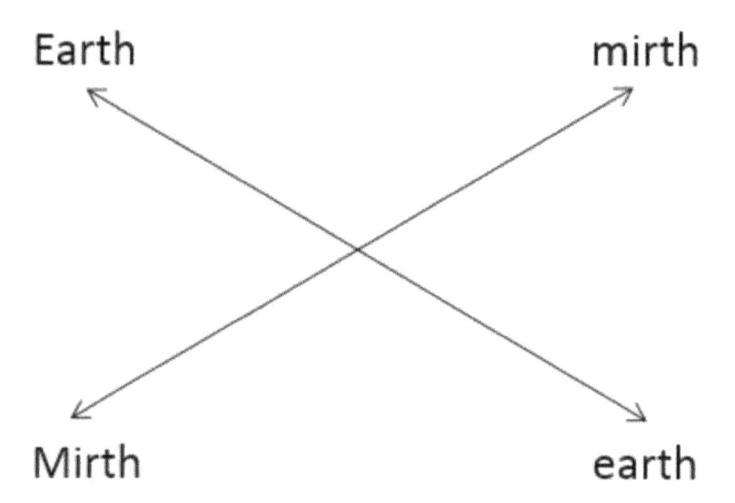

Figure 7.1. Earth-mirth mandala

repetitions of Earth and mirth meet, their differences dissolve. Repetition here does not hold the function maintaining that "there is no longer anything but language" in Roland Barthes's much-discussed words,[34] nor that one is faced merely with a kind of material surface of signs as G. Douglas Atkins is quick to argue in *T. S. Eliot Materialized*.[35] Its function here is precisely to melt the word surfaces into a still point of enormous vibrancy, as has been seen in the case also of other mandalic structures and poetic elements discussed in the present book. Meaning arises not from realistically "transparent" words that act as a window into the "real" world, to put it another way, but the meaning becomes participant in that actuality *beyond* words *in which* words find their real presence. This means, however, that the presence is real. The actual therefore combines the subjective and the real, the perceiver and the perceived, in a way that is ultimately as magical as it is immeasurable. However, to deny facts and reality puts up an unnecessary barrier between humanity and actuality for precisely these reasons.

Still, at first glance, deconstructive "infinite semiosis" may appear to have everything to say about the Earth-mirth mandala, given that the mandala bases itself on the difference between the signs "Earth" and "mirth." Returning for a moment to one of the "original" insights that Derrida and deconstruction bring (despite his numerous and intriguing subsequent claims not to be associated with the latter term), one may in deconstructive spirit insist that the supposed significance of the two signs, even here in *Four Quartets*, features within a set of differences and deferrals. Just as (say) the signs "bath" and "path" take their meaning not from some intrinsic connectedness with the presence of that which they refer to in the world, but rather to the agreed-upon, tiny difference between their acoustic and visual forms, so do "Earth" and "mirth" rely for their meaning on a very similar, relatively slight difference in sound and appearance. In the case of "bath" and "path," the only difference on the level of sound is the plus or minus, presence or absence, of voice in the first letter of each, namely "b" or "p." The rest is the same. *Their meaning relies on a convention of differences between signs on a linguistic plane*. They are therefore caught in and carried by the infinite conventional differences that they themselves, in part, carry as part of the system of sign-making. This, more or less, is the deconstructive view, based on Derrida's very careful and much-discussed close reading of Saussure's seminal course in general linguistics.

In this view, "Earth" and "mirth" differ purely on the basis of the omission of an "m" on the level of sound, and relatively diverse differences on the level of the sign's visual appearance. They, too, carry and are carried by a chain of differences that persistently defer an original moment of their return to connection with the actual presence of the meaning that they supposedly refer to.[36] But to refute this weary, paralyzing point is easy as soon as one sees signs as more than objects of re-presentation (signifiers) set in a system of rational relations to each other. In the case here, they visually and hence non-phono-centrically relate themselves to an ancient and fresh archetype, the mandala. And mandalas come into consciousness from unconscious depths that may or may not find expression in English or another language. One would have to refute the very existence of dream images to refute this. Mandalas are a meaning unto themselves to which language may on occasion successfully relate itself. For, as dreaming clearly indicates, the unconscious hardly differentiates *in the re-presented manner of linguistic categories*: it can in a struggling manner differentiate in this way only when it comes to individual consciousness. In other words, the unconscious does not in itself honor the differences between yesterday, today, tomorrow: it is "always now," it is timeless. Mandalas pertinently point exactly into this timelessness even as it becomes conscious and necessarily differentiated.

In other words, as soon as one gives value to meaningful materials such as mandalas, seeing these as images presenting in consciousness valuable symbolic energies, the nihilistic argument that violently insists on signifiers as the sole access point to meaning evaporates. Deconstructive "infinite semiosis" must therefore assume stark nihilism about certain values in order to maintain its apparently all-encompassing truthfulness. Taking Eliot's playful, joyful Earth-mirth mandala seriously gets rid of "infinite semiosis," reconnecting the time-bound sign with timeless origins of meaningfulness. And even if deconstructionists were able to continue to "prove" that one has used "mere" words to say this, hence apparently staying within the deconstructive chain, they have not added much to anything. For now it becomes a matter of belief in meaningful values, about which deconstruction struggles to say anything affirmative. It must deliberately distort such values in order to remain relatively true to itself.

In contrast, the Earth-mirth chiasmus embodies on the linguistic level the wholeness of being, without which there is no being. To return to Derrida's disdain toward forms of unity, the theory of evolution, though this admittedly involves a huge jump in the argument, delightfully proves that I am of a kin with mammals, even insects, since we physically and livingly share unfathomable depths of shapes and experiences. We are "living in the living seasons," the "time of coupling of man and woman / And that of beasts."[37] The phrase "And that of" indicates difference, and the dancing rhythm of embodied context indicates how that difference emerges from an enormous unity within which coexistence enjoys participatory magic, the magic, that is, within which difference breathes.

Is the denial of this worth the outcome? Besides this concern, it is further worrisome that by insisting so adamantly that evolution is stupid for the reason that it insists on a biological family tree, Derrida is plainly construing his critique to suit his case. There has to be difference at every cost, and evolution itself flies out the window. It is not enough to dismantle the spiritual claims of Genesis by showing up its ineptitudes and contradictions. Though evolution is neither flawless nor unlimited, again because it tends to reduce at once the sense of matter, mind, and presence, denial of its truth is about as helpful as is other forms of denial, such as denying that Earth is round or that the Holocaust is a historical fact. Worse, in this surprising attack on evolution, Derrida philosophizes badly. If we carefully take the distance between the ant and the cat, the distance between the cat and the lamb shrinks considerably, and so forth. The relativity of the distances already indicates that they are not simply infinite in each case, that there is tapering in the direction of a beginning, and that evolutionary thought does not simply view different animals as belonging to a homogenous blanket. It is acute study of differences over a long, painstaking time that has led scientists to crack open the nut of the theory that places the evolutionary family tree at its center. It is hard for those in the humanities to imagine just how painstaking and patient the effort has been. As a lepidopterist, I have had a mere taste of the tenacity that is necessary to do so, a form of tenacious doing that comes to fruition only *across generations*. It has taken a very long time indeed for humanity to discover that, as Eliot's poetry formulates it, the sea tosses up "hints of earlier and other creation: / The starfish, the horseshoe crab, the whale's backbone."[38] These are no less than hints of *evolution*, indicating that we are kin with the apparently most basic forms in existence. The progression from starfish through horseshoe crab (a very ancient living creature indeed) to whalebone (closer to us, wonderfully mammalian, familial) is in fact not only scientifically satisfying, but poetic. When a milkweed butterfly drifts past me with cells in its amber wings reflecting sunlight and diaphanously allowing it to splash through, I am sometimes brought to tears of joy or goosebumps of astonishment or utter peace of sensing being, not least because I know that flying past me is an impossible form brought about by millions of years of incredibly painstaking, patient chipping away by Earth. There goes my sister, reminding me of who I am, I think as this living mandala floats on. In any event, it is clear even here when it comes to horseshoe crabs and ancient history that Eliot knew nature, that he had a keen sense for it that went beyond his sailing of perilous waters and his amateur ornithology.

And then again it is in poetry, especially poetry as compelling and lasting as Eliot's, that the evolutionary sense of unity finds multivalent and colorful expression, in contrast to reductionist materialism. Briefly consider again the bestiary spanning his oeuvre, ranging from the anemone to the hippopotamus, all arranged in unique affective relations with human speakers in the poems. Being desperate enough within a context of modern indifference, for instance, one comes to wish with Prufrock to be a pair of ragged claws scuttling across silent seas, being perhaps something of an animated writer working across empty pages. Or one is moved, and so is the reader, as indicated, by a crab grabbing a stick. There is the reciprocal integrity of interconnecting human and otherly experience on the planet.

But it is not only on the material level of evolutionary discourse that Derrida forces his sense of the non-originality of origins. As I have been intimating, the problem spills over into the world of poetry. For, it is true that animals also appear in human relations in Derrida's work, albeit then at an "infinite distance" on which he insists in denial of evolutionary material reality, as indicated here. It is equally true that Eliot's poetic embodiment of these kinds—kinds being the exact word, having to do with kin—of relationships resonate on deeper levels of experience, because they are *embodied* in poetry in rich sounds and images that underscore our kinship with the animal kingdom and its rich and subtle forms of noise, music, and seeing-in-images, as expounded in Aaron Moe's *Zoopoetics: Animals and the Making of Poetry*.[39]

This is a rich materiality that denies neither unity nor difference. There is something familiar, family-like, about the crab's grabbing of the stick. The enormous difference between crab and human speaker, (once more) finely rendered in the poignancy and pathos of the image in its piercingly timed context of the poem, is precisely what makes the unity so striking, indeed almost unbearable. In short, the combination of difference and unity makes the image *deep*, in the sense of touching rooted nerve-ends. Does "infinite semiosis" allow enough room for this kind of non-skepticism in unity, also on the level of poetry? It does not appear to be the case, because it prefers to pretend that our postmodern differentiation overbears the supposedly clumsy unities of the past. Perhaps one should therefore not be taken aback by the fact that Derrida's one-sided emphasis on denial of evolution entails a counter-one-sidedness, for this is often the case when it comes to one-sidedness of all kinds. A very angry man tends to be too kind on occasion, so that his kindness will make us feel uncomfortable, and a very nihilistic man will tend to champion his positivity too much on occasion. A different passage of this same essay in which he denies evolutionary familiality claims a peculiar isolation for its author, Derrida, who says that, "as for the other category of discourse," that is, discourse not restricted to Western metaphysical aloofness from animals,

> found among those whose signatories are first and foremost poets or prophets, in the situation of poetry or prophecy, those men and women who admit taking upon themselves the address of an animal that addresses them, before even having the time or the power to take themselves off [*s'y derober*], to take themselves off with clothes off or in a bathrobe, I know of no *statutory representative* of it, that is to say no subject who does so as theoretical, philosophical, or juridical man, or even as citizen. I have found no such representative, but it is in that very place that I find myself, here and now, in the process of searching.[40]

One way of reading this passage, perhaps the dominant way, is that Derrida places himself in the position of which he finds no representative. He is the theoretical man that as citizen and statutory representative represents that poetic, prophetic voice that communicates the animals nakedly, as they are naked. It is "in that very place that I find myself," as he states, "in the process of searching." It is as if he wants to place himself in total singularity in the most important position of his intellectual tradition. Besides the implausibility and even attractive immodesty of this positioning, one asks oneself why such extreme isolation from the *poets* is necessary. Are poets not also citizens with statutory citizenship and philosophical prowess as they give voice to animals? Are they not the ones, in fact, who would dare to say that the lizard, butterfly, and orchis are our countrymen, while plainly stating the prayer reading "In the name of the Bee— / In the name of the Butterfly— / In the name of the Breeze—Amen"[41]—*Amen*!? Amen: so be it, this is affirmation.

Eliot's "The Hippopotamus" illustrates how poets are able to use the very sounds that connect humanity with its animal roots in the most positive sense, as has been illustrated. By careful placement of lower and higher pitched sounds in contrast and at just the right moments of the line break, the poet is able to change an important recognition into a special experience. The poem's argument that modern life is out of touch with its animal materiality becomes a wholly different experience that gets in under the reader's skin, as argued, on levels that any form of theorizing cannot reach, simply because any piece of theory is still very far away from the levels of immediate skill that it takes to create a convincing poem. This, while the philosophical powers of Eliot's poetry are considerable, evoking deep thought about one's position and dispositions in modernity. And the poetic embodiment of his poems can be found, moreover, on affective bodily levels especially: there where meaning and concreteness meet. And lest I be misunderstood, as may likely be the case, I am not making of genre an absolute. There is poetic energy in theory, and theoretical energy in poetry. A piece of theory can give as much pleasure as a piece of poetry. But there is also a considerable set of differences between the two forms, and the poem is primary in time, as well as in depth of skill. Put blandly, Derrida has not successfully composed line breaks on the level that Eliot has, *with the result that*, should there be poetry in his theory, it is not yet poetry in its primary fullness, and in this sense his isolated searching is unnecessarily fruitless. He could therefore have treated poetry with greater respect, looking again at the actual lines, including them in his work on poetry, giving them the embodiment in thoughtful discourse to the limited extent that it is possible. To the degree that he *does* allude to poetry, for instance in terms of Alice's cat throughout his piece, the piece is enlivened, of course. But he could have treated poetry with the greater sense of responsibility that comes with responsiveness and flexibility in the face of meaningful art.

The danger when theory claims to function on the same level as poetry like this, however inadvertently or cunningly, is the undermining of the artistic delight and profundity of poetic experiences and energies of communication, as though theory really could replace the space occupied by poetry. And it is again theory's massive emphasis on secondariness in our time and the concomitant nihilistic emphasis away from classical art works that induces this confusion and neglect of meaningful worlds. For, if all is mere difference, there is no difference between the profound, the profoundly moving capacities of art, and the undeniable pleasures of reading theory.

My sense upon careful reading is that this dubious insistence on the extent of difference is the reason why Said is cautious about adopting a broadly deconstructive approach. "Indeed," he says, "it has always seemed to me that the supreme irony of what Derrida has called logocentrism is that its critique, deconstruction, is as insistent, as monotonous, and as inadvertently systematizing as logocentrism itself." In similar vein he says that even "the disciplined skepticism of post-modernist theory can be grooved like a boring train ride."[42] He does not give examples of what he has in mind, but the image readily springs to mind of *différance*, the infinite deferral of meaning into further instances of difference slogging along like a locomotive on a predictable philosophizing track, while the passenger increasingly finds the predictability of the systematic way in which the movement occurs, unsatisfactory. The disciplined skepticism of postmodern theory is therefore always on the brink of becoming the same old set of differences, leading to responsive inflexibility. Each mirror in Gerontion's wilderness of mirrors is sliced into smaller and smaller further mirrors, and this is supposed to be refined. But Eliot's poetry resoundingly warns that somewhere on this track of insisting on difference right back into the origins of being, healthy skepticism turns into parading and then incarcerating cynicism. Since the origin can only be named, and since it always already needs its supplement in signification, the argument more or less goes, its absence supposedly becomes wholly pervasive. But this is to forget modern poetry and even the poetic potentials of the evolutionary family tree too readily. And ultimately, it is to underestimate the persistent presence of meaningfulness. One wonders what has happened over the years to Derrida's exemption of Pound and Mallarmé from the logocentric drift of modernity.

The patient work against the new monotony of poststructuralist surplus has always already begun in the various mushroomings of ecocriticism overall. And since communication is a kind of action, as I believe it to be, a relative green activism has been prevalent not only in textual ecocritical studies, but in poetry over many generations and nationalities. As citizens these men and women have been doing work that is more profound even than

Derrida's theorizing. One thinks instantly of the Chinese river and mountain poets who have laid refreshing little poetic footpaths into perceiving the fresh enormity of Earth's now-moments; Robert Pogue Harrison's notion that *logos* is that which ties us in with the ecosystem; David Abram's valuable work on the alphabet; even Derrida's attempt to link his project with animal rights,[43] and much more. One however continues to think of, respond to, the many excellent poets who have woven ordinary human signs into the presencing of nature.

One outcome of these recognitions that one is forced to turn to is, of course, that the concerns about the secondariness that now characterizes "literariness" are healthy. They involve necessary and vital skepticism toward the double poststructuralist notion that skepticism belongs only to it, as if all modes of thought and skepticism that came before it were somehow slightly naive in their affirming assumptions. That is, as mentioned in preceding chapters, it is necessary also to be skeptical about the skepticism of postmodern disciplines, as Said rightly advocates. There is by now a range of work that has been done in this regard, such as work by Raymond Tallis, Umberto Eco, Valentine Cunningham, and Terry Eagleton. Perhaps even more valuable in respect of placing or locating deconstruction are "smaller," astute passages on a less "grand" scale such as Glen Lentricchia's suggestion that by now deconstruction has boiled down to that which it supposedly goes against, another professionalized, indeed highly refined and complicated, method of close reading.[44]

The secondariness in current discourse may further have to do with the relative marginalization of poetry in our day, especially serious poetry, in favor of narrative. This may be the result of a theorizing continuum that marginalizes the potential of increased understanding—however tentative and incomplete—of the vital connections between signs and Earth. For, at its root, meaningful understanding of being on Earth once more enjoys mythopoetic, charged ontological values: wonderment, reflection, elation, spontaneity, and a sense of the earthly magic of being around, certainly also in sound and sight, of which poetry has a willingness to offer masterful embodiment. In Eliot's case, as indicated, the powerful nuances of celebrating these Earth values range from the awe-inspired liberty of Marie's going down a slope on a sled to the careful mandalic structures in *The Waste Land* and *Four Quartets*.

When it comes to theorizing, it is therefore a pity, among other things, that Yuri Lotman's notion of the semiosphere[45] has not had the ubiquitous impact that "infinite semiosis" has had. For, Lotman's term always beckons in the direction of the vital and permeable barrier uniting semiosphere and biosphere, and the need to acknowledge the meaningful transgression of these limits that poetry is able to achieve. Eliot's direct and indirect evocations of the vital connections between poetic signs and earthly meanings are just one important example of this. Derrida's implication that in our time the theoretician, indeed he himself, has come to occupy a position as important as if not more important than the poet in expressing animality, is to replace the supposed "violent hierarchies" of the past with one that is even more violent. It denies too much of the unforgettable skill through which a poetic voice as indelible as Eliot's is able to take the reader along into deeper understanding of what it means to live concretely on the planet.

It is therefore vital for new materialism to use its initial window of impetus carefully to think about our inheritances of deconstructive, poststructuralist, postmodern ways of thinking and going about differentiation. The sobering thought that Eliot brings into this discussion is, again, that every sign may involve necessary refinement, *but it equally may involve another bit of added distance away from the existence of the authentic jellyfish.* One foresees a paradoxical direction toward signs that increase with knowledge of the potential violence of that increase: signs that decrease in this sense. They may decrease thus in the manner of John Keats's negative capability toward greater understanding of what sparrow-hood entails,[46] or the silence of singing and singing of silence that permeates Cummings's poetry—electric-yet-peace-giving saturation of Earth-experience in which signs are utterly aware of their resonant limits within Earth—or in many of the other extant, current, or future forms of such decrease. Theoretical signs may, of course, do so by *following* the poetry in the various ways available to it, adding signs that are aware of the unnecessary distances and complications that they may create. Part of such following is that theoretical discourse continues to know what its secondariness means with a view to respect for and incorporation of poetry.

Somewhere in this discussion of "infinite semiosis" one must come to Derrida's infamous, famous, dreaded notion that "there is nothing outside the text." I want to start by pointing out that the mere fact that this phrase has enjoyed such considerable resonance in our semiotic day is in and of itself significant, even before one says anything about its validity or otherwise. As "Gerontion" has already suggested, the deserts of vast eternity to come for modern humanity in the twentieth century would be semiotic, that is, semiosis would be at the heart of modern humanity's greatest difficulties of coming to meaning. It is only in such a context that the notion of nothing outside the text could have such bewildering and celebrated impact. It is fair to say that for many centuries prior to the twentieth the very notion of this would have seemed preposterous. Life is spiritual, yes, and certainly concrete, and so on. These our forebears surely believed, but not that life is linguistic in a general textual manner at its point of delivery, and in those moments that matter.

A crucial restlessness arises from Derrida's "there is nothing outside the text," because this maxim misappropriates a very deep understanding, ultimately beyond words, of what it means to be on Earth. Even its apparently more correct, later translation makes little sense: "there is no outside-text."[47] However ironical, metaphorical, or Adamically parading this postulate may yet turn out to be, it will always already evoke rightful suspicion that it overlooks something that is at once obvious, important for survival, delicate, and outside text. This does not imply that one has not said this, or that it cannot be said. Saying that an outside text exists does not boil down to undercutting the argument. For, one knows not only in terms of saying or texts. One's body knows in its way, and it is not textual, to name a very important example. The wrestling about this that has gone on with Derrida over decades now seems somewhat ridiculous in the face of this knowledge.

More importantly, as shown here, Eliot's elusive textuality is able to catch up with the textual elusiveness of the plainly deep connections between humans and Earth. For instance, his poetry embodies the important insight, as inferred here, that one can be trapped in either biology or language—more probably in both—through disconnection between real presence and matter. It embodies the condition, too, that connection between real presence and matter shatters the opposites and their concomitant one-sidedness and barrenness, as has been illustrated amply here. Meaningful connection with flesh and blood is vital to the existence of language, in other words. But this implies that respect of distance, overcome in the love of connection, where text ends and the authentic jellyfish begins, living its life in its own world.

In a thought experiment, if I were to post a maxim on the same level of boldness as Derrida's "no outside-text," it would consequently read that there is "almost no text." But this is not an anti-climax, not even for the most ardent scholar soaked in words alone. For, I have existed long enough to know that active matter, active energy, Cosmos, the song of my cells, the piano key pressing back sensuously as I press it, the immensity and complexity of this beautiful Earth, the hours of playing with one's children, the biodiversity within which I live, the connecting Eros of experience, the collective unconscious on which my (linguistic) ego floats as a thin wafer on the ocean,[48] and much more, mean that textuality is a very small part of experience indeed. My body has intelligence of its own, connecting me to Earth and Cosmos, within which intelligence breathes my ego and its (partly linguistic) comprehension.

I believe this comes close to the intelligent scale of Merleau-Ponty's phenomenology as set out among others by Said (see chapter 6 of the present book), and the enchanting work of the more recent new materialist, David Abram. It is certainly also true to the thought of Carl Gustav Jung. I boldly add my voice to these voices, having survived the stimulating advent of the coming of theory and the linguistic turn—with some admiration for the liberations that that turn brought about, still intact. And even though I have "delivered" these remarks in written language here, it is plain to see that behind, below, within, around, and above them, there is a delicate enormity of non-textual, dynamic materiality and mind that is not in need of language in order to mediate its immediacy. It is the immensity of the hippopotamus's fleshly being that enjoys the first meaning. Again, this does not mean that language is secondary to it, but rather that *it* (Earth) becomes humanly conscious, which consciousness occurs partly, importantly, and liberatingly in language. However, that very liberation is at stake if we continue to insist on infinite difference as the main modus of human understanding.

To be sure, admitting to textuality's relative smallness of scale makes its impact and importance all the more visible. But then again it cannot afford to pretend that there is no outside-text, since that would be to give up too much of its enlivening resonance with all that is not text. I mention that the smallness of the scale of textuality is relative, because, from within textuality, everything in one sense or another does appear textual, particularly after hours and hours of careful reading and writing! If the chemist sees the whole world as consisting of chemicals, the semiotician now sees the whole world as consisting of signs—and both are right within their contexts, and wrong in every other sense.

However, it appears that the semioticians strangely take their understandable mistake to the point of pretending that it literally is the case that infinite semiosis is the basic point of life's delivery.[49] "There is no outside-text," this too-famous maxim, does reflect a problem of our day and age. It is a many-clawed problem ranging from material reductiveness to consumerist ennui and semiotic starvation. And it is preceded by the dwindling Gerontion, the match-stick glutton Prufrock, and the hope embodied in the holy hippopotamus—wholly hippopotamus—a hope that has never really left us behind.

There is therefore a real choice to be made by new materialism between the linguistic turn and its own turning. It can never be an absolute choice, not only because that is now impossible in our culture, but especially because this will just lead anew to two sets of unbearable one-sidedness, as if only signs or only matter matter. Snow's famous "two cultures" will return to their original splitting, and clearly this is not desirable. Western civilization has taken this blind, destructive turn into two sets of one-sidedness too often now. For, surely it is only in the name of a certain one-sided ignorance about the relationships between humanity and Earth, including those between language and the meaning of concreteness, that the one-sided destruction of habitat and the natural quality of life continues. That is, we could not continue to destroy Earth in the most barbaric way if we were honest about the barbarism, and a great part of the rationalization that "allows" us to continue to mask the barbarism is, of course, the many words we produce to gloss over the situation. One has in mind an ecocritical version of Fredric Jameson's political unconscious.[50] The latter will gloss over tears, blood, and pain with "sense-making" wholes, addresses, semiotic gauze. For this reason above all it is necessary to consider the material turn seriously, even in understandably playful manner in some respects. The material turn should turn to concrete origins. With Abram I again agree that it is necessary, however patiently, to rub signs back into their magical ringing with Earth.[51] The alternative is to continue getting bogged down in the struggle with the two sets of one-sidedness that I have been outlining in these pages: material reductionism and infinite semiotic neurosis that has to deny material unity and evolution by insisting on infinite distances. Eliot's poetry reveals that the two things are sides of a valueless coin, while the loss of value is the direct result of the disconnection from matter that arises through the loss of corporeal belief, that is, the loss of acknowledging and experiencing what I have termed the real presence of concreteness, even and especially in its poetic linguistic forms.

Already the one-sidedness of material reductionism is being contested rather well outside deconstructive discourse and any notion of "infinite semiosis." For instance, it seems that positivist biological thought is reaching the point of its limits, the point of "abandoning the standard assumption that evolution is driven by exclusively physical causes,"[52] as the philosopher Thomas Nagel distinctly argues without falling into vitalist pitfalls or the tyrannies of differentiation. It is now the turn of literary experts to question the one-sidedness of semiotic reductionism, which paradoxically resides in its proclivities toward infinite differentiation. In all this, new materialism comes before one of its particular challenges, brought into strange and compelling light by Eliot's poetry. Will new materialism merely amount to a continuation of the reign of postmodernism and "infinite semiosis"—and that kind of postmodernism that insists on discarding modernism, to boot? Or does its explicit differing from the linguistic turn entail an advance away from the constraints, ennui, cynicism, and one-sided tyrannies of poststructuralist differentiation? As an initial response to this non-rhetorical question, consider how "Gerontion" ends with a coda that includes the whole poem, like the outermost layer of an onion:

> Tenants of the house,
> Thoughts of a dry brain in a dry season.[53]

Drought within drought here does not enjoy the arithmetic that states that a minus multiplied by a minus gives a positive. There is no plus in this situation, because Gerontion, like the modern Pharisee, is trapped between two sets of one-sidedness, as mentioned. As in *The Waste Land*, the complement that would unify the opposites into seasonal and other integrity, is lacking. There is therefore no continuity, only infinite repetition that may appear eternal, while it contradictorily sets up the most terrible limits of enmeshment in relational linguistic objects, in this instance the image of houses containing houses that contain the former houses, and so on (indeed, so on).

At the outset of the argument here I mention that greater maturity in critical doing will balance this kind of skepticism with affirmation. How, exactly, is the deep skeptical imposition of "infinite semiosis" immature? A valuable answer resides in Laurence Coupe's work. Part of what is enjoyable about Coupe's discourse is his ability to be simultaneously sensitive and plain, occasionally entertaining rightful horror and staunch frankness. His work enters that line of thought where responsiveness to nature grows as if by itself into responsibility to nature, certainly also on the level of theoretical discourse and its preoccupations with "infinite semiosis," which he refers to as the "semiotic fallacy."[54] He cites an instructive Buddhist anecdote according to which, for the monk Ching-yuan, mountains and waters first were just mountains and waters, then they no longer were mountains and waters, and then they became mountains and waters again. First one ignorantly assumes nature is just around for one's use (nature is "just" nature), then one recognizes that it is totally other, because it appears to one as existing only as constructs of one's mind (nature is no longer nature), and then one recognizes that it has complete existence and independence of its own, to which one is radically related. In this third stage, Ching-yuan understands that "it is mistaken to take nature for granted and try and subsume within his own mental operations. The point is to learn from nature, to enter its spirit."[55] (This moves closely to what I have been terming Eliot's and modernism's sense of threeness.) On the platform of this story, Coupe suggests that getting stuck at the "referential fallacy," the infinitely semiotic idea that signs are at most only re-presented referents to natural actualities, while this is our only or main point of access to those actualities, is immature. On the one hand, he writes,

> the scepticism of theory has proved salutary: too often previous critics assumed that their preferred works of literature told the "truth" about the world. On the other hand, it has encouraged a heavy-handed culturalism, whereby suspicion of "truth" has entailed the denial of non-textual existence. It is a mistake easily made, perhaps, once one has recognised the crucial role language plays in human sense-making. But it should still be pointed out that, in failing to move beyond the linguistic turn, theory has been stuck in Ching-yuan's second stage of enlightenment. In seeking to avoid naïvety, it has committed what might be called "the semiotic fallacy." In other words, it has assumed that because mountains and waters are human at the point of delivery, they exist only as signified within human culture. Thus they have no intrinsic merit, no value and no rights. One function of green studies must be to resist this disastrous error.[56]

In its way, this book resists this disastrous error by reading Eliot's poetry with its equal measures of skepticism about the human linguistic ability to reach into nature, and its affirmation of that ability. Soberly, there probably are positions to be avoided as a consequence of this recognition. Rationalism without emotion or real thought, thought without everyday experience, progressive destruction of Earth without contemplation and non-action, drought without relief, and culture without meaningful integrity with and within the Earth process; these are the corrupted conditions to be avoided by positively critiquing the one-sided "triumph" of signifiers referring to yet more signifiers. Such a "triumph" replaces, in each of its motions, the awareness of earthly continuity and agency with the mandate of postponement and exquisite, immaturely exciting, "eternal" removal from earthly real presence. In Kate Soper's passionately drastic, realistic, and admirable image: "In short, it is not language which has a hole in its ozone layer; and the real thing continues to be polluted and degraded even as we refine our deconstructive insights at the level of the signifier."[57]

Surely at the level of poetry one may theorize that Eliot's "infinitely gentle / Infinitely suffering thing"[58] is nothing else than semiotic humanity suffering from cosmological disconnection. His ability to embody this on the level of the signifier is compellingly green. He knows, with the global warming cultural specialist Bill McKibben, that nature's "independence *is* its meaning; without it, there is only us."[59] Nature can make one feel lonely, but without non-human nature in which we participate, we are very lonely indeed. One thinks in contrast to this of the extraordinary connections between oneself and Earth's otherness, as Thoreau does in striking awe of *contact* on Mount Ktaadn in the Maine Woods.[60] But if there is only us, the mermaids will not sing to us, and we will as yet have no other Earth symbolism with which to reconnect ourselves meaningfully to matter. In all of this, the infinitely dry thoughts in a dry epistemological season literally, physically are no longer able to hide their devastating poverty, their nature of an absence with claws, their willingness to consume wild Earth, only to replace it with an arid world of empty semiotic houses within houses, husks within husks. Will this absence also dominate new materialism, as it in part seems to desire?

NOTES

1. Umberto Eco, *The Limits of Interpretation* (Bloomington: Indiana University Press, 1990), 38.
2. Eco, *Limits of Interpretation*, 38.
3. Laurence Coupe, "General Introduction," *The Green Studies Reader: From Romanticism to Ecocriticism*, ed. Laurence Coupe (London: Routledge, 2000), 2–3.
4. Jewel Spears Brooker, *Mastery and Escape: T. S. Eliot and the Dialectic of Modernism* (Amherst: University of Massachusetts Press, 1994), 89.
5. Brooker, *Mastery and Escape*, 89.
6. Brooker, *Mastery and Escape*, 93.
7. Brooker, *Mastery and Escape*, 94.
8. T. S. Eliot, *Collected Poems 1909-1962* (New York: Harcourt Brace, 1991), 29.
9. Brooker, *Mastery and Escape*, 95.

10. Brooker, *Mastery and Escape*, 96, 97.
11. Brooker, *Mastery and Escape*, 100.
12. Brooker, *Mastery and Escape*, 100.
13. Eliot, *Poems*, 29.
14. Eliot, *Poems*, 30.
15. Murray Stein, *Jung's Map of the Soul: An Introduction* (Chicago: Open Court, 2001), 64.
16. Brooker, *Mastery and Escape*, 106.
17. Eliot, *Poems*, 31.
18. Eliot, *Poems*, 31.
19. See Norman Friedman, *(Re)Valuing Cummings: Further Essays on the Poet 1962-1993* (Gainesville: University Press of Florida, 1996), 4.
20. Eliot, *Poems*, 4.
21. Eliot, *Poems*, 29. See Brooker, *Mastery and Escape*, 91.
22. Edward Said, *Reflections on Exile and Other Essays* (Cambridge: Harvard University Press, 2002), 267.
23. Iain McGilchrist, *The Master and His Emissary: The Divided Brain and the Making of the Western World* (New Haven: Yale University Press, 2012), 209.
24. Jacques Derrida, "The Animal That Therefore I Am (More to Follow)," trans. David Wills. *Critical Inquiry* 28.2 (Winter 2002), 415.
25. Derrida, "Animal," *see* 405, 407.
26. Derrida, "Animal," 401.
27. Derrida, "Animal," 402.
28. Arthur O. Lovejoy, *The Great Chain of Being* (Cambridge: Harvard University Press, 1964), 195.
29. Kate Soper, *What Is Nature? Culture, Politics and the Non-Human* (Oxford: Blackwell, 1995), 38.
30. Noam Chomsky, "French Intellectual Culture and Post-modernism," discussion held at Leiden University in the Netherlands on 14 March 2011, https://www.youtube.com/watch?v=2cqTE_bPh7M, retrieved 19 October 2014.
31. Eliot, *Poems*, 191, 194.
32. Eliot, *Poems*, 183.
33. Slavoj Zizek, "Nature Does Not Exist," https://www.youtube.com/watch?v=DIGeDAZ6-q4, retrieved 23 October 2015; Slavoj Zizek, "Love Is Evil," https://www.youtube.com/watch?v=hg7qdowoemo, retrieved 23 October 2015.
34. Roland Barthes, *The Pleasure of the Text*, trans. Richard Miller (London: Jonathan Cape, 1976), 9.
35. G. Douglas Atkins, *T. S. Eliot Materialized: Literal Meaning and Embodied Truth* (New York: Palgrave, 2013), iv, 52. Atkins's reading is useful, but he blandly refuses in connection with Eliot's poetic relationship with Earth one or two aspects that are crucial to its life: the element of immersion in physical being, the Buddhist element, and mystical depth. Though he denies that Eliot is puritan, he is perhaps guilty of attempting to cleanse the materialism of his poetry from perceived "non-Christian" aspects.
36. Jaques Derrida, *Of Grammatology*, trans. Gayatri Spivak (Baltimore: Johns Hopkins University Press, 1997), 157, 163.
37. Eliot, *Poems*, 183.
38. Eliot, *Poems*, 191.
39. Aaron Moe, *Zoopoetics: Animals and the Making of Poetry* (Lanham: Lexington Books, 2014), 10.
40. Derrida, "Animal," 383.
41. Emily Dickinson, *The Letters*, ed. Thomas H. Johnson (Cambridge: Belknap Press, 1958), 21.
42. Said, *Exile*, 128, 267.
43. David Hinton, *Mountain Home: The Wilderness Poetry of Ancient China* (New York: New Directions, 2005), 5; Robert Pogue Harrison, *Forests: The Shadow of Civilization* (Chicago: University of Chicago Press, 1993), 200; Derrida, "Animal," 395.

44. Joe Moran, *Interdisciplinarity* (London: Routledge, 2002), 93.
45. Yuri M. Lotman, *Universe of the Mind: A Semiotic Theory of Culture* (Bloomington: Indiana University Press, 1990), 133.
46. John Keats, "Letter to John Bailey," http://www.john-keats.com/briefe/221117.htm, retrieved 25 February 2015.
47. Jacques Derrida, "There Is No Outside-Text," http://en.wikiquote.org/wiki/Jacques_Derrida, retrieved 25 February 2015.
48. James Hollis, *Under Saturn's Shadow: The Wounding and Healing of Men* (Toronto: Inner City, 1994), 29.
49. Coupe, "Introduction," 3.
50. Fredric Jameson, *The Political Unconscious: Narrative as a Socially Symbolic Act* (Ithaca: Cornell University Press, 1981), 110.
51. David Abram, *The Spell of the Sensuous: Perception and Language in a More-Than-Human World* (New York: Vintage, 1997), 273.
52. Thomas Nagel, *Mind and Cosmos: Why the Materialist Neo-Darwinian Conception of Nature Is Almost Certainly False* (Oxford: Oxford University Press, 2012), 52.
53. Eliot, *Poems*, 31.
54. Coupe, "Introduction," 3.
55. Coupe, "Introduction," 1.
56. Coupe, "Introduction," 2.
57. Soper, *What Is Nature?* 151.
58. Eliot, *Poems*, 15.
59. Bill McKibben, *The End of Nature* (New York: Random House, 2006), 48.
60. These are Thoreau's unforgettable words as he recognizes the meaningfulness of being in connection with stone on Mount Ktaadn in the Maine Woods: "Talk of mysteries! —Think of our life in nature, —daily to be shown matter, to come in contact with it, —rocks, trees, wind on our cheeks! the solid earth! the actual world! the common sense! Contact! Contact! Who are we? where are we?" Henry David Thoreau, *The Maine Woods* (University of Virginia Library: Electronic Text Center, 2000), 40.

Conclusion

Where Does the Truth of New Materialism Lie?
A Response Based on Eliot's Poetry

Ecopoetic examination of Eliot's oeuvre shows that poetry tends to return to Earth almost inevitably, for it has not been thought that Eliot or other modern poets have too much to do with it, while the preceding pages involve the necessary modification of this superfluous impression. Perhaps the most important aspect of Eliot's particular Earth-engagement is how his poetry rediscovers in a singular manner the way that leads from nihilism to that vibrant nothing from which vibrant something continues to emerge: the still point that is that moving no-thing (neither from nor toward), and the immaculately specific dance of all some-thing.

An obvious inference from this intriguing situation is that the theoretical study of literature may have drifted so far away from engagement with great art, that it may well have missed one or two imperative insights that modern poetry offers. The first of these is that the ongoing theorizing of which new materialism forms part may patiently have to write its way back into literature at large, and poetry in particular. It would have been a greater and more revealing pleasure, for instance, to read Said while encountering in his texts actual passages from Eliot's poetry when he eagerly critiques or dismisses the figure, and this might have rescued him from some of his culture studies aberrations.

Theory's drifting away from literary art is by now considerable. It reflects itself in habits that have combined into secondary jargon with "the blind weight of a tidal wave."[1] Some of these habits include simply eliding great literary art, reducing its authors to ideological pulp, focusing with great deliberation on secondary materials, or pretending that there is no distinction between the great and the secondary. In the process, "infinite semiosis" very nearly becomes a flat, literal phenomenon, especially in the sense that the "production" of more signs is staggering, while most of the articles or books that contain them have just about as much staying power as the newsflash.[2]

There are subtler ways of "subverting" (that stock poststructuralist word!) the aesthetic. In their introduction to new materialism, Dana Phillips and Heather I. Sullivan dichotomize the "savory and unsavoury," as well as the "appetizing and disgusting." They rightfully argue that both must be included in new materialism. On this basis they conclude that including these opposites into one's discourse amounts to moving "beyond questions of aesthetics," again rightfully calling as a consequence on an interdisciplinary approach to new materialism.[3] However, their point gives the unnecessary impression that aesthetics avoid such things as the unsavory and the disgusting. Modern aesthetics of Eliot's kind have long since been including opposites such as those mentioned, showing that the aesthetic should not be confused with the artificial, the ugly-denying, or the decorative. I have focused on the example of "Dung and death" in the present book, as well as Lil's abortive habits, the polluted Thames, Madame Sosostris's bad cold, and more. For Eliot these ugly, non-"pohetic" realities are part of what should be incorporated into aesthetic worlds. His insistence on the hoarse inflections of the hippo during mating comes to mind again along with numerous other examples ranging from the radical inclusion of the carbuncular clerk in serious poetry to Prufrock's fear of the horrors of sex, and so forth.

Other examples abound in modern poetry. For example, Cummings's poem "POEM,OR BEAUTY HURTS MR. VINAL," (the lack of spacing after the comma is typical of the poet, and not an error here), is one of his searing satires of American emphasis on hygiene to the point of denying organic reality.[4] Mr. Vinal presents that part of modern humanity that lives by way of a combination of artificiality (vinyl) and an anal refusal to participate at all in the actuality of organic life; again, a Prufrock of sorts. He gets hurt by the poem, precisely because it is not "aesthetic." Often it is the truly aesthetic poem that hurts most those pretenses toward a world so clean, so laterally continuous in its superficiality, as to be, by all pretenses, devoid of all disgust. Poetry does not only unmask this, but also goes a step further in its inclusivity. It equally often shows that the non-aesthetic is beautiful. The entire history of poetry may be seen as the constant checking of balances as poems become just too pretty, calling upon counter-poetry that elevates the reader by entering or incorporating the supposedly "ugly" that has been marginalized by a flood of pretty-pretty "poems." Shakespeare's oeuvre of sonnets *in toto* is just one major example of this.

At the opposite end of this, theorizing itself often becomes glib, flat, artificial, organics-denying. In some respects its secondary tendencies only *aspire* to the appearance of detritus. Its jargon is after all quite polished and prosaic and, in this way, limited also with a view to claiming waste-status, albeit that ironically it may turn out to be so much secondary pulp despite itself in the instances of many pieces of writing. Perhaps the excessive focus on waste within new materialism is a reaction to this initial dilemma of its coming-about. That fixation has by now gone far beyond Jane Bennett's initial, illuminating appreciation of a random collection of waste objects. And the affirmative tone of her work seems to have been diluted in literary studies. Yet there is much to affirm in synthesis of Eliot's poetry and new materialism. In her introduction to the latter, the new material specialist Serenella Iovino refers to Patricia Yaeger's question: "how liquid are we?"[5] We have seen that for Eliot we are virtually entirely liquid if we are to be completely human. We are immersed in the stream of changing life. We have furthermore seen his concern for the Thames polluted by a new culture that simply ignores its connections with nature. Objects are artificially afloat where flow itself should be the overriding impression.

Iovino continues her liquid imagery, saying that in order to understand new materialism, "we have to start with a plunge in its theoretical premises."[6] This seems innocent enough. Literary studies now always pays the obligatory nod in the direction of "theorizing first." There can be no naked reading of the poem, so to speak. I would suggest simply that this plunging into theorizing—which does not guarantee an objectivity superseding critical reading of a poem, since a theory often is little more than a new viewfinder among many others[7]—should not involve the strategic elision, mentioned above, of great literary art. For, if it is true that "the main focus of the 'material turn' is the refusal to talk of matter in reductionist and essentialist terms,"[8] as she points out, then poetry has for centuries been an ally for new materialism, and new materialism should mine it as such. There is perhaps no other discourse that brings one's immersion in earthly life into sharper focus, readily and magnanimously celebrating Earth in ways that do not reduce it to "mere" matter.

A great poem further carries significant instances of the "material-semiotic agencies" that Iovino refers to.[9] The poem's materiality is not simply a question of dead matter printed on dry mash. It soon evokes sound patterns and visual ones that bring with them profound meanings and visceral responses such as gooseflesh, not least by way of material-semiotic forms such as rhythm, meter, rhyme, iconic images. This means that on the micro-scale of the page, the poem embodies the largeness and minutiae of earthly existence on its (Earth's) many scales, including its all-inclusive macro-scale. Eliot's employment of *Da* in blank space is just one example of this. Moreover, since the reader co-creates the modern poem especially, an impression will be gained of significance organizing itself into patterns in the manner of *autopoiesis*, thus miming the magic of "living matter organizing itself in auto-regulated patterns," to cite further from Iovino.[10] The emergence of being from non-being as embodied in Eliot's poetry remains perhaps the prime example of such *autopoiesis*. After all, what is it that makes *autopoiesis* creative, and not simply repetitive? It is the feeling and knowledge of the now-here emerging from nowhere, the specific from the universal, the time-ous from the timeless, and their continuing combination in poetic experience.

This indeed includes, in Eliot's case especially, the "being embodied" of discursive practices.[11] As demonstrated here, poetry is first and foremost a poetic embodiment of language, and he excels at this. "If knowledge [or poetry] is an embodied practice, the knower and the known are mutually transformed in the process of knowing, and new levels of reality emerge."[12] The collaborating co-creator of modern poems such as Eliot's, as has been demonstrated here, too, strikingly similarly gets involved in a poetic becoming, a performative reading act that unfolds in the mind's eye as much as on the levels of emotion and bodily response, leading to a linguistic-bodily perception that alters the realities of one's outlook, perhaps however slightly. At the very least, meeting the excellent art work is like meeting a new person, tangibly, viscerally, imaginatively. But the overall effect of the changes that occur via or within these apparently small pockets of energy (as in the case of an individual's perception altered by an embodied poem) cannot ultimately be followed or measured: they may well become huge, or huge energies may well hinge on them. For instance, over generations apparently minor things like Sanskrit fragments find enormous impact not only in India, but in modern English via Eliot's poetry, given that *The Waste Land* in particular has been studied extensively now for nearly a century at too many institutions to mention, and in too many minds influencing other minds, to number.

The extent to which Eliot's poetry anticipates new materialism is therefore remarkable. His poetry dexterously, anachronistically participates in the "refusal to talk of matter in reductionist or essentialist terms,"[13] to mention this just once more. At one extreme of his oeuvre, those who do reduce matter to mere matter end up in Prufrock's dilemma. Those who participate in its agentic, changing essence become elevated to the extent of their participation, such as the hippo, or the speaker and reader of *Four Quartets*. And ultimately, there is only the participation, only the dance, only the immersion, only the dissolving, as even Prufrock must eventually know by drowning.

Eliot's poetry, as promised in his prose (as we have seen), works radically against mechanism to rediscover remnants and ultimately whole patterns of organic aliveness, directly or indirectly. A similar sentiment works in new materialism, which absolves "matter from its long history of attachment to automatism or mechanism" in Bennett's words, cited by Iovino in her context of presenting a new mode of literary thought.[14] The outset of the present book mentions how important the sacred Earth process is for Eliot as opposed to a mechanized view that would reduce it to a mere site of myopic utility, that is, an inert site that only "makes sense" when manipulated in the name of one-sided, intentional human agency. The etymological connection between *materia* (matter) and *Mater*, the ur-Cosmos or ur-Womb, to which Iovino[15] further points, is enriched entirely by Eliot's oeuvre, as has been made abundantly clear in this book. The matter with Prufrock and the Prufrockians that may be carrying out a modern lifestyle is dislocation of matter, disconnection from it, and the disenchantment of experience.

In not being entirely postmodern in some regards, though postmodernism is unthinkable without him, Eliot would agree further with Iovino who insists that human and natural biology palpably are not human constructs (how has it come about that one would even have to make this obvious point so emphatically, one wonders?). They are powerfully semiotic, but not constructed by language: language is one aspect of communication, and the nonhuman world brims with meaning in which humanity participates.[16] This is exactly how Eliot's poetry presents humanity's connection with Earth. Perhaps it has to do with the commonsensical realization that humanity has always been at once outside and entirely part of the Earth process,[17] which also happens to underpin Eliot's Earth sense to the point at which that outside and inside dissolve in the sheer-ness of existence, so to speak. To be alive, as *Four Quartets* says, is to know that "where you are is where you are not."[18] It is your being-within Earth, which you are not, that forms no little part of the clear, mysterious experience of existence. This is true on more than one level. To be here, one has to be preceded by forefathers and foremothers who happened to use Sanskrit: in being here, one is there, where one is not. *The Waste Land* embodies this notion. The poem's existence comes from where the poem is not, namely its Sanskrit roots. But it is the entering of this knowledge that the poem is about, so that where it is not becomes where it is.

Earth precedes and includes one's existence in this way and in many others. It is important to know the profundity of this situation. In Kate Soper's words, again, one "accords value to what is created by natural processes rather than by artificial human ones."[19] Poetry enjoys the freedom to say it more immediately, as in Cummings's excellent phrase, "A world of made / is not a world of born."[20] Much of the living magic of being alive continues to reside in this natural independence from human processes. Absolving from the long history of mechanism sets one free to realize Earth's independence: the freedom in which one happens to participate. Eliot's poetic expression of this freedom is crucial to the enjoyment of his poetry.

New materialism, Iovino goes further, does not see culture and nature, as well as subject and object, as mere juxtapositions, but as "a circulating system."[21] Reconciled among the circles of the stars and the seasons, *Four Quartets* shows (by embodying it in paradoxical poetic cycles that dissolve into circularity, or are immersed in it) that human meaningfulness enters and comes from the same continuing cyclical emergence, along with animals such as the boarhound, and constellations such as Herakles,[22] a cluster pattern recognized over the span of more than one civilization in human history, traditionally viewed as an animated, kneeling figure with a humanoid shape and a quadrangle-mandala at its center.

Dissolving entrenched linguistic barriers, his poetry shows that ontological barriers (between noun and verb, as indicated) "are not preexisting as such," to employ Iovino's words.[23] Instead, the unified pre-existence of all permeates the now-moment in cycles. Eliot thus moves on from an inherited Western grammatical ontology of supposedly fixed properties into a dissolving ontology of change and creativity. One infers that the new material insistence on these kinds of boundaries that *change* and *become* rather than being handed down like static things most probably has mytho-poetic roots. New materialism, I think, is in fact more mytho-poetic than it has so far been able overtly to announce.

Resonating with Andrew Pickering, who focuses on the new materialism of scientific practice, Iovino writes of the "dance of agency" in which social and material elements mangle—or melt in a more refined process—resulting in "new, unexpected configurations."[24] In Eliot's poetry, as demonstrated, this is writ large. The continuing unfolding of life itself, as it unfolds like the lotos, is in every moment an astonishing and apparently impossible becoming: there is only the dance, the dance of all that is, down into the minutest detail of emergence. We dance with the petrel and the porpoise, the wave and the dust stirring in a rose bowl.[25] According to this, even the most ordinary thing—a rock, a wave, the wind—is utterly extraordinary by virtue of the dance of agencies.

An important further part of her new material delineation occurs when Iovino briefly discusses David Abram, who makes the beautiful point that the body is a sensitive threshold through which the world experiences itself.[26] Eliot's poetry plays upon the full modern spectrum of this important notion. As has been shown, the disembodied Prufrock scuttles like a pair of lost claws across the ocean, unable to connect the meaningful and the concrete like the mermaids do. Drastically clouded by his preoccupation with slipping signs, his body fails as a threshold into experience. At the other end of Eliot's spectrum in *Four Quartets*, upon having come to the point of connecting exhaustively with life's pattern, its cyclical flow of changes at once stabilizing and destabilizing,[27] the speaker (and reader) perceives the invisible movement of the wind as it wrinkles on the water between two waves. These are just two examples of Eliot's poetic rendition of the body as a *limen* of awareness.

At the conclusion of her introduction to new materialism, Iovino asks: "what about texts as matter?"[28] I hope to have shown in this book that the matter of the text is not simply the so-called "cold artifact," the stack of pages containing little black ants of printed markings. Those ants—perhaps they should be referred to rather as potent little black dragons that enter and claw into the nerves—always promise visceral life, imaginative and affective experience, and it simply takes a willing reader to make this happen. In the case of Eliot the results really are intense—he has not been viewed as one of the most impacting poets for nothing. He draws charged attention to the text as vibrant matter, for instance, by arranging clusters of printed material in very deliberate fragmentary configurations that make one aware anew of the blankness of the page, the play between characters and blank space, and the potential meanings of this. I hope to have done justice to this in the present book, in the further hope of beginning to provide one answer in response to Iovino's question above.

In what is fast becoming a fairly standard new material strategy, a different ecocritic, Serpil Opperman, introduces new material discourse by referring to waste. Citing an editor's column by Patricia Yaeger (as does Iovino), she posits that we are born into a world strewn with detritus. She reminds one that junk and rubbish often are subjects for postmodern photography and painting.[29] But the modern Eliot anticipates these developments: in a sense, he makes them possible along with his fellow modern artists, breaking down the barriers between high and popular, "wasted" culture—as portrayed best in general perhaps by Michael North's book *1922: A Return to the Scene of the Modern*. Somehow, Eliot makes of popular materials striking poetry, and it is of equal importance that he gathers the detritus of Sanskrit fragments into modern patterns. John Elder refers to *The Waste Land* when he says that the "principle affirmed" by Eliot's and Snyder's poetic views is that "culture must be understood in terms of a dynamic continuity," which includes decaying fragments of Sanskrit as part of renewed cycles of experience.[30] In other words, the poet is a cultural worker willing to dig into bits and pieces of cultural waste in order to establish (the prospect of) new growth.

When Opperman further argues that postmodern art "radically challenges the subject/object, nature/culture, and human/animal binaries,"[31] again one is reminded of how modern artists most radically induce these still-current trends. Almost every modern art work or poem points out the volatility of all "objective" perception in terms of subjectivity. Cummings persistently visits the boundaries between nature and culture, as well as human and animal, only to dissolve them in a singular osmotic manner again and again. In the case of Eliot here, we have seen how *Four Quartets* gets rid of hierarchies between human worlds and natural worlds. We have also seen how Prufrock's subjectivity alters his entire objective world into a delicately suspended, and also drastically volatile, subjective one.

More examples could be cited of how modern poetry and Eliot's show that things "are always in excess of their subject-object duality," to cite thus from Opperman.[32] The nonhuman is "uncanny," writes Opperman, because it performs an act beyond human control.[33] In Eliot's poetry, the more-than-human enjoys similar agency, and indeed even the absence of (human) meaning turns into a tiger with claws, as has been indicated. On the other hand, the moderns also know that exceeding the subject-object boundary in a certain way leads to the relief of transcendence, enchantment, full or full-empty (the Afrikaans is *volledige*) participation.

Opperman continues to make the Saidian or general culture studies point that material practices such as physical forces in natural and social life spaces "are always co-extensive with discursive practices (power, race, gender, class, ethnicity, identity, language, narrative, etc.)"[34] By now this is a stock response of culture studies, which allows it to focus on areas supposedly much wider than literary art. There is comfort and value in this, but also discomfort. Since we are literary scholars, what about literature as a valuable phenomenon to be studied closely? In poetry, as we have seen, for instance, the co-extensiveness between material practices and Earth delve into wholly other, perhaps more literary terrains than the stock string of gender, race, et cetera (important as these can be): connection, disconnection, love, feeling, dislocated language, and even the loss of a sense-making perception of "me and my story."

That is, in many ways *The Waste Land* begins precisely where narrative ends: Europe has torn itself apart, destroying the direction of its history, and Eliot responds with the "mythical method"[35] akin to a kind of Darwinian search among myriads of language "fossils" for historical roots that are meaningful. Hence the arrangement of Sanskrit detritus takes on also *this* significance, of bringing poetry to bear where history-stories have been cut off, like wires standing on end, wires that no longer have the capacity to carry the familiar story-currents. It is this a-narrative sense that gives rise to one of the most important novels of the twentieth century, James Joyce's *Ulysses*, as Eliot foresees.[36]

In short, focus on literature has much to say about the co-extensions between materiality and narrative, but not necessarily in the skeptical way (skeptical toward literature) readily assumed by culture studies. It is not farfetched to insist, as demonstrated in chapter 6, that culture studies led Said astray in coming to terms with Eliot *as poet*. The "broadness" and "freedom" of the culture studies response have *their* limitations, ironically at the point at which literary art and poetry begin.

Another problem with Opperman's new materialism is her championing of postmodernism in contention with modernism. She says that non-dualistic epistemic practice "is truly postmodern, insofar as it constitutes a radically new point of departure from realist epistemologies and modernist ontologies."[37] Opperman does not indicate whether she has in mind literary modernism or other forms of it, but champions of postmodernism tend to present a "false analogy" between literary modernism and positivist practices in other disciplines, while Fredric Jameson's notion that the postmodernist crisis in representation begins in modern literature, is more pertinent in the world of literature.[38] Since there is the risk of this misunderstanding, it is important to point out again that Eliot's modern poetry *is* a radical ontology of volatile non-dualistic practice. In "A Wilderness of Mirrors" Jewel Spears Brooker and Joseph Bentley give an excellent exposition of this historical fact.[39] Indeed, the real change from Cartesian dualism to dialectical flexibility comes with modern art, including all its poets, ranging from Eliot to Cummings and from Marianne Moore to Wallace Stevens.

"The old conceptions of matter as stable, inert, and passive physical substance, and of the human agent as a separate observer always in control," Opperman continues, "are being replaced here [in new materialism] by the new posthumanist models that effectively theorize matter's inherent vitality."[40] Yes, and it is the modern literary revolution against static dualism, its heroic replacing of realism with actuality, where these notions have their beginnings in literary studies. On another day, perhaps, one can contend whether stability and *inertness* belong to the same problematic field, as she implies here. Surely there is stability in the sense of change so slow or so unnoticeable in everyday life that things are solid enough; equally surely, this does not mean that matter is inert.

And it is equally true, having read Eliot's poetry from a perspective informed by new materialism, now to say that it anticipates the new material complexity of "intertwined practices of knowing and becoming" in Opperman's phrase.[41] *Four Quartets* is no less than the poetic embodiment of such intertwining. Again and again the poem *shows* (rather than says with finality) that knowing cannot be final or static: that the only knowing worth knowing is that which continues to become. Among other things, that is why beginning and end continue to dissolve in the poem, and it is the reason why Eliot combines Christian and Buddhist positions in his poetry.

When Opperman further insists that new materialism, with postmodernism as its continuous ally, poses "a serious challenge of [to?] logocentric thought,"[42] she may as well have been speaking about modern literature and indeed the vast movement of modern art in general. As indicated in preceding pages here, perhaps the most serious break away from logocentrism in Western history comes from modern art, and modern poetry in particular, as acknowledged by Derrida. I would therefore advocate modern poetry as a natural ally to new materialism, apparently unlike Opperman. However, I would go further and be more skeptical about her assumption that "postmodernism becomes a natural ally for ecocriticism."[43]

If this is so, why the need for announcing the movement of new materialism, which at least *questions* the linguistic turn? To the extent that postmodernism and the linguistic turn are one and the same, new materialism is in fact everything but its natural ally. I would not go as far as to say that it is its natural foe, but neither is it simply a question of one happily flowing into or from the other. There are important complexities and contentions to be enjoyed. Does a view that proposes a radical difference between signs and matter, *as well as* their compelling combination, not challenge one or two non-referential postmodern "assumptions" about the nature of the relations between nature and the making of signs?

Though Opperman does not define what she means when she therefore insists on a "lateral continuum" between ecocriticism and postmodernism,[44] one should perhaps be cautious toward it. In more than one way, literary studies, including its culture studies elements, is still recovering from the "lateral continuum" imposed on it by the deconstructive spirit: I have in mind again how deconstruction sees language as a monotonous continuum of *différance*. It therefore always already has to complicate depth and meaningfulness, in the nihilistic spirit, despite its many illuminations. The glittering surface of signs *as little more than a surface* uncomfortably reminds of Saul Bellow's "nihilism without the abyss";[45] there is too little awe about depth in the general deconstructive/ poststructuralist/ postmodern mood.

To return for the moment to Iovino's new material introduction: it speaks of the "posthuman" that "replaces the human/ nonhuman dualism and overcomes it in a more complex and dialectic dimension."[46] To my mind, this accurate and sensitive formulation leaves the door wide open for the entrance of modern poetry into the new material discussion. Eliot's threeness is an example of this: dualism and its hierarchies dissolve into the meaningfulness of participation. This is a form of transcendence, to be sure, and the word "overcoming" does fit its case, since one is able to move through and beyond a sterile separation between opposite energies. In another sense, though, the transcendence of threeness is not an "overcoming." It is not a renewed subjugation of one opposite condition by another. For instance (as indicated), *The Waste Land* powerfully critiques the male domination that goes with patriarchy, since patriarchy leads to sterile separation between opposite energies. It achieves nothing less than showing how patriarchy diminishes female *and male* experience in equal degrees; and in *Four Quartets* the duality is overcome, without new dominance.

This "complex dialectic" moves beyond dualism into connection, immersion, dissolving, giving credence at last to the poetic aspect of all agency. So to speak, Eliot's poetry somehow manages to avoid the positivist Cartesian split that the moderns inherited from the past, *as well as* the "nihilism without the abyss" that would come in postmodernism. His poetry manages to avoid the flat, counting spirit that holds that "anything goes as long as it is consumable or consumed" of some postmodern practice. It has not been mentioned, but it is obvious that the latter threatens a new strategic dualism, a dualism that would insist in rejecting and denying its modern roots.

This brings into focus Opperman's "rejection of hierarchical orders,"[47] which she ascribes exclusively to ecocriticism and postmodernism. It is not always clear what is meant by this, neither in postmodernism, nor in Opperman's discussion. On the one hand, if it means the rejection of the hierarchy that maintains that objectivity and objects are important, whereas subjectivity is of no importance, then she is entirely correct—but then, again, modern literature comes strongly into the picture. The same is true if she has in mind the violent hierarchies of culture versus nature and male versus female. If, on the other, she has in mind that no literature can be better than other literature—that primary artistic literature, for example, is not more important than secondary trash literature—then one should pause to consider the situation more carefully. Is the fact that Opperman proposes new materialism and the reading of her text and others that she mentions in her writing, not always already a choice? Does it not claim: "read this"? Is it not always already exclusive?

Consider that the matter of hierarchy is fundamental to her argument for choosing postmodernism above modernism: if "there is one thing that ecological postmodernism and ecocriticism have in common, it is the rejection of hierarchical orders. Moreover, they both endorse renewed forms of imaginative interaction with the material world."[48] But to *reject* something is to establish a hierarchy. This is preferable, that not. To *endorse* something else is to begin to entrench the new hierarchy of preferences. And renewed forms of imaginative interaction with the material world, once more, is *not* something that postmodernism in many of its poststructuralist and deconstructive modes endorses; rather, it elides such engagement strategically, being afraid of being seen to commit the "referential fallacy,"[49] the notion that signs have to do with a world that exists over and above signs (of which signs are part). Meanwhile, such imaginative interaction occurs most intensely, upliftingly, and thought-provokingly in many of the excellent literary works of the past—in their presence; that is, in the manner of news that somehow stays substantial news in a world flooded by blips of culture that simply come and go, instantly.

I am not suggesting that the idea that art can be of a major or minor nature involves an absolute hierarchy, since the importance attached to works clearly shifts over time. And yet the difference is a reality. Even when postmodernism prefers the secondary, it posits the existence of the primary. One does not have an absolutely free flowing of textual materials. Alas, some articles are included in journals, others rejected. More importantly, some classical works of literature—the *Tao Te Ching* and *Four Quartets* (in their admittedly different domains, but also in their intertextual connection)—enjoy remarkable powers of recurrence. Even more importantly, when one investigates for oneself whether such texts really do reward reading—whether to one's taste, or not—one will find that they carry within them a near-inexhaustible capacity for rewarding close examination and reflection in their relations to life.

I would not go as far as to classify works persistently and hurriedly into major or minor categories. The game soon becomes tedious if pursued too persistently, and one does not always know in one's own time what will last, and what not. And the classification can be used to hide prejudices. In some respects the modern artists in their intellectual and/ or personal mode are guilty of such mistakes. Sexism is rampant in Eliot's time, and he alas appears to have partaken in it. But in his great poems, once more, he overcomes sexism, which is no little part of the reason why we pay any attention to him in the first place.

Moreover, when it comes to the actual classification of art in their time into major and minor categories, Eliot is remarkably right for the most part. He knows in his time that W. B. Yeats is a great poet; that Marianne Moore's excellence will continue (as it has done for instance in the poetry of Elizabeth Bishop); that James Joyce has changed the nature of prose forever; that Ezra Pound is a mountainous figure of his century (for instance, the oriental influence is given its first huge impetus by Pound, and it continues in the work of J. D. Salinger, Allen Ginsberg, Gary Snyder, to name some). What makes this all the more remarkable, of course, is that in their time the modern artists suffer from the severest possible rejection of their works, not only by the general public but most pertinently by heavy-weight critics. In a recent review of a book comprising the reviews over time of Eliot's poetry, with reference to the earlier critical reception especially, Frank Kermode has reiterated the question that Eliot had to confront from critics in his day: "Why didn't he commit suicide?"[50]

Wrong as modern artists and Eliot certainly were, then, I would not discard entirely with their major and minor categories. I would view them as flexible, hoping that there will be the assurance that they are not used as excuses for ideological prejudices to the greatest extent possible. In short, I would say that major works of literary art exist. To dispense with all hierarchies is from this perspective neither possible nor desirable. Nor does Opperman herself practice it, though she strongly preaches it. The dilemma is that the strong kind of preference that she holds for one kind of literature (the postmodern) comes at a potentially high price within her ecocritical context for another kind—modern literature. In appearing to demolish hierarchy, she erects hierarchy.

Still subtler hierarchies characterize her work and that of postmodernism, especially in the mode of defending itself against modernism. One of these is that discourse becomes more important than literary art. The discourse furthermore strategically refuses to delve closely into great literary art, occupying important space where the discussion of it might have taken place. But sometimes the work that champions postmodernism in these ways will undercut itself, and the undercutting can be illuminating. For instance, with a view to the "lateral continuum" between postmodernism and ecocriticism, Opperman attempts to give a *basic* definition of what new materialism is about: "basically," she writes,

> material ecocriticism interweaves postmodern and ecological voices in a shared project of constructing new ecocritical discourse which attempts to theorize a dynamic world of becoming comprised of nontotalizable multiplicities, assemblages, networks, and mangles of material and discursive practices always engaged in vital intra-actions.[51]

The abundance of nouns, verbs, and adjectives in this sentence is abstract in the grammatical sense, making it hard to follow what new materialism "basically" amounts to. Though also abstract in some sense, however, the reading of Opperman's article suddenly lights up when she cites from literature, in this instance, John Fowles. The new material "onto-tale tells us that 'matter is eternal life,' and that 'everything is unique in its own existing,'" she writes in citing this green novelist and essayist.[52] The article becomes concrete and vivid in this moment, by virtue of giving that formidable other—the good artistic writer—his own voice within a theoretical context. For a moment the article further becomes richly polyphonic, dialogical, heteroglossial, in Mikhail Bakhtin's democratic spirit.[53] The imperative of including primary literary artistic material into theoretical discussion thus speaks for itself.

Opperman follows up on the Fowles citation to say that "narratives and discourses have the power to change, to re-enchant, and create the world that come[s] to our attention,"[54]—and so does poetry especially, of course. But then she quickly returns to her insistence on the privileging of postmodernism. The re-enchantment comes "to our attention only through the foregrounding of ontological concerns which is common to many post-modernist writers, such as John Fowles, whom I quoted above."[55] It is perhaps necessary to point out that this is one-sided. On the one hand, Fowles is not readily classifiable like that. Modernist traits abound in his work, *including* the trick of the unreliable narrator entering the story in *The French Lieutenant's Woman*, preceded by similar maneuvers in Vladimir Nabokov's *King, Queen, Knave* already in 1928,[56] and indeed Eliot's masking of personas and appointment of various voices giving rise to an outlining of modern unreliability in *The Waste Land* in 1922. The literary boundary between modernism and postmodernism is amorphous. A heavy-handed new hierarchy based on that boundary does not do justice to this literary reality. Thus Opperman's new material view shows that it is simplistic to maintain that postmodernism can get away from modern dialectics; postmodernism presupposes its sources in modernism.

In his compelling book *What Ever Happened to Modernism?*, Gabriel Josipovici gets a grip on the relative smugness with which Marxism and what he terms "the post-Modern" evade modern art as if it no longer matters. He accedes that Marxism has a point that modern art reflects "a social as much as an artistic crisis." But does this crisis have an obvious solution? he asks, suggesting that we are still within the curve of that crisis. He further agrees with the post-Modernist that "Modernists do occasionally give the impression that they are fighting old battles with inadequate tools."[57] But he expresses concern: "the anxiety, not to say obsession, evinced by the Modernists betrays, the post-Modernist suggests, an unwarranted belief in Truth and Self. There are, however, he argues, many truths and many selves," while "the angst expressed by these writers shows how much they were still in thrall to now outdated notions which had long been dear to Western thought but which we have now thankfully laid to rest."[58] As I have been trying to point out in this book, what we now have is something akin to modernism without angst or awe, while the sense of a certain differentiating "manyness" that has to replace notions such as Self is not entirely possible or innocent. By ignoring the modern artistic struggle (and its solutions within modern art) one misses the point that the travails of the modernists

> are so intimately bound up with their achievements that it feels simply impertinent to condescend them, as [Marxist and post-Modern] responses do, as though *we* understood what was wrong with *them* and could set them right with a remark or two. They laid their lives on the line, after all, and though we might feel that they were misguided we should think twice before presuming to tell them they were wrong.[59]

Of course telling them that they are wrong by now comes across not necessarily in passionate (if vague) distancing as in Opperman's case, but mostly through the elisions that I have been outlining here, as if modern poetry and art in fact are *passé*. Part of the problem with this is that one begins historically to see modernism for what it is not:

> in order to understand that there are good reasons for the difficulties they encountered in getting their work not just published but written, and that these difficulties are part and parcel of what makes them rewarding to read, we have to try and see Modernism not from without [. . .] but from within.[60]

Let it be said in response to this that the ecopoetic impetus provides a singular and important way of seeing modern poetry from within. For, the history of poetic changes from Romanticism to modernism and postmodernism are not one-sided or even simple when viewed from the ecopoetic angle. Robert Langbaum demonstrates how the Romantic ideal and the pathetic fallacy continue in modern poetry—a nature poetry after all—in unique new ways, including greater distance from and emphasis on the natural other, in order to create greater empathy with it.[61] James Longenbach illustrates how modernism turns out to be what Romanticism wants it to be, namely a "'diminished' Romanticism," in the positive sense that the modern poets focus on smaller phenomena, controlling smaller poetic worlds characterized also by a certain brevity and minimalism. They are self-conscious about the hugeness of subject and scope that the Romantics entertain.[62] The historical continuities between these movements, from a perspective interested in Earth, are therefore as striking as are the discontinuities.

And in a sense, as Longenbach already suggests in 1999, postmodernism is what modernism wants it to be: a movement that is self-conscious about and hides away from Truth and Self, to employ Josipovici's phrase in this regard. Yet the self-consciousness about these things, wherever it occurs, betrays its opposite: the potentials and actualities of those large energies (Self and Truth), *including* the recognition of their loss. It is in other words not at all certain that huge awareness—such as awareness of wholeness, which puts individual phenomena in brighter contrast—belongs clearly or purely to the past. To say for instance (with Fowles and Opperman) that matter is eternal, and that everything is unique in its own existing, brings the relief of tasting life's largeness in a world besotted with tiny tastes and little differences to the extent of deliberately denying and/ or avoiding wholeness. Fowles's beautifully large statement indeed penetrates from within postmodernism *into* modernism (since it sets the chiasmus between the eternal and the specific in motion) and *into* Romanticism (since it is huge). This is no little part of its enchantment.

Josipovici, like any good modern critic, is aware of the modern artists' shortcomings, but he correctly maintains that this hardly provides reason for scorning their work: "one can easily lose patience," he notes,

> with Kafka's masochism and his self-centredness, with Picasso's egotism and Beckett's elegant, almost mannered, expressions of despair. Reading Waugh taking pot shots at Picasso and Wittgenstein, or Larkin and Amis laughing at Virginia Woolf and E. M. Forster, is refreshing—we don't, after all, want to worship them, or any artist. But unfortunately what we get is not simply a criticism of what these artists were like as human beings or of the adulation they evoked in this or that coterie; *it slips all too easily into a response to their work* (emphasis added).[63]

I, too, am concerned that modern poetry and Eliot's especially make too much of their "Situation," staying on the brink of a new sentimentality at home not in sweetness, but in sighs of despair. For this reason the renewed discovery and expression in this poetry of vibrancy in full-emptiness excites one. But this discovery has been obscured, first by a wave of New Criticism that ignores the connections between modern poetry's vivid orientalism and its sense of Earth, and then by a postmodern wave that either doubts links between signs and Earth too much, or doubts links between modernism and postmodernism. These links have been abused on a general scale to the extent that the postmodern doubt about modern art has slipped into a response to the work, instead of recognizing the enormous potential of the art to inform postmodern positions, including the ecopoetic one (to the extent that it is or is not postmodern). The present book hopes to have shown, as a subset of this broader concern, that Eliot's grappling with the difficulties of his day does not simply end in world-weariness about concrete existence on the planet. Instead, it finds the enchantment of immediate experience related to the first condition of earthly existence, being-and-non-being. For, modern art is "a response by artists to that 'disenchantment of the world' to which cultural historians have long been drawing our attention," in Josipovici's words again.[64] Prufrock's problem and the underlying theme of *The Waste Land* connect with this loss of enchantment with the world. This phrase, "disenchantment of the world," continues Josipovici,

> was given currency by the sociologist Max Weber in the early years of the twentieth century. In *The Protestant Era and the Spirit of Capitalism* (1904) and in later essays, he argues that the Reformation was part of a historical process "the disenchantment of the world" (*die Entzauberung der Welt*), whereby the sacramental religion of the Middle Ages was transformed into a transcendental and intellectualised religion, which led to the disappearance of the numinous from everyday life.[65]

In other words, the "transcendental" ironically becomes the procedure through which one is enabled to "*de-magic*" the world (the meaning of *Entzauberung*), and the process of removing the magic comes about through an intellectualized disconnection from corporeal meaningfulness. The study of Eliot's poetry indicates that this is as much an illness as is the tendency deliberately to "mystify" the world. In his poetry it is very much the numinous in everyday life—its meaningful absence and presence—that Eliot is after, as has been seen here, and his poetic transcendence is everything but an intellectualized stripping away of the numinous from everyday life. In this particular context, Josipovici points out that Maurice Merleau-Ponty suggests in terms of painting that the primal time of our childhood is always there,

> waiting to be rediscovered by the artist. Of course there is no guarantee that it will be and no clear sense of what it is that is waiting to be rediscovered, but one thing is certain: it has to do with a dialogue between us and the world, a dialogue conducted through the medium of our art.[66]

The primal time of our childhood, our first ground of experience with its seamless integrity of being and non-being, things appearing from nowhere and returning to it, and so forth, is very much there in Eliot's mind and poetry, too, as has been demonstrated in respect of fragments and blank space as much as with a view to Marie on the sled, the moment of a crab grabbing a stick, and so on. There is in all of Eliot's art the spontaneity, even in reading it again, of not knowing exactly where it is going, thus mediating the dialogue between us and the world, between us and the predictable but also unpredictable Earth process as the now moment evolves on the brink of the future to come. It is a rare occasion when the reading of Eliot does not make the fragments, pauses, and silences in the poem vivid. And so, as grownup as his themes most certainly are for the most part, the poems hardly ever lose sight of their childlike ground.

This *poetic* form of new materialism, which knows the dynamic agency of being and non-being, sheds light on its theoretical form, involving such large questions as to why anything exists at all, and how the relations between the numinous and the supposedly everyday, concrete realities of being come about. On the scale of literary studies, it certainly involves the role of poetry and the mytho-poetic in the new material advance, starting with the recognition that canonical literature is of the utmost importance to its maturation, while poetry and the mytho-poetic have to do with the sacredness of being that is imperative to getting along with Earth—at least, from a poetic perspective. Perhaps in this way poetry could be said to make itself obsolete from the discussion. If it does, however, the discussion seems immensely the poorer.

We end up with a mystery that is in no need of explanation or mystification, since it clearly is a mystery, or it is a *clear* mystery. The numinous-and-ordinary, plainly numinous, perception of the actuality of earthly existence comes into focus. Has this sacred mystery, this mytho-poetic experience, or this secular perception of the deep meaningfulness of *being* here and now, received clear illumination anywhere? It most certainly has. One has simply to turn to Earth, without preconceptions, and see its unique phenomena in all their here-ness, there-ness, or suchness engaging in what Martin Heidegger calls "a kind of presuppositionless awe over the sheer fact of existence."[67]

Or one has to turn simply to poetry, and in this instance, Eliot, to find the clear mystery expressed in the manner of the charged, singular communication that comes with excellent poetic art—and then perhaps attempt to write a response to it that is responsive and worthwhile. It is therefore the poetry that I wish to conclude with, by citing again one or two of the clearest, brightest, feather-light, and paradoxical formulations in Eliot's oeuvre of the actual, alive mystery:

> Except for the point, the still point,
> There would be no dance, and there is only the dance.[68]

The cycles of life, very much earthly life, that one dances through as the still point continues to carry the dance, means that one comes to a place, again and again, where one sees the moon rising for the first time, or feels the frost under one's feet crisply all over again, as forms of the first love that has never changed and is full of change:

> We shall not cease from exploration
> And the end of all our exploring
> Will be to arrive where we started
> And know the place for the first time.[69]

NOTES

1. George Steiner, *Real Presences* (Chicago: University of Chicago Press, 1991), 24.
2. Steiner, *Real Presences*, 26.
3. Dana Phillips and Heather I. Sullivan, "Material Ecocriticism: Dirt, Waste, Bodies, Food, and Other Matter," *ISLE: Interdisciplinary Studies in Literature and Environment* 19.3 (Summer 2012), 447.
4. E. E. Cummings, *Complete Poems 1904-1962* (New York: Liveright, 1994), 228.
5. Serenella Iovino, "Stories from the Thick of Things: Introducing Material Ecocriticism," *ISLE: Interdisciplinary Studies in Literature and Environment* 19.3 (Summer 2012), 449.
6. Iovino, "Thick of Things," 450.
7. Steven Earnshaw, *The Direction of Literary Theory* (Hampshire: Macmillan, 1996), 113.
8. Iovino, "Thick of Things," 450.
9. Iovino, "Thick of Things," 450.
10. Iovino, "Thick of Things," 450.
11. Iovino, "Thick of Things," 455.
12. Iovino, "Thick of Things," 455.
13. Iovino, "Thick of Things," 450.
14. Jane Bennett, *Vibrant Matter: A Political Ecology of Things* (Durham: Duke University Press, 2010), 3; Iovino, "Thick of Things," 453.
15. Iovino, "Thick of Things," 453.
16. Iovino, "Thick of Things," 454.
17. Kate Soper, *What Is Nature? Culture, Politics and the Non-Human* (Oxford: Blackwell, 1995), 21.
18. T. S. Eliot, *Collected Poems 1909-1962* (New York: Harcourt Brace, 1991), 187.
19. Soper, *What Is Nature?* 16.
20. Cummings, *Poems*, 554.
21. Iovino, "Thick of Things," 454.
22. Eliot, *Poems*, 177.
23. Iovino, "Thick of Things," 454.
24. Iovino, "Thick of Things," 455.
25. Eliot, *Poems*, 190, 175.
26. Iovino, "Thick of Things," 459.
27. *See* Iovino, "Thick of Things," 453; Karen Barad, *Meeting the Universe Halfway: Quantum Physics and the Entanglement of Meaning and Matter* (Durham: Duke University Press, 2007), 151.
28. Iovino, "Thick of Things," 460.
29. Serpil Opperman, "A Lateral Continuum: Postmodernism and Ecocritical Materialism," *ISLE: Interdisciplinary Studies in Literature and Environment* 19.3 (Summer 2012), 460.

30. John Elder, *Imagining the Earth: Poetry and the Vision of Nature* (Urbana: The University of Illinois Press, 1985), 229.
31. Opperman, "Lateral Continuum," 461.
32. Opperman, "Lateral Continuum," 461.
33. Opperman, "Lateral Continuum," 461.
34. Opperman, "Lateral Continuum," 462.
35. T. S. Eliot, *Selected Prose*, ed. Frank Kermode (London: Faber & Faber, 1980), 177–178.
36. Eliot, *Prose*, 175, 178.
37. Opperman, "Lateral Continuum," 463.
38. Pericles Lewis, *The Cambridge Introduction to Modernism* (Cambridge: Cambridge University Press, 2010), xix; Eric Hayot, *Chinese Dreams: Pound, Brecht,* Tel Quel (Ann Arbor: The University of Michigan Press, 2007), 12.
39. Jewel Spears Brooker and Joseph Bentley, *Reading* The Waste Land: *Modernism and the Limits of Interpretation* (Amherst: University of Massachusetts Press, 1990), 19.
40. Opperman, "Lateral Continuum," 456.
41. Opperman, "Lateral Continuum," 463.
42. Opperman, "Lateral Continuum," 468.
43. Opperman, "Lateral Continuum," 463.
44. Opperman, "Lateral Continuum," 460.
45. Saul Bellow, *Ravelstein* (New York: Penguin, 2001), 219.
46. Iovino, "Thick of Things," 459.
47. Opperman, "Lateral Continuum," 464.
48. Opperman, "Lateral Continuum," 464.
49. Laurence Coupe, "General Introduction," *The Green Studies Reader: From Romanticism to Ecocriticism*, ed. Laurence Coupe (London: Routledge, 2000), 2.
50. Frank Kermode, "Why Didn't He Commit Suicide?," review of *T. S. Eliot: The Contemporary Reviews* by Jewel Spears Brooker, http://www.lrb.co.uk/v26/n21/frank-kermode/why-didnt-he-commit-suicide.
51. Opperman, "Lateral Continuum," 468.
52. Opperman, "Lateral Continuum," 469.
53. Mikhail Bakhtin, "Heteroglossia in the Novel," *Bakhtinian Thought: An Introductory Reader*, ed. Simon Dentith (London: Routledge, 1995), 208–209.
54. Opperman, "Lateral Continuum," 469.
55. Opperman, "Lateral Continuum," 470.
56. Vladimir Nabokov, *King, Queen, Knave*, transl. Dmitri Nabokov (New York: Vintage, 1989), 153.
57. Gabriel Josipovici, *What Ever Happened to Modernism?* (New Haven: Yale University Press, 2010), 8.
58. Josipovici, *Modernism?* 7.
59. Josipovici, *Modernism?* 8.
60. Josipovici, *Modernism?* 8.
61. Robert Langbaum, *The Modern Spirit: Essays on the Continuity of Nineteenth and Twentieth Century Literature* (London: Chatto & Windus, 1970), 104.
62. James Longenbach, "Modern Poetry," *The Cambridge Companion to Modernism* (Cambridge: Cambridge University Press, 1999), 104, 122, 125.
63. Josipovici, *Modernism?* 7.
64. Josipovici, *Modernism?* 11.
65. Josipovici, *Modernism?* 11.
66. Josipovici, *Modernism?* 96.
67. Soper, *What Is Nature?* 47.
68. Eliot, *Poems*, 177.
69. Eliot, *Poems*, 208.

Bibliography

PRIMARY TEXTS

Eliot, T. S. *Collected Poems 1909-1962.* New York: Harcourt Brace, 1991.
———. *The Waste Land* (Norton Critical Edition). Ed. Michael North. New York: W. W. Norton, 2001.

SECONDARY TEXTS

Abram, David. *The Spell of the Sensuous: Perception and Language in a More-Than-Human World.* New York: Vintage, 1997.
Ackroyd, Peter. *T. S. Eliot: A Life.* London: Hamish Hamilton, 1984.
Albright, Daniel. *Quantum Poetics: Yeats, Pound, Eliot, and the Science of Modernism.* Cambridge: Cambridge University Press, 1997.
Atkins, G. Douglas. *T. S. Eliot Materialized: Literal Meaning and Embodied Truth.* New York: Palgrave, 2013.
Augustine. "From *Confessions*." In *The Waste Land* (Norton Critical Edition), 58. Ed. Michael North. New York: Norton, 2001.
Bakhtin, Mikhail. "Heteroglossia in the Novel." In *Bakhtinian Thought: An Introductory Reader*, 195–224. Ed. Simon Dentith. London: Routledge, 1995.
Barad, Karen. *Meeting the Universe Halfway: Quantum Physics and the Entanglement of Meaning and Matter.* Durham: Duke University Press, 2007.
Barron, James. "Beethoven May Not Have Died from Lead Poisoning, After All." http://www.nytimes.com/2010/05/29/arts/music/29skull.html?_r=0.
Barthes, Roland. *The Pleasure of the Text.* Trans. Richard Miller. London: Jonathan Cape, 1976.
Baudrillard, Jean. *The Ecstacy of Communication.* Trans. Bernard and Caroline Schütze. Ed. Sylvére Lotringer. New York: Semiotext(e), 1988.
Bellow, Saul. *Ravelstein.* New York: Penguin, 2001.
Bennett, Jane. *Vibrant Matter: A Political Ecology of Things.* Durham: Duke University Press, 2010.
———. "Artistry and Agency in a World of Vibrant Matter." https://www.youtube.com/watch?v=q607Ni23QjA.

Bergman, Charles. "Nature Is the Story That We Live: Reading and Teaching 'The Ancient Mariner' in the Drake Passage." *ISLE: Interdisciplinary Studies in Literature and Environment* 19.4 (Autumn 2012):661–680.

Berlin, Brent. "Tapir and Squirrel: Further Nomenclatural Meanderings towards a Universal Sound-Symbolic Bestiary." In *Nature Knowledge: Ethnoscience, Cognition, and Utility*, 119–127. Eds. Glauco Sanga and Gerhardo Ortalli. Oxford: Berghahn, 2003.

Berry, Wendell. *Life Is a Miracle: An Essay against Modern Superstition.* Berkeley: Counterpoint, 2001.

Bevis, William W. *Mind of Winter: Wallace Stevens, Meditation, and Literature.* Pittsburgh: University of Pittsburgh Press, 1988.

Blackmur, R. P. "Between the *Numen* and the *Moha*: Notes towards a Theory of the Novel." *The Sewanee Review* 62.1 (Jan-Mar 1954):1–23.

———. "Notes on E. E. Cummings's Language." In *Critical Essays on E. E. Cummings*, 107–125. Ed. Guy Rotella. Boston: Hall, 1984.

Blake, William. Letter to the Revd. Dr. Tusler, 23 August 1799. http://www.unc.edu/~kastone/pagelinkletter.html.

———. *The Complete Illuminated Books.* New York: Thames & Hudson, 2001.

Bloom, Harold. "Deciphering Spinoza, the Great Original." Review of *Betraying Spinoza: The Renegade Jew Who Gave Us Modernity* by Rebecca Goldstein. *New York Times*, 16 June 2006. http://www.nytimes.com/2006/06/16/arts/16iht-idside17.1986759.html?pagewanted=all&_r=0.

Bowers, C. A. *Critical Essays on Education, Modernity, and the Recovery of the Ecological Imperative.* New York: Teachers College Press, 1993.

Brooker, Jewel Spears. *Mastery and Escape: T. S. Eliot and the Dialectic of Modernism.* Amherst: University of Massachusetts Press, 1994.

Brooker, Jewel Spears and Bentley, Joseph. *Reading* The Waste Land: *Modernism and the Limits of Interpretation.* Amherst: University of Massachusetts Press, 1990.

Buell, Lawrence. "The Ecocritical Insurgency." *New Literary History* 30.3 (Summer 1999): 699–712.

Chinitz, David E. *T. S. Eliot and the Cultural Divide.* Chicago: University of Chicago Press, 2005.

Chomsky, Noam. "French Intellectual Culture and Post-modernism." https://www.youtube.com/watch?v=2cqTE_bPh7M.

Cooper, J. C. *An Illustrated Encyclopaedia of Traditional Symbols.* London: Thames & Hudson, 2013.

Coupe, Laurence. "General Introduction." In *The Green Studies Reader: From Romanticism to Ecocriticism*,1–12. Ed. Laurence Coupe. London: Routledge, 2000.

Cummings, E. E. *A Miscellany Revised*, ed. George James Firmage. London: Peter Owen, 1966.

———. *Complete Poems 1904-1962.* New York: Liveright, 1994.

Dalai Lama. *Beyond Religion: Ethics for a Whole World.* London: Rider, 2011.

Derrida, Jacques. *Of Grammatology.* Trans. Gayatri Spivak. Baltimore: Johns Hopkins University Press, 1997.

———. "The Animal That Therefore I Am (More to Follow)." Trans. David Wills. *Critical Inquiry* 28.2 (Winter 2002): 369–418.

———. "There Is No Outside-Text," http://en.wikiquote.org/wiki/Jacques_Derrida.

Dickinson, Emily. *The Letters.* Ed. Thomas H. Johnson. Cambridge: Belknap Press, 1958.

Dinerstein, Eric. *The Kingdom of Rarities.* Washington: Island Press, 2013.

Dostoevsky, Fyodor. *The Brothers Karamazov.* Trans. Richard Pevear and Larissa Volokhonsky. New York: Farrar, Straus and Giroux, 2002.

Dwivedi, A. N. *T. S. Eliot: A Critical Study.* New Delhi: Atlantic Publishers, 2002.

Earnshaw, Stephen. *The Direction of Literary Theory.* Hampshire: Macmillan, 1996.

Eco, Umberto. *The Limits of Interpretation.* Bloomington: Indiana University Press, 1990.

———. *The Name of the Rose.* Trans. William Weaver. Boston: Mariner, 2014.

Edwards, Michael. *Towards a Christian Poetics.* Grand Rapids, Mich.: Eerdmans, 1984.

Elder, John. *Imagining the Earth: Poetry and the Vision of Nature.* Urbana: The University of Illinois Press, 1985.
Eliot, T. S. *After Strange Gods: A Primer of Modern Heresy.* London: Faber & Faber, 1934.
———. *Selected Prose.* Ed. Frank Kermode. London: Faber & Faber, 1980.
Felstiner, John. *Can Poetry Save the Earth? A Field Guide to Nature Poems.* New Haven: Yale University Press, 2009.
Forster, E. M. *A Room with a View.* London: Penguin, 1990.
Friedman, Norman. "Post Script" [to "E. E. Cummings and the Modernist Movement"]. In *Critical Essays on E. E. Cummings*, 174–175. Ed. Guy Rotella. Boston: Hall, 1984.
———. *(Re)Valuing Cummings: Further Essays on the Poet 1962-1993.* Gainesville: University Press of Florida, 1996.
Frye, Northrop. *Northrop Frye on Twentieth Century Literature* (Collected Works of Northrop Frye, Volume 29). Ed. Glen Robert Gill. Toronto: University of Toronto Press, 2010.
Galetti, Dino R. "Looking for a Logic in Derrida: Assessing Hurst's 'Plural Logic of Aporia.'" *Journal of Literary Studies/ Tydskrif vir Literatuurwetenskap* 26.3 (September 2010): 84-109.
Gardner, Helen. *The Composition of Four Quartets.* New York: Oxford University Press, 1978.
Garrard, Greg. "Nature Cures? Or How to Police Analogies of Personal and Ecological Health." *ISLE: Interdisciplinary Studies in Literature and Environment* 19.3 (Summer 2012): 494–514.
Gifford, Terry. "Recent Critiques of Ecocriticism." *New Formations: Earthographies: Ecocriticism and Culture* 64 (Spring 2008): 15–24.
Gioia, Dana. "Can Poetry Matter?" http://www.theatlantic.com/past/docs/unbound/poetry/gioia.htm.
Glotfelty, Cheryll. "Introduction: Literary Studies in an Age of Environmental Crisis." In *The Ecocriticism Reader: Landmarks in Literary Ecology*, xv-xxxvii. Eds. Cheryll Glotfelty and Harold Fromm. Athens: University of Georgia Press, 1996.
Gold, Matthew K. "The Expert Hand and the Obedient Heart: Dr. Vittoz, T. S. Eliot, and the Therapeutic Possibilities of *The Waste Land.*" *Journal of Modern Literature* 23.3–4 (Summer 2000): 519–533.
Goodrich, Celeste. *Hints and Disguises: Marianne Moore and Her Contemporaries.* Iowa: University of Iowa Press, 1989.
Grenander, M. E. and Rao, K. S. Narayana. "The Waste Land and the Upanishads: What Does the Thunder Say?" *Indian Literature* 14.1 (March 1971): 85–98.
Harrison, Robert Pogue. *Forests: The Shadow of Civilization.* Chicago: University of Chicago Press, 1993.
Hayot, Eric. *Chinese Dreams: Pound, Brecht, Tel Quel.* Ann Arbor: The University of Michigan Press, 2007.
Hellerstein, Nina. "Calligraphy, Identity: Scriptural Exploration as Cultural Adventure." *Symposium* 45.1 (Spring 1991): 329–344.
Hinton, David. *Mountain Home: The Wilderness Poetry of Ancient China.* New York: New Directions, 2005.
Hollis, James. *Under Saturn's Shadow: The Wounding and Healing of Men.* Toronto: Inner City, 1994.
Hopkins, Gerard Manley. *The Major Poems.* Ed. Walford Davies. London: Dent, 1979.
Iovino, Serenella. "Stories from the Thick of Things: Introducing Material Ecocriticism." *ISLE: Interdisciplinary Studies in Literature and Environment* 19.3 (Summer 2012): 449–460.
Jameson, Fredric. *The Prison-house of Language: A Critical Account of Structuralism and Russian Formalism.* Princeton: Princeton University Press, 1972.
———. *The Political Unconscious: Narrative as a Socially Symbolic Act.* Ithaca: Cornell University Press, 1981.
Josipovici, Gabriel. *What Ever Happened to Modernism?* New Haven: Yale University Press, 2010.
Jung, Carl Gustav. *The Archetypes and the Collective Unconscious.* Trans. R. F. C. Hull. Princeton: Princeton University Press, 1990.

———. *Modern Man in Search of a Soul.* Trans. W. S. Dell and Cary F. Baynes. London: Routledge, 2002.

———. *The Earth Has a Soul: C. G. Jung on Nature, Technology & Modern Life.* Ed. Meredith Sabini. Berkeley: North Atlantic, 2008.

———. "Commentary on *The Golden Flower.*" http://carljungdepthpsychology.blogspot.com.

Kalsched, Donald. *Trauma and the Soul: A Psycho-Spiritual Approach to Human Development and Its Interruption.* London: Routledge, 2013.

Kearns, Cleo McNelly. *T. S. Eliot and Indic Traditions: A Study in Poetry and Belief.* Cambridge: Cambridge University Press, 2008.

Kearns, George. *Guide to Ezra Pound's Selected Cantos.* New Brunswick: Rutgers University Press, 1980.

Keats, John. "Letter to John Bailey." http://www.john-keats.com/briefe/221117.htm.

Kenner, Hugh. *The Invisible Poet, T. S. Eliot.* London: Methuen, 1965.

Kermode, Frank. "Why Didn't He Commit Suicide?" Review of *T. S. Eliot: The Contemporary Reviews* by Jewel Spears Brooker. http://www.lrb.co.uk/v26/n21/frank-kermode/why-didnt-he-commit-suicide.

Kern, Robert. *Orientalism, Modernism, and the American Poem.* Cambridge: Cambridge University Press, 1996.

Kerridge, Richard. Review of *Ecocritical Theory: New European Approaches*, eds. Axel Goodbody and Kate Rigby; *Environmental Criticism for the Twenty-First Century*, eds. Stephanie LeMenager et al. *ISLE: Interdisciplinary Studies in Literature and Environment* 19.3 (Summer 2012): 595–598.

Kolodny, Annette. "Unearthing Herstory." In *The Ecocriticism Reader: Landmarks in Literary Ecology*, 170–181. Eds. Cheryll Glotfelty and Harold Fromm. Athens: The University of Georgia Press, 1996.

Kozain, Rustum. "Review: *Bodyhood* by Leon de Kock." https://groundwork.wordpress.com/2010/10/19/review-bodyhood-leon-de-kock.

Langbaum, Robert. *The Modern Spirit: Essays on the Continuity of Nineteenth and Twentieth Century Literature.* London: Chatto & Windus, 1970.

Lao Tzu. *Tao Te Ching: The Richard Wilhelm Edition.* Trans. H. G. Ostwald. London: Arkana, 1987.

Leavis, F. R. "The Significance of the Modern Waste Land." In *The Waste Land* (Norton Critical Edition), 173–184. Ed. Michael North. New York: Norton, 2001.

Leibniz, Gottfried. *The Philosophical Works of Leibniz.* Ed. George Martin Duncan. New Haven: Tuttle, Morehouse & Taylor, 1890.

Lewis, Pericles. *The Cambridge Introduction to Modernism.* Cambridge: Cambridge University Press, 2010.

Longenbach, James. "Modern Poetry." In *The Cambridge Companion to Modernism*, 100–129. Cambridge: Cambridge University Press, 1999.

Lotman, Yuri M. *Universe of the Mind: A Semiotic Theory of Culture.* Bloomington: Indiana University Press, 1990.

Lovejoy, Arthur O. *The Great Chain of Being.* Cambridge: Harvard University Press, 1964.

Lovelock, James. *The Vanishing Face of Gaia: A Final Warning.* New York: Basic Books, 2009.

Mahler, Gustav. *Symphonie No. 2: Auferstehungs-Symphonie* [Resurrection Symphony]. Cond. Leonard Bernstein. New York Philharmonic, 1988.

Marvell, Andrew. *The Complete Poems.* Ed. Elizabeth Story Donno. London: Penguin, 2005.

McGilchrist, Iain. *The Master and His Emissary: The Divided Brain and the Making of the Western World.* New Haven: Yale University Press, 2012.

McKibben, Bill. *The End of Nature.* New York: Random House, 2006.

McMahan, David. *The Making of Buddhist Modernism.* New York: Oxford University Press, 2008.

Miner, Earl. "Pound, Haiku, and the Image." In *Ezra Pound: A Collection of Critical Essays*, 115–128. Ed. Walter Sutton. Englewood Cliffs: Prentice-Hall, 1963.

Moe, Aaron. *Zoopoetics: Animals and the Making of Poetry.* Lanham: Lexington Books, 2014.

Moody, A. D. "A Cure for a Crisis of Civilization?" In *The Waste Land* (Norton Critical Edition), 240–246. Ed. Michael North. New York: Norton, 2001.
Moore, Marianne. *Complete Poems*. New York: Penguin, 1991.
Moran, Joe. *Interdisciplinarity*. London: Routledge, 2002.
Müller, Max F. *The Upanishads*. Delhi: Motilal Banarsidass, 1969.
Nabokov, Vladimir. *King, Queen, Knave*. Trans. Dmitri Nabokov. New York: Vintage, 1989.
Nagel, Thomas. *Mind and Cosmos: Why the Materialist Neo-Darwinian Conception of Nature Is Almost Certainly False*. Oxford: Oxford University Press, 2012.
Nietzsche, Friedrich. *The Antichrist*. Trans. H. L. Mencken. New York: Knopf, 1924.
Opperman, Serpil. "A Lateral Continuum: Postmoderism and Ecocritical Materialism." *ISLE: Interdisciplinary Studies in Literature and Environment* 19.3 (Summer 2012): 460–475.
Ovid. *Metamorphoses*. Gutenberg e-Text. Trans. Henry Riley. www.gutenberg.org/files/21765/21765-h/files/Met_IV-VII.html.
Oxford English Dictionary, http://www.oed.com.nwulib.nwu.ac.za.
Penny, William Kevin. "Dialect of the Tribe: Modes of Communication and the Epiphanic Role of Nonhuman Imagery in T. S. Eliot's *Four Quartets*." *Harvard Theological Review* 108.1 (January 2015): 98–112.
Perl, Jeffrey M. and Tuck, Andrew P. "The Hidden Advantage of Tradition: On the Significance of T. S. Eliot's Indic Studies." *Philosophy East & West* 35.2 (April 1985): 116–131.
Phillips, Dana. "Is Nature Necessary?" In *The Ecocriticism Reader: Landmarks in Literary Ecology*, 204–221. Eds. Cheryl Glotfelty and Harold Fromm. Athens: University of Georgia Press, 1996.
———. *The Truth of Ecology: Nature, Culture, and Literature in America*. Oxford: Oxford University Press, 2003.
———. "'Slimy Beastly Life:' Thoreau on Food and Farming." *ISLE: Interdisciplinary Studies in Literature and Environment* 19.3 (Summer 2012): 532–547.
Phillips, Dana and Sullivan, Heather I. "Material Ecocriticism: Dirt, Waste, Bodies, Food, and Other Matter." *ISLE: Interdisciplinary Studies in Literature and Environment* 19.3 (Summer 2012): 445–447.
Pound, Ezra. *ABC of Reading*. New York: New Directions, 1987.
———. *Cantos*. London: Faber & Faber, 1990.
Qian, Zhaoming. *Orientalism and Modernism: The Legacy of China in Pound and Williams*. Durham: Duke University Press, 1995.
Rainey, Lawrence. *The Annotated* Waste Land *with Eliot's Contemporary Prose*. New Haven: Yale University Press, 2006.
Ransom, John Crowe. "Waste Lands." In *The Waste Land* (Norton Critical Edition), 167–170. Ed. Michael North. New York: Norton, 2001.
Russell, Sharman Apt. *Standing in the Light: My Life as a Pantheist*. New York: Basic Books, 2009.
Said, Edward. *Orientalism*. London: Penguin, 2003.
———. *Reflections on Exile and Other Essays*. Cambridge: Harvard University Press, 2002.
Shakespeare, William. *The Globe Illustrated Shakespeare*. Ed. Howard Staunton. New York: Gramercy, 1979.
Sharma, A. K. "The Relation between Buddhism and the *Upanishads*." *The Monist* 38.3 (July 1928): 443–447.
Snyder, Gary. *The Real Work: Interviews and Talks 1964-1979*. New York: New Directions, 1980.
———. *A Place in Space: Ethics, Aesthetics, and Watersheds*. Berkeley: Counterpoint, 1995.
Sole, Kelwyn. "Our Literature Needs Incisive Criticism, Yes, But on Exactly Whose Values Will It Be Based?" http://www.mg.co.za/article/2011-03-04-our-literature-needs-incisive-criticism-yes-but-on-exactly-whose-values-will-it-be-based.
Soper, Kate. *What Is Nature? Culture, Politics and the Non-Human*. Oxford: Blackwell, 1995.
Sri, P. S. *T. S. Eliot, Vedanta and Buddhism*. Vancouver: University of British Columbia Press, 1985.
Stein, Murray. *Jung's Map of the Soul: An Introduction*. Chicago: Open Court, 2001.

Steiner, George. *After Babel: Aspects of Language and Translation.* London: Oxford University Press, 1975.
———. *Real Presences.* Chicago: University of Chicago Press, 1991.
Stevens, Wallace. *Collected Poems.* London: Faber & Faber, 1990.
Surette, Leon. *The Birth of Modernism: Ezra Pound, T. S. Eliot, W. B. Yeats and the Occult.* Montreal: McGill-Queens University Press, 1994.
Terblanche, Etienne. *E. E. Cummings: Poetry and Ecology.* Amsterdam: Rodopi, 2012.
Thoreau, Henry David. *The Maine Woods.* University of Virginia Library: Electronic Text Center, 2000.
University of Toronto Representative Poetry Online. http://rpo.library.utoronto.ca/
Van Heerden, Ernst. "Dood van die Akkedis" [Death of the Lizard]. *Groot Verseboek* [Great Book of Poems]. Ed. André P. Brink. Cape Town: Tafelberg, 2008.
Vendler, Helen. [Review of E. E. Cummings's *Complete Poems 1913-1962*]. In *Critical Essays on E. E. Cummings*, 99–105. Ed. Guy Rotella. Boston: Hall, 1984.
Waldau, Paul. "Buddhism and Animal Rights." In *Contemporary Buddhist Ethics*, 81–112. Ed. Damien Keown. Richmond: Kurzon, 2000.
Webster, Michael. "'singing is silence:' Being and Nothing in the Visual Poetry of E. E. Cummings." In *Form Miming Meaning: Iconicity in Language and Literature*, 199–214. Eds. Max Nänny and Olga Fischer. Amsterdam: John Benjamins, 1999.
Williams, William Carlos. *The Collected Poems* (Volume 1). Eds. A. Walton Litz and Christopher MacGowan. New York: New Directions, 1986.
Wilson, Edward O. *On Human Nature.* Cambridge: Harvard University Press, 2004.
Woolf, Virginia. *Jacob's Room.* London: Penguin, 1992.
Wordsworth, William. *Collected Poems.* London: Wordsworth Editions, 1995.
Yeats, W. B. *Yeats's Poetry, Drama, and Prose.* Ed. James Pethica. New York: W. W. Norton, 2000.
Zizek, Slavoj. "Nature Does Not Exist." https://www.youtube.com/watch?v=DIGeDAZ6-q4.
———. "Love Is Evil." https://www.youtube.com/watch?v=hg7qdowoemo.

Index

Abram, David, 177, 179, 183n51, 190; and the spell of the sensuous, 107
absolute, 68, 124; etymology, 124
Ackroyd, Peter, 148–149
actuality, 12, 128
actual life, 6
affirmation, 7, 8; of life's value, 8; of location, 62; of place, 64; as recognition, 8
affirming location, 68
Albright, Daniel, 92, 109n1, 109n3, 109n4; *Quantum Poetics: Yeats, Pound, Eliot, and the Science of Modernism*, 92
American: guilt, 6; Transcendentalism, 6
ancient Earth, 20. *See also* Earth
ancient natural past, 44
Anesaki, Masaharu, 144
art as art, 108
Atkins, G. Douglas: *T. S. Eliot Materialized*, 169, 182n35
Augustine's *Confessions*, 53; sexual promiscuities, 53
authenticity, 92
authority without connection, 80
autopoiesis, 187–188
awareness of nowhere, 116

Barthes, Roland, 160, 169
being, 102, 117, 127; belongs to Earth, 102; that comes from Non-Being, 126; -and-nothing, 128

belief, 20; and concrete existence, 16
Bellow, Saul: *Ravelstein*, 40, 48n19
Bennett, Jane, 124, 188; *Vibrant Matter*, 128, 129n30, 130n39, 130n40
Blackmur, R. P., 139; and New Criticism in America, 139
Blake, William, 8, 29n18, 59, 87, 89n56
blank space, 83, 116
body, 190; as a threshold into experience, 190
Bradley, F. H., 82
Brooker, Jewel Spears, 19, 29n57, 36, 67, 129n2, 141, 149; absence of God in *Gerontion*, 160; matter is "mater," 36; *Reading* The Waste Land, 149; structure of *Gerontion*, 157; thought experiment, 67; "A Wilderness of Mirrors," 193
Buddhism, 20, 21, 25
Buddhism-Taoism-Zen, 21
Buddhist: participation, 20; perceptions of Earth, 23; sense of life, 72; strand, 20; tradition, 18, 82

Christian and Buddhist: notions, 126; religious imagining, 8
Christianity, 18
classical literature, 63
climate change, 62
"close reading," 1
co-existence, 7, 53

211

communication, 20; about earthly emplacement, 20
completeness, 117
concrete existence, 4, 25, 136, 142; on Earth, 9
concreteness, 34, 71
connection, 12, 36, 150; essential to love, 32; between humanity and concrete being, 17; between signs and Earth, 62; with matter, 91; with a vibrant Earth, 19
consciousness of co-existence, 73
Conrad, Joseph, 140
contemporary psyche, 31
cortesia, 7
continuation, 116
Coupe, Laurence, 26, 180, 181n3
creatures of immersion, 91
crisis in ecocentrism, 3
critical theory, 147
critics, 135; theories of meaningless of Eliot's Sanskrit elements, 135–136
cultural origins, 69
culture: and Earth converge, 139; and nature, 19; studies, 25–26, 132, 133, 141, 146–147, 155, 192
culture-nature: boundary dissolves, 109; connection, 41, 68, 104; unity, 41
Cummings, E. E., 10, 13, 29n25, 65n21, 130n35, 134, 146, 148; boundaries between nature and culture, 191; celebration of being within non-being, 115; imagery, 109; poetry, 10, 79, 83, 119, 134, 176

Dalai Lama, 13, 29n33; *Beyond Religion: Ethics for a Whole World*, 13; inclusivity, 13; secularity, 13
Darwin, Charles, 74, 77
Dayadhvam, Sympathize: command, 76
death and rebirth, 116
deconstruction, 175
deformation of humanity, 17
Derrida, Jacques, 26, 30n72, 147, 148, 163, 166, 173, 175, 182n24–182n27; and animal rights, 175; and deconstruction, 169; and difference, 165, 166, 170; and evolution, 164–166, 167, 170, 171–173; *Of Grammatology*, 147, 153n63, 182n36; "nothing outside the text," 176–177
desert, 57; images, 56; place of spiritual testing, 61; symbol of pitiless democracy, 61; within, 58
desertification, 45, 57, 58; within, 59
desertified images, 60
desertscapes, 56, 61, 62; disturbing icon of isolation, 56
desire, 53; as root cause of human suffering, 54
difference between saying and the said, 119
differences, 91, 165, 174
differentiation, 7, 82, 155, 163, 166; incorporated into the new materialism, 157; interdependent with wholeness, 7; master of wholeness, 7; as a set of tyrannies, 26
disconnection: from earthly being, 34; from matter, 43, 179; of meaning, 32; between pagan and modern sense of the Thames, 53; from the planet, 71
dislocating language, 54
dislocation, 23, 26, 32, 51, 80; and fragmentation, 7; of great literature, 64; of matter, 189; from the natural world, 58; of signs and nature, 63
disorientation: and connections to matter, 32; levels, 38
dissociation from nature, 60
dissolving, 150
distance: and integrity, 164; and space, 12
distant and immediate past, 10
distortions, 119
divorce, 32
Dostoevsky, Fyodor, 42; ignorant courage of the Fool, 42
dynamic wholeness, 7
dynamism of existence, 85

Eagleton, Terry: *After Theory*, 106
Earth, 1, 5, 9, 11, 42, 52, 58, 63, 87, 175, 181. *See also* ancient Earth; is change, 9, 23; connection, 21; continues, 146; creation, 4; definition, 14; dissolves opposites, 117; how Eliot sees its meaning, 9; exploitation, 17, 18; human participatory change, 9; and humanity, 2, 16; and humans, 120; induces

changes in others, 4; mirth mandala, 168, 169; as motion and change, 9, 85; moves without human agency, 4; not as an object, 9; as objects, 85; and ocean, 43; process, 2, 10; suggests a wiser materiality, 59; as unfathomable, 43; values, 175

Earth-as-process, 23

earthly: being-and-non-being, 85; change, 4, 123

Earth's: cycles, 123; independence, 189; movement, 134; poetic mystery, 127; vibrancy, 84, 87

Eco, Umberto: *The Limits of Interpretation*, 106

ecocritical: praxis, 1; skepticism, 62; theory, 1

ecocriticism, 1, 2, 4, 8, 63, 105, 108, 155, 174; concerns, 42; Glotfelty's definition, 2; inherent skepticism, 63; macrocosmic development, 3; and postmodernism, 194; response to non-connection with nature, 47

ecocritics, 106

ecological: "crisis," 31, 38, 71; health, 44; skepticism, 4

ecology, 54

ecopoetic findings, 25

Edwards, Michael, 70, 136; and Sanskrit, 136

Elder, John, 131

Eliot, Thomas Stearns (T. S.), 1, 114–115; brings simultaneity into focus, 135; Buddhist sensibility, 18; the Christian, 20; contrasts the ancient and the new, 72; creates porous effects of dissolving, 113; cultural world of "between," 21; desertscapes, 46; directness by way of indirectness, 16; dissolving ontology of change and creativity, 190; eco-*logos*, 5, 11, 16, 135; emphasis on Earth, 20; essay on James Joyce's *Ulysses*, 75; expression of *wholeness*, 6; generational awareness, 10; *The Idea of a Christian Society*, 161; *immersion* in existence, 24; insistence on "*dislocation*," 2; and Jung, 44; later poems, 46; later prose, 20; major poems, 7, 8; making of the new Buddhism, 22; notion of dislocation, 51; and philosophy, 142; as poet, 192; poet must be more allusive to dislocate language, 51; poetic city, 54; poetic reinvention of Buddhism, 22; poetic tradition of value created by natural processes, 17; realism, 14; relationship with nature, 1; reverence for Earth, 13; revitalizes the (lotos) rose, 134; and sexism, 141; and Snyder, 18; spiritual presences in poetry, 20; thought-becoming-poetry, 14; two worlds, 5; use of skepticism, 8; world-weary nihilism, 16

Eliot's: affirmative connection, 103; art, 201; break with everyday grammar, 86; Buddhist skepticism, 115, 136; central aesthetic values, 87; central linguistic dilemma, 75; connections between poetic signs and earthly meanings, 175; development as a poet, 128; dissertation on Bradley, 137; dynamism of the now moment, 139; Earth-engagement, 185; Earth-mirth mandala, 170; Earth sense, 189; eco-*logos*, 131; elusive textuality, 177; embodying Earth-experience, 107; first condition of earthly existence, 200; fractured language, 84; fragmentation, 61–62; grappling with the difficulties of his day, 200; ideogrammatics, 148; impersonal theory of individual poetry, 127; mandalic structures, 167–168; oeuvre of the actual, alive mystery, 201–202; orientalism, 74, 129, 131, 136–137, 142; poetic form of the new materialism, 201; poetic voice, 55, 146–147; poetry, 5, 6, 84, 87, 116, 141, 148, 171, 179, 188, 190, 191, 194, 200–201; prose, 57, 79; regard for Moore's poetry, 105; religious imagination, 91; sense of Christianity, 96; sense of location, 64; sensibility of the *absolute*, 124; skepticism, 107, 136; student essay "*Degrees of Reality*," 137; text as vibrant matter, 191; themes, 201; use of oriental influences, 126; use of skepticism, 128; warning about "material progress," 58; wholeness, 163

English poetry, 62

enmeshment, 24, 91
ennui, 36
entanglement, 91
entomological imagery, 40
environmentalist skepticism, 63
Europe's early history, 67
evolution, 164–165, 166, 171. *See also* Derrida, Jacques
existence, 20, 124

fear, 81; and threeness, 81
Felstiner, John, 134; poems and nature, 134
Fisher King, 81
Fool, 42
forms of great poetry, 133
Forster, E. M.: *A Room with a View*, 86, 89n54
fourness, 76
Four Quartets, 6, 9, 10, 11, 20, 42, 67, 73, 114, 116, 117, 120, 125, 136, 167, 189. *See also* Eliot, Thomas Stearns (T. S.); advocates ignorance as a way to understanding, 126; centrality of the word "rose," 121; coexistence of opposites in concrete actuality, 103; conclusion, 102; concrete access to existence on Earth, 14; connecting with life's pattern, 190; continuation, 103; darkness, 83; a *dissolving grammar*, 122; dissolving of signs into Earth process, 25; dynamism, 85; earthly acceptance, 67; and earthly existence, 126; fire and rose, 122; fragments embody dislocation, 67; freedom, 12; hierarchies between human and natural worlds, 191; immersion in life, 103; immersion linked to cyclical returning, 101; informative mandalas, 69; invokes the lotos flower, 121; journey into existence, 122; land and soil, 67; lotos rose, 125, 126; natural images, 12; nature of all movement, 10; newness of our moments on the planet, 124; oxymoron/ still point, 148; pattern, 120, 126; patterns of flow, 99; poem of active location, 23; resonances of Christianity and Buddhism, 122; secular sense of holiness, 14; sense of continuity, 103; sense of immersion, 99, 103; sense of soil, 19; shows that knowing cannot be final, 193; the still point, 10, 118; stillness and dance, 10–11, 11; unity of man and woman, 100; words enact their dissolving, 125–126
fractured ontology of ordinary experience, 51
fragmentary imagery, 80
fragmentation, 8, 24, 26, 52
fragments, 58, 68; as icons, 56; mime the concrete experience, 56; sense of wholeness, 68; signify dis-location, 56
Frazer, James G.: *The Golden Bough*, 74
Freud, Sigmund, 77, 160; reductive analytical-materialist thought, 77
Friedman, Norman, 119, 147

Garrard, Greg, 8, 28n17, 62, 107; ecocritical limits of sceptical thought, 8; and ecocriticism, 8, 62, 107; and new materialism, 62
Genesis and the fall of humanity, 39
"Gerontion," 2, 3, 26, 157–163, 179. *See also* Eliot, Thomas Stearns (T. S.); absence of spiritual truth, 159; concreteness and signs, 158; connection with the Earth, 2; continuity is central to modern existence, 167; despair, 2; differences in sameness, 160–161; disconnection occurs, 158; distancing from the miraculous, 159; and the Freudian house, 160; imagery of the onion, 157; infinite repetition, 179; infinite semiosis, 159, 163; love, 158; nature's continuation and indifference, 161; notion of infinite difference, 162; proliferation of sign worlds, 157; and the spider's web, 161
global: climate change, 57; warming, 23, 57, 71
Glotfelty, Cheryll, 2, 3
great literary art, 7
grounded life, 18

Harrison, Robert Pogue: *Forests: The Shadow of Civilization*, 59, 65n24
hell of powerlessness, 80

hermeneutic loop, 2
hippopotamus, 87, 92
"The Hippopotamus" (1920), 8, 24, 92, 92–94, 173. *See also* Eliot, Thomas Stearns (T. S.); aquatic imagery, 97; belief turned into a form of neutral materialism, 94; centering on the values of matter, 96; and the church, 95, 96, 96–97; critique of materialism, 93; disconnection from Earth, 94; immersion, 97; irony, 95; loss of significant soil, 97; and nature, 95; sermonizing tone, 94; size-sound symbolism, 94–95, 96
history of poetry, 186
holiness of matter, 87
"The Hollow Men," 10, 51, 83. *See also* Eliot, Thomas Stearns (T. S.); extreme fragmentation, 52; linguistic dislocation, 52
"holy," 13; perception of Earth, 18
human: dislocation from Earth, 62; immersion in concrete changes, 10; inheritance, 44; language, 4; perception, 12; semiosis, 4; signs, 4; understanding, 178
humanity, 37, 81, 124; and Earth, 2, 81, 178, 189; loss of meaning, 37; modern materiality, 44; movement away from superstition, 37
humility, 19
humus, 19
hypernature, 6

The Idea of a Christian Society, 16, 17, 20; connections between religion and nature, 16; engagement with Earth, 16
immersed in one's existence, 113
immersion, 10, 24, 91, 98–99, 102, 105, 150; in being on Earth, 24; as a condition of existence, 104; and dissolving, 128; equality of inside and outside, 104; and flow, 102; linked to cyclical returning, 101–102; in one's actual being, 91; in poetry, 24; where time and timelessness meet, 104
inauthenticity: of modern material existence, 92
inclusivity, 13. *See also* Dalai Lama

indirectness, 22–23; of dislocating language, 64
industrial civilization, 17
"infinite semiosis," 3, 26, 84, 151, 155–156, 176. *See also* signs; challenged, 156; imagery, 157; limits, 157; patterns and values, 156
inner and outer worlds of being, 92
intersection: of time and timelessness, 119, 120; of place and placelessness, 120
Iovino, Serenella, 187, 188–189, 189, 202n5; "material-semiotic agencies," 187
ISLE: Interdisciplinary Studies on Literature and Environment Summer 2012, 6. *See also* Phillips, Dana

Jameson, Frederic, 193; political unconscious, 178, 183n50
jellyfish, 91, 104, 104–105; experience, 119; lives its earthly wholeness, 91; mandalic being, 105
jester, 42. *See also* Fool
Josipovici, Gabriel, 199, 200, 203n57; and Marxism, 198
Joyce, James, 196
Jung, Carl Gustav, 44, 45–46, 49n34–49n36, 49n40, 49n41, 49n43, 77, 177; and Eliot, 44, 160; and the archetype of the wise child, 79; oriental influence in the occident, 137; and the psyche, 45; understanding through life, 137
Jungian therapy, 44
juxtaposition of Sanskrit and English, 123

Kafka, Franz, 114
Kearns, Cleo McNelly, 123, 129n26, 129n27; Indic survey of Eliot's project, 123
Kerridge, Richard, 24, 30n73, 107; and theory, 107, 108
King Tereus. *See also* Philomela legend: Eliot alludes to the legend, 53; rape of Philomela, 53; used his power against the female world, 53

lack: of instinct in modern man, 46; of love, 80; of meaningful connection, 80

language, 4, 54, 73, 91, 114, 140, 178, 189; -as-boundary dissolves, 113; as "breath," 24; creates a context of presencing, 113; mediates experience, 113; mingles with that vibrant nowhere from whence things emerge, 114; -nature wholeness, 113
Lao Tzu's "spatial limitations," 119
laughter, 32
layers of differentiation, 43
Leavis, F. R., 22, 30n67, 74, 135; response to Sanskrit in *The Waste Land*, 144; and *The Waste Land*, 144, 151n10
Liebniz, Gottfried, 115
linguistic: connections with concreteness, 32; embodiment, 56; nature of experience, 3; turn, 4–5, 42; worlds, 5
linkages with nature, 38
literary: art, 6; discussion, 63; studies, 107, 108, 155; theory, 105
literary movements, 47; ecocriticism, 47; postmodern infinite semiosis, 47
location, 7, 23, 62, 67, 150; is not a static destination, 87; or place, 2
logocentrism, 147
loss of connection, 43; with nature's real presence, 43
loss and rediscovery of location, 48
loss of wisdom, 81
Lotman, Yuri: semiosphere, 175
lotos rose, 117, 134; *See also Four Quartets*
love: and connection, 32
"The Love Song of J. Alfred Prufrock," 31, 54, 57. *See also* Eliot, Thomas Stearns (T. S.); Prufrock; absence of a father figure, 46; argument analysis, 26; lack of contact with Earth, 47; mermaid image, 43; poetic impact, 44
Lovelock, James, 58; wisdom to live with Earth, 58

machine-like disconnection, 16
Mahler, Gustav: Second Symphony, 55, 65n16
major works of literary art, 196
Mallarmé, Stéphane, 147, 148
mandalas, 69, 170; symbols of cosmological centering, 70

mandalic: centered lines, 69; *Da*, 71, 86; pattern, 71; structure, 74, 84
marginalization of poetry, 175
Marvell, Andrew, 33, 48n5; erotic metaphor, 33; poem, 33
Marvellian metaphor, 33
material: existence, 33; progress, 17; reductionism, 166; skepticism, 27; unity, 179; world, 35
materialism, 9, 39
materiality, 39; of experience, 3
matter, 5, 31, 32, 33, 35, 54, 178; of belief, 40; meanings, 32, 33; as problem, 33
McMahan, David, 21, 30n62; *The Making of Buddhist Modernism*, 20–21
meaning, 39, 40; of Earth, 32
meaningful relationships, 41
meaningfulness, 33, 124, 174; of being, 201; of existence, 144; of participation, 194
memory, 55
Merleau-Ponty, Maurice, 139; and Eliot, 139; meaning of existence, 139
mermaid image, 43
mermaids, 92
metaphors, 33, 34
modern: art, 86, 200; audience, 33; consciousness, 44; humanity, 20, 37; literature, 63, 196; material psyche, 31; poetry, 8, 58, 86, 115, 116, 119, 125, 134, 150, 185–186, 194, 198; poets, 13, 113; time, 42; urban existence, 53
modernism, 198, 198–199; and postmodernism, 197
Moe, Aaron: *Zoopoetics: Animals and the Making of Poetry*, 172
moha, 142; of cloudy or bodily knowing and instinctive uncertainties, 137
Moody, A. D., 74, 135, 144; and Eliot's Sanskrit, 145
Moore, Marianne, 13, 104–105, 115, 196; poem "A Jelly-Fish," 104–105
motifs of immersion, 87
movement, 11

Naagaarjuna, 142, 144; and reality, 142–143
Nagel, Thomas, 179
natural: resources, 17; science, 6

nature, 20; as a process, 9
nature of modern experience, 52
nature's: changing timelessness, 42; destruction, 59; spirit, 58
new material: context of vibrant matter, 87; ecocriticism, 23; perspective, 128; sensibility, 19
"new materialism," 3–5, 6, 7, 8–9, 23, 25, 151, 155, 156, 163, 181, 189; in its culture studies, 132; and the "dance of agency," 190; and differentiation, 176; and dissolving of signs, 127; and ecocriticism's inherent skepticism, 63; and Eliot's poetry, 188, 190; finds affirmation in great literature, 86; focus on waste, 187; great literature and its affirmation, 105; and literary art, 133; and poetry, 128, 193; skepticism about nature, 62; silence is vibrant, 124; theoretical inheritance, 26
Nietzsche, Friedrich, 88n30; *Wille zur Macht*, 80
nihilism, 114, 144
nothing, 115, 116, 117, 124
nothing-as-nihilism, 114
notion : of false, mechanistic "goodness," 73; of nothing in literature, 114; of wholeness. See wholeness
now-here-nowhere, 10, 115, 119
nowness, 115, 120; of being, 120
numen: connection with concrete existence (*moha*), 142; of illumination, 137; sacred awareness of Earth, 142
"objective correlative," 9

oneness, 76, 82
openness, 116
Opperman, Serpil, 191–192, 196, 202n29; and hierarchical orders, 195; literary modernism, 192; matter's inherent vitality, 193; new materialism, 192, 193, 195, 197; and postmodern art, 191, 193, 197
opposites, 117
oriental philosophies, 18
orientalism in modern poetry, 163

pagan roots of European history, 18
parody of crucifixion, 40

participation in life, 39
patriarchal cruelty, 53
perception, 9; of existence, 36
Phillips, Dana, 6, 28n11, 63; criticism, 6; cynicism, 6; ecocriticism, 28n10; and modern aesthetics, 185; skepticism, 6
Philomela legend, 52, 80; in Ovid's *Metamorphoses*, 52; raping and closeness to Earth, 52
philosophy, 142
physical Cosmos, 34
poems, 1; analysis, 1; eco-*logos*, 2; examination of meanings, 1; internal level, 2; meanings within the world the poem creates, 2
poet: dislocates language, 51; forced into extreme levels of indirectness, 51
poetic: experience of being, 113; fragmentation, 7; interaction, 134; language, 124; traditions, 51
poetry, 105, 125; and earth, 2; linguistic concreteness in sound and pattern, 14
postmodern: condition, 42; ecocritical skepticism, 7; narrative, 7; theory, 174
postmodernism, 3, 7, 43, 179, 195, 196, 199
poststructuralism, 3, 155; postmodernism, 155
Pound, Ezra, 13, 56, 59–60, 79, 125, 126, 196; arid ideograms, 60; *Cantos*, 56, 59, 60, 65n28; desertscapes, 59, 60; fragmentation, 61; perspective on landscape, 59–60; translucencies, 125
poverty of the collective soul, 59
power, 80
"Preludes" (1917), 38, 54, 97. See also Eliot, Thomas Stearns (T. S.); material troubles, 36; pronouns dislocate the poem, 36; unclear personas, 36
primitive : energies, 44; societies, 19
procedures of dislocation, 56
process of coexistence on Earth, 72
profit, 17
progress, 17, 19
prose, 105
Prufrock, 2, 31, 92, 127. See also Eliot, Thomas Stearns (T. S.); "The Love Song of J. Alfred Prufrock" ; all-consuming barbarian, 35; awkward

orientation in life and love, 32; becomes immune to experience, 151; bland surname, 31; connection with physical existence, 31; as central consciousness, 31; comedy of concrete engagement, 42; desertscape of meaninglessness, 62; disconnection from matter, 2, 23; disconnected love song, 36; disconnection with Mater, 36; dislocation, 23, 35, 42; failed materialism, 23; finds only severed objects, 45; from furniture wholesalers' name, 31; inability to love, 32; life and meaningfulness, 33; and loss, 43; materiality, 31; the matter with Prufrock, 35; meaning and nature dissociation, 42; nature of the modern lifestyle, 23; needs immersion in concrete being, 45; perceptions of existence, 36; poetic embodiment of ecopoetic loss, 48; proof of his existence, 31; prototype of bored postmodern consumer, 35; prototype of "political correctness," 39; rock solid proof of his existence, 31; sense of expansion and contraction, 37; severed objects, 35; signs swamp his existence, 31; static uncertainty, 33; surname, 31; swamped by objects, 45; three material levels, 36; traits of modern human being, 31; victim of disconnection from concreteness, 32; waste in and of a lifetime, 42; within his disconnected world, 34; world in a collection of discrete objects, 35

Prufrock's. *See also* "The Love Song of J. Alfred Prufrock": body, 45; death, 45; dehumanization, 43; dilemma, 41; drowning, 92, 97–98; entomology, 39–40; existence, 56, 98; "greatness," 45; hunger for significance, 56; inability to locate Earth's spiritual presence, 43; infinite semiotic shallowness, 46; life enjoys no real presence, 45; loss of subjective-objective integrity, 41; matter, 41, 42; moments of weakness, 42; peculiar materialism, 41; sense of the mermaids, 43

psychology : of modern Earth engagement, 44
pure metaphor, 33

rape: and Earth-rape, 23
rationality, 63
"real presence," 6, 12, 23, 26, 87, 115, 124, 155; of nature, 125
"Real World," 142
reality, 14
reason: becomes one-sided, 57; and progress, 57
re-bind connections with unfolding Earth, 19
recombination, 7; and location, 7
reduction of meaningfulness, 62
reductionism: in literary studies, 5; loss of spiritual perception, 5; in material science, 5
religion, 13; Sanskrit roots of the word, 19
religious and philosophical life, 67
renewed identity, 43
restoration, 23
"Rhapsody on a Windy Night," 12, 55, 98; disconnection, 98; immersion, 98; portrayal of meaninglessness, 98
Ricks, Christopher, 32; improbable "Love Song" of Prufrock, 32
rose object: and change, 114
Romanticism, 199
Rousseau, Jean Jacques, 18, 44

sacred: Earth process, 188; sense of Earth, 53
Said, Edward, 25, 30n75, 74, 125, 131, 138–142, 146, 149–150, 175. *See also* culture studies; and classical art, 146; and concreteness of ordinary life, 138; condemnation of modern poetic orientalism, 138; culture studies aberrations, 185; and deconstruction, 163; and Eliot as a critic, 139, 141; and Eliot's poetic orientalism, 138, 144; and Eliot, Yeats, and Pound, 140–141; and the emergence of feminist writers, 141; global influence on orientalism, 131; and the modern poets, 150; and modern poetry, 131; *Orientalism*, 138, 152n31; praises Blackmur, 139–140

Sanskrit, 72, 81. *See also* Eliot, Thomas Stearns (T. S.); benediction of *shantih*, 78; commands, 81; elements, 73–74, 136; and English, 70, 71; fragments, 67, 133; metaphor of primitive speech, 70; patterns, 74, 75, 77, 145, 146; semantics, 135; syllable, 69; threeness, 84

scientific: "essence," 40; reductionism, 62

self-recognition, 32

semiosphere, 25, 175. *See also* Lotman, Yuri

semiotic reductionism, 179

sense of place, 27, 84

sensitivity : as self-delusion, 39

sex, 41; becomes material, 54; earthly and mystical connection, 53; vital connection with Earth is dislocated, 54

sexism, 18

Shakespeare's sonnets, 186

shantih, 143

shared world of human experience, 142

signs, 25, 33, 127, 155, 175, 178, 194; and blank space, 128; become bottomless, 42; and Earth, 84, 175, 200; "Death," 88n4; dissolve, 116, 119; dissolve into the earth process, 10; in their earthly context, 67; as infinite, 5; leading to awareness, 116; and nature, 116; are only signs, 62; part of something greater than themselves, 116; as self-referring husks, 62

Sino-English, 125

skepticism, 5, 8, 74, 143–144, 174, 175; and affirmation, 7, 8, 22; and agency, 8; as avenue into affirmation, 8; in ecocriticism, 7; about existence, 80; as a form of cynicism about existence, Earth, and literary art, 5; as a kind of recognition, 8; postpones judgment of facts and phenomena, 5

Snow, Charles Percy (C. P.) : "two cultures," 155, 178; nature in ecocriticism, 155

Snyder, Gary, 13, 17, 29n34, 29n47, 120, 131, 196; Eliot's sense of roots, 68, 69; holy perception of Earth, 18

"soil-erosion," 17, 57

Soper, Kate: and postmodernism, 162; *What Is Nature? Culture, Politics and the Non-Human*, 162

Spears Brooker, Jewel. *See* Brooker, Jewel Spears

spiritual, 24; aloofness from matter, 24; perception, 5

stair, 55, 56; as metaphor of ascendancy, 55

Steigler, Bernard, 128, 130n32, 130n33

Steiner, George, 5, 28n15, 30n61, 130n37; defines real presence, 12, 23; *Real Presences*, 5, 106, 108, 156; view of matter, 5

Stevens, Wallace, 135; poem "The Glass of Water," 135; poetry, 108

stillness and motion, 11

stretched soul, 37

substance exists, 63

suspended time, 54

taking from Cosmos, 39

Taoist notion of being, 118

text, 34

Thames, 16. *See also The Waste Land*; of Edmund Spenser, 16; nymphs from pagan past, 53; pollution, 16; presence as an ancient natural place, 16

things change, 114

Thoreau, Henry David, 63, 181, 183n60

threeness, 76, 79, 82, 84, 109, 145–146, 180, 194; and its actuality, 120; and reality, 82

theoretical study of literature, 185

theorizing, 106

theory: and poetry, 173–174

thunder, 71; "diluted," 71

time: dislocated from any sense of eternity, 54; fragments, 55; images, 54; as a knife that severs, 55; lack of satisfactory time, 54

transcendence, 109; and linguistic "dissolving," 109

tree metaphor, 9; Christ's mandalic cross, 9

twoness, 76, 82

un-being, 6; and being, 126

understanding, 38

unity, 47, 76, 82, 91; of being-and-nothing, 117; of disparate things, 83; of dynamic elements, 9
universal significance, 38
universe, 38
urban tension, 37

Van Heerden, Ernst, 39, 48n17
verbs, 9
vibrant: emptiness, 27, 118; matter, 27, 84; unity of vibrant matter, 118
violence, 80; to women, 84
vital: connection with matter, 91; kind of nothing, 115

Wagner's opera *Tristan and Isolde*, 53
wasteland(s), 77, 84; of disconnection, 32; for family and children, 32; from human progress, 32
The Waste Land (1922), 7, 9, 14, 20, 51, 57, 59, 68, 74, 82, 85. *See also* Eliot, Thomas Stearns (T. S.); active blank space, 133; affirmation of existence, 136; comic wholeness, 83; continuity is central to modern existence, 167; critiques male domination, 194; desertification, 59; desertscapes, 18, 23, 67, 71; dire individual and collective situation, 70; disconnection between holiness and Earth, 16; dislocating language, 51, 52; dramatization of threeness, 77; embodies location in mandalic patterns, 23; Fisher King legend, 120; flow of existence, 10; fragment/ blank space, 148; healing, 78; joy of emplacement, 15; immersion, 99; importance of nature, 16; inability to reconcile opposite conditions, 75; kingfisher image, 120–121; and Leavis's criticism, 144–145; Lil's bar scene, 138; linguistic dislocation, 51; mandalic patterning, 71; mandalic Sanskrit, 109; mental act of counting, 77; in modern fragmented time, 53; moment of charged nothing, 135; mythological narrative structure, 75; pattern points to earthly location, 68; pollution, 16; rape of Philomela, 18; reality is beyond words, 143; real places in London, 15; recognition of Sanskrit roots, 68–70; return to/ of wholeness, 71; Sanskrit fragments, 133, 136, 144, 188; Sanskrit mandalic structure, 68, 69, 70; sense of place, 15; *shantih* benediction, 78; shaping toward moral maturity, 72; tension between opposites, 116; third dimension beyond twoness, 78; title evokes issues of place, 67; underlying theme, 200; vital connection with matter, 91
wave of New Criticism, 199–200
wholeness, 7, 19, 63, 78, 81, 82, 83, 84; and its absence, 7; and differentiation, 7; is dynamic and open, 19; opposites dissolve into Earth's continuation, 91
Williams, William Carlos, 13, 83, 115; celebration of being within non-being, 115; poems, 134, 151n7
wisdom, 81
Woolf, Virginia: *Jacob's Room*, 86, 89n53
Wordsworth, William, 43, 49n30; sonnet "The world is too much with us . . . ," 43
worlds of good and evil, 54

Yeats, W. B., 13, 59, 65n34, 114, 148; desertscapes, 59, 60; and Eliot and Pound, 140–141; fragmentation, 61; "The Second Coming" (1921), 56, 60–61

About the Author

Etienne Terblanche teaches and researches English poetry and literature at the Potchefstroom Campus of the North-West University, South Africa. In 2012 he published a well-received monograph titled *E. E. Cummings: Poetry and Ecology* under the flag of Rodopi Publishers (Amsterdam/New York) in the series Literature, Culture and Nature. Various articles on the ecological aspect of modern poetry have flowed from his pen. His ecocritical interest embraces iconicity studies, a Jungian approach, and Taoism. A new article is forthcoming on butterfly dialectics in modern poetry within *ISLE: Interdisciplinary Studies in Literature and Environment*. Etienne lives in sweet thorn savannah with his beloved wife and four children in Potchefstroom, writing poetry of his own in his mother tongue, Afrikaans. His first volume of published poetry, titled *Kronkelmandala* (Meander-Mandala), is due at Protea Books in 2016. His interest in butterflies takes him out into the South African veld, where he is able to shed some of the nature deficit disorder that office life induces and connect joyfully with Earth.

Lightning Source UK Ltd.
Milton Keynes UK
UKHW012342150722
405892UK00009B/277